Will you control your anger— or will your anger control you?

- Why do some people seem angrier than others?
- What affects your own emotional trigger?
- Why do you express your anger in a hurtful or nonhurtful way?
- How can you control your most powerful feelings— especially your anger?

Don't stay mad. Start reading! *PRESCRIPTION FOR ANGER* may be your Rx to change self-defeating behavior, master your emotions, discover the joy of personal fulfillment, and triumph over everyday provocations to anger.

PRESCRIPTION FOR ANGER

ABOUT THE AUTHORS

Gary Hankins holds a Ph.D. in Counseling Psychology from Georgia State University. He is a nationally known consultant to and seminar leader in the areas of anger, stress, and communication for businesses, schools, law enforcement agencies, mental health agencies and institutions. In addition, he teaches part-time at Willamette University, continues his private counseling practice, and is a popular, often requested speaker to television and radio audiences.

As a counselor, Dr. Hankins has devoted his life to helping others discover and clear away the blocks that keep them from experiencing the life they deserve.

Carol Hankins received her degree in sociology from Portland State University. A social worker with extensive experience, she has been on the staff of several hospitals and long-term care facilities.

PRESCRIPTION
FOR ANGER

Gary Hankins, Ph.D., with Carol Hankins

WARNER BOOKS

A Time Warner Company

*To Carol, my wife and best friend, for her
devotion, guidance, and unconditional love
—and to my daughter, Michelle, for her
patience, understanding, love, and support.*

Except for references made to myself and members of my immediate
family, all of the names and identifying characteristics of people
described in this book have been changed to preserve their privacy.

WARNER BOOKS EDITION

Cover design by Diane Luger

This Warner Books Edition is published by arrangement with the authors.

Warner Books, Inc.
1271 Avenue of the Americas
New York, NY 10020

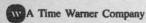A Time Warner Company

Printed in the United States of America

First Warner Books Printing: January, 1993

10 9 8 7 6 5

ACKNOWLEDGMENTS

I'd like to thank the staff and patients at Oregon State Hospital, as well as my colleagues, clients, and students who, in their own special ways, have helped to stimulate many of the ideas expressed in this book. I'm particularly thankful to my friends and colleagues Brett Rogers, Ph.D., for listening to my ideas and providing valuable feedback, and John Cochran, Ph.D., for sharing his expertise about forensic psychology and the extremely self-serving personality.

I'm very grateful to Carol Fischer and Cheryl Kilbourn for reading and rereading the manuscript in its early stages of development. They provided many positive and deeply appreciated editorial suggestions. I'm particularly thankful to Susan Suffes, my editor at Warner Books, for her belief in what I was trying to communicate. Susan's editing clarified my message and greatly enhanced the readability of this manuscript. I'm also grateful to Dave Adamson and Chuck Laiti for the care, creativity, and artistic skill they used in creating the illustrations and diagrams.

To my daughter, Michelle, I extend my heartfelt appreciation for her unwavering support and encouragement throughout the duration of this project. It is with pride and pleasure I have included her creative ideas.

I'm especially grateful to my wife, Carol, for the outstanding work she has done as researcher, typist, and co-writer of this book. I am extremely thankful for the dedication, commitment, perseverance and self-discipline she demonstrated from inception to completion of this book, and for her ability to transform my thoughts and ideas into a finished product.

CONTENTS

PART THREE: Techniques for Coping with Angry Feelings and Angry People

INTRODUCTION

Every day, millions of people become angry. Whether directed inwardly or toward others, anger can be felt and expressed as genuine anger, or it can take on many forms and mask a variety of emotions. In fact, anger is at the heart of at least 80 percent of the problems for which people seek professional therapeutic advice.

Underneath many feelings of anger are profound feelings of helplessness. The typical apology for angry outbursts is, "I'm sorry, I didn't mean to do that, but I was so angry I just couldn't help myself." It is not uncommon to want to humiliate, punish, or get back at the person who provoked your anger and left you feeling powerless. Unfortunately, the harder you try to hurt those who provoke your anger, the more intense your anger becomes. And the more intense your anger becomes, the more you get caught up in a destructive cycle of anger, hurt, and helplessness.

Prescription for Anger is *not* a wonder drug; rather, it contains key insights and easy-to-learn techniques. When combined with your willingness and commitment to put these insights and techniques into action, *Prescription for Anger* will enable you to cope more effectively and more constructively with angry feelings and angry people. Additionally, it will help you regain your sense of personal power and control over your reactions to anger-provoking situations.

Part 1 demystifies anger by discussing its advantages and disadvantages and presenting the constructive choices you can make whenever you are angry.

Part 2 discusses the major factors that contribute to the individual differences in people's reactions to various provocations. These include the impact of certain aspects of the environment, the influence of other people, and the angered person's own innate and acquired characteristics.

Part 3 describes a variety of constructive ways to cope with many kinds and causes of angry feelings and angry people. The effectiveness of each of the techniques is verified by the results of over twenty years of research that has established what is and what is not effective in actually reducing people's anger.

Physicians maximize the effectiveness of medications they prescribe by carefully adjusting the type and quantity according to each patient's needs. They take into consideration the specific ailment, age, weight and possible interactive effects that medication may have with any medication the patient may already be taking. Likewise, you can maximize the effectiveness of any anger management techniques you choose from part 3 by selecting those most appropriate for your particular needs and always using them in combination with the self-awareness technique described in chapter 21.

Although most people are able to regain their physical well-being by following their physicians' advice, there are some people who require extended and comprehensive professional intervention in order to overcome their particular disease or disabilities. Similarly, most people will be able to regain their emotional balance and self-control by following through, on their own, with the anger management techniques described in part 3. There are, however, some segments of the population who require professional intervention in order to learn how to cope with and control their anger. These include people who have poor impulse control, those who are under medical and/or psychological treatment for neuroses, psychoses, or mood disorders, and those who have severe personality disorders. Thus, part 4 contains some additional techniques and guidelines for professionals to follow when working with people who require special interventions.

Just as some people are beyond the help of even the most advanced medical technology, some people are beyond the scope of *Prescription for Anger*. This book is not designed for those who have severe brain damage, retardation, neurosis, or psychosis.

Perhaps you are having difficulty managing your anger. Maybe you're experiencing difficulty coping with someone else's mismanaged anger, such as an abusive spouse, an ill-tempered boss, or an angry child. If so, *Prescription for Anger* can help you! Whether you read it on your own, as part of a discussion group, or as a supplement to therapy, *Prescription for Anger* can help you gain the insights and develop the skills you need to cope constructively and effectively with angry feelings and angry people.

PART ONE

What Is Anger?

CHAPTER ONE

Clearing up the Confusion

"I don't want to eat my broccoli, and I'm not going to eat it!" the seven-year-old girl boldly declared. "I said you *will* eat it, and that's final!" retorted her father. Frustrated by her father's insistence, the girl screamed, "I won't eat it and you can't make me!" Giving his daughter a murderous glance, the father rushed up out of his chair, picked her up by her shoulders, pinned her against the wall, and roared, "DON'T YOU EVER GET ANGRY IN THIS HOUSE AGAIN!" As he stormed out of the room, she slid down the wall to the floor.

Even though it has been more than twenty years since my friend witnessed that interaction between his father and little sister, he still feels confused about anger. Is it wrong to be angry, as his father said? Or is it okay to be angry, as his father demonstrated?

Unfortunately, my friend is not the only one who is confused about anger. Millions of Americans are. Perhaps you are, too.

Parents, teachers, clergy, mental health "experts," magazines, newspapers, books, radio, television, and movies present an overwhelming variety of messages about anger. The answers to the following questions are typical of the conflicting opinions given by the "experts."

Is anger a *valuable* emotion?

". . . anger can be a constructive emotion that helps resolve hurts and differences between people, improves their understanding of one another, and gives their relationships a firmer base." (Albin, 1983)

. . . or a *worthless* emotion?

"Getting angry is simply a discharge of emotions and does not lead to growth." (Lazarus and Fay, 1975)

Is it *okay* to be angry?

"We need to feel that anger. Accept it, for it is part of our emotional makeup, put there by God." (Stoop, 1982)

. . . or is anger a *sin*?

"Anger is one of two universal sins of mankind." (LaHaye, 1982)

Is anger *unavoidable*?

". . . anger is part of being human. It is a basic and necessary emotion." (Stoop, 1982)

. . . or can anger be avoided?

"Anger is not 'only human.' You do not have to possess it. . . . While the expression of anger is a healthy alternative to storing it up, not having it at all is the healthiest choice of all." (Dyer, 1976)

So, What Reputation Does Anger Really Deserve?

Anger is a normal, natural emotion that, in itself, is neither good nor bad. Instead, its value is determined by how you choose to respond to it. It is up to you to decide whether anger will be a negative or a positive emotion in your life.

When you channel the energy generated by your anger into constructive endeavors, anger can *stimulate* many worthwhile activities. Channeled into destructive actions, anger can *drain* your energy. Many athletes have benefitted from the extra energy they derive from a moderate amount of anger. However, when that anger becomes too intense, or is not properly controlled, it becomes a distraction, leaving the athletes feeling emotionally, physically, and mentally drained and exhausted.

Depending on how it is expressed, anger can either *open* new channels of communication or *block* its flow altogether. Constructive communication of anger *alerts* others to your needs, thereby creating an opportunity for reconciliation and support. Destructive communication of anger has just the opposite effect. It *deters* others from caring about your needs and increases their desire to respond in equally hurtful ways.

When you are self-aware, the arousal of anger can be your *internal indicator* that it is time to regain your sense of personal control by taking positive action to resolve the conflict, or by finding a constructive way to cope with your angry feelings. The arousal of anger also serves as an *emotional trigger* that you can respond to by trying to regain control in destructive ways. These often include trying to intimidate others with aggressive behavior, or manipulate them with passive-aggressive behavior.

When you choose to express your anger in a destructive manner (swearing, name-calling, hitting, kicking, breaking something, or giving someone the "silent treatment") anger becomes a destructive emotion. But when you choose to channel the energy derived from your anger into constructive activities (communicating your needs in a nonhurtful manner, completing a worthwhile project, striving to correct a problem such as social injustice, drunk drivers, neighborhood crime, etc)., then anger is a positive emotion.

Constructive Uses of Anger	Destructive Uses of Anger
• Stimulates	• Drains
• Opens communication	• Blocks communication
• Alerts others	• Deters others
• Indicates need for positive action	• Triggers destructive action

Converting Angry Feelings into Positive Actions

Learning how to manage your anger is similar to learning how to master a particular sport. The more skillful you are at using the basic techniques, and the more capable you are at *blending* those techniques together, the more success you will experience.

The year I coached a high school basketball team, one of my players set the state record for the most points scored in a single game. Unfortunately, the night our "star athlete" set that record, he ignored his defensive responsibilities, and we lost the game. But, on other nights when he concentrated on contributing to the defensive as well as the offensive aspects of the game, utilizing a combination of his defensive and offensive skills, our team's chances of winning were greatly enhanced.

As you begin the process of learning how to manage your anger, you may prefer to start by learning just one or two of the techniques described in part 3, then adding more as your comfort level increases. By combining several of the techniques, you'll gain even more control over your anger.

If Anger Is Neither Good nor Bad, Why Do Some People Try to Avoid It?

When one of my clients (who was scowling and sitting slumped in her chair) objected to my comment that she seemed angry about something, I explained that her body language and tone of voice indicated to me that she was angry. Infuriated by my confrontation about her anger, she bolted out of her chair, pounded her fist on my desk, and shouted, "I'M NOT ANGRY! I'VE NEVER BEEN ANGRY IN MY LIFE, AND I'M NOT ANGRY NOW! I'M JUST UPSET!"

Many people try to deny that they are feeling angry, or they try to talk other people out of their anger, because they associate anger with loss of control. How many times do you hear comments like these?

"I was so angry all I could do was scream!"

"If I had thought about it I would have behaved more rationally, but I was so angry I just hit him before I knew what I was doing."

"He was so angry there was no stopping him, he kept cussing and ranting and raving something fierce!"

Loss of control often leads to feelings of frustration, confusion, embarrassment, guilt, hurt, and/or helplessness. Indeed, many physical, emotional, and mental hurts have resulted from uncontrolled anger, as evidenced by the frequency of strained employee-employer relations, on-going tensions in public and private schools, our nation's high divorce rate, and the millions of child- and spouse-abuse victims (including more than 3,500 women and children who die each year as a result of that abuse). Uncontrolled anger is frequently responsible for triggering criminal activity and international conflict.

The Positive Power of Anger

In contrast to the destructive power of *uncontrolled* anger, *controlled* anger provides the energy for some of the most constructive activities imaginable. The nonviolent resistance movements led by civil rights leaders Dr. Martin Luther King, Jr., and Indian leader Mahatma Gandhi demonstrate how anger can be used in controlled and constructive yet powerful ways to *help* others.

Yes, anger is a very powerful emotion, but as you will see in the next chapter, *you can control that power.*

CHAPTER TWO

Anger: Chance or Choice?

Can someone *make* you angry, or do you *choose* to be angry? Actually, it depends on the situation and your perception of the situation.

Situation 1

You are walking along a busy sidewalk. Suddenly a stranger slugs you in the stomach while his accomplice steals your wallet.

Situation 2

Your spouse informs you that he (or she) is no longer interested in going to the play you were planning on seeing together in two weeks.

In situation 1 you had no control over what was happening to you. If you were the victim, would you feel angry?

Although situation 2 included at least three options (missing the play, going by yourself, or seeing it with a friend), if you were the one with your heart set on going to the play, would you feel angry?

In situations where you are accustomed to having the control and it is suddenly and forcefully taken away, *you can be made to be angry.* On the other hand, in situations where your control is merely threatened, you can *choose* whether to be angry.

Is Anger Management the Art of Avoiding Anger?

If learning to control your anger were as simple as choosing not to feel angry at any time or at anyone you could eliminate the need to improve your anger management skills. But it's not that simple. According to the research of Karl Pribram, M.D., professor of neuropsychology at Stanford University's School of Medicine, anger is a chosen response in some situations and an automatic reaction in others. Anger is a natural, normal emotion. You may be able to decrease the frequency of your anger, but you cannot always avoid it.

So, Is Anger Manageable Only Under Certain Conditions?

Regardless of whether your anger is an unavoidable reaction or the result of a conscious choice on your part, you can always begin the process of controlling your anger by asking yourself the following three questions.

1. How intense will your anger be?
2. How long will you be angry?
3. What will you do with your anger?

You may not always be able to control *when* you are going to feel angry, but your responses to these three questions will determine the outcome of your anger. You can always decide how intense your anger will be, how long you will hold on to your angry feelings, and whether the outcome of your anger will be positive or negative. The cycle of wife abuse, described in the next chapter, illustrates how the *consequences* of your anger are often a direct result of the *choices* you make when you are angry.

One common response to anger is retaliation. Retaliation is the act of expressing hurtful and angry feelings in ways that inflict those same feelings on someone else. Retaliation, if allowed to run wild, continues the anger-retaliation-more-anger cycle. You can, however, avoid that destructive cycle by choosing to express your anger in constructive, healing ways.

Angry feelings are a natural, normal, inevitable part of life. You can't always choose when you're going to feel angry. But you can choose how intense your anger will be, how long your anger will last, and what you are going to do with your anger. By making those three choices, *you* can control the power of anger and determine what the consequences of your anger will be.

CHAPTER THREE

The Cycle of Abuse: An Example of Choosing Destructive Expressions of Anger

The outcome of anger in abusive relationships is not only violent, all too often it is deadly. The National Coalition Against Domestic Violence reports that 66 percent of all marriages involve at least one instance of wife abuse; each year at least 6 million women are severely beaten by their spouses, and of those women, 1,500 die as a direct result of spouse-inflicted injuries. According to statistics reported on the September 17, 1991, airing of the television program *20/20*, 200 women are physically attacked by their husbands every hour; two-thirds of all battered women are told by their mates that they intend to kill them; and as a response to those threats, approximately 600 women kill their battering husbands each year. The cycle of violence appears to be never-ending. The good news is: the cycle can be stopped. The bad news is: there are many barriers to breaking out of the cycle. Before looking at some of the major barriers to leaving a battering relationship, and how to stop the cycle of abuse, let's look at the role anger plays in perpetuating the battering cycle, who gets abused, the significance of control, and the emotional consequences of abuse.

How Does Uncontrolled Anger Perpetuate the Cycle of Abuse?

The battering cycle typically consists of:

1. a slow buildup of tension
2. the actual battering
3. the husband apologizing and showering the wife with kindness and promises of no more abuse (the "hearts and flowers" stage)

Abused women appreciate the kindness and affection given to them by their mates during the "hearts and flowers" stage. Even though their painful feelings of hurt, helplessness, and anger usually linger long after their physical injuries have healed, the majority of battered women who seek relief from abuse in shelter homes say that they would prefer to return to their partners if their relationships could be free of abuse. The thought of divorce or being alone often seems more threatening to battered women than does the prospect of returning to their abusive relationships. Without realizing what they are doing, battered women often justify their decisions to stay with their mates with thoughts such as, "My parents and religion have always said divorce is wrong. If I got a divorce, how could I face my friends and relatives? And what about the embarrassment it would cause him? How would the kids and I make it without his financial support? How can I leave when I need him so much? I'm sure he could change, if only... After all, it always makes him more abusive when I try to leave. I'm afraid he's serious when he says he'll kill me if I go. I can't stand his abuse, but I can't stand the thought of being alone. I feel so trapped. I thought I deserved more than this, but at least there are times when he says he loves me. Who else would ever want me? Besides, he needs me . . . how would he survive without me?''

Traditionally, men have been regarded as the perpetrators of violence. However, in most abusive relationships, both the man and the woman contribute to the escalation of conflict that results in violence. Battered women *never* deserve to be abused, nor are their partners ever justified in being abusive. But in most battering situations, the woman needs to assume at least partial responsibility for the abuse she receives. Without self-awareness of their own hurtful expressions of anger, these women may be increasing the abuse they receive. Some women become so furious with their abusive mates that they retaliate with physical or emotional violence of their own, which further escalates the violent relationship. However, most battered women attempt to hide their hurt, resentment, bitterness, hate, and rage by holding it in, because they feel traumatized by and afraid of their mates' retaliatory violence. When a woman doesn't assume any responsibility for her own hurtful expressions of anger (no matter how subtle they may be), or for her role in the abusive relationship, the cycle of abuse intensifies. Failure to accept some responsibility for the abusive relationship may lead battered women to become blind to some of the rational options that could help them break out of the abusive cycle. When they deny their anger and turn it inward, irrational options such as suicide or homicide begin to emerge. When battered women try to suppress their anger and rage, it often erupts anyway, despite their best efforts to hide it. Battered women often perpetuate the battering cycle by letting their hurt and anger ''leak out'' in subtle ways. Their need to ''get even'' may be manifested by pouting, giving their mates angry looks, rolling their eyes (indicating disbelief), contradicting or arguing with their mates, feigning illness to avoid having to interact with them, or ''forgetting'' to do something they've promised to do. (See chapter 4 for a more extensive list of passive-aggressive behaviors.) When a battered woman refuses to accept responsibility for her own behavior she often uses a double standard, claiming that her hurtful retaliations are justified even though her mate's are not.

A battered women can perpetuate the cycle of abuse by either knowingly or unknowingly expressing her anger in ways that weaken her mate's feelings of self-worth or self-control. When she does this, it usually leads to her mate's expressions of anger being even more destructive and abusive. The more frequently couples are abusive with each other, the more habituated they become to the abuse and the more intense it gets. By expressing anger in demoralizing ways, and not moderating the intensity or the duration of it, both the batterer and the battered person perpetuate the destructive cycle of abuse.

NOTE: In some relationships, the husband (or mate) may have a severe personality disorder, such as the Extremely Self-Serving Personality (ESS), and be very emotionally detached (as describe in chapter 42). An ESS husband is so self-centered that he believes he has the "right" to do whatever he wants to his wife (or partner). An ESS thinks of his partner as his personal property and believes that she deserves to be abused whenever he doesn't get his way. Thus, the partner of an ESS may be abused no matter how constructively she manages her anger or how well she controls it.

Who Gets Abused?

Unfortunately, many people still hold on to the myth that all battered women are basically weak, dependent people who lack education, job skills, and family support. In reality, battered women come from all socioeconomic levels. Abuse does not discriminate. Having a character flaw is not a prerequisite for abuse. Abuse can happen to anyone.

Battered women come from a wide range of intellectual, emotional, economical, and psychological levels. Women who are mentally retarded or have a severe personality disorder don't have the same innate capacity to recognize their options and make healthy choices for themselves as do well educated, securely employed, self-assured women. Individual differences influence how a woman responds to abuse when it occurs, how she copes with the abusive relationship, and how easily she is able to recognize and respond to her options.

The Significance of Control

In most abusive relationships, the issue of control is one of the most important underlying factors. Most men who batter their mates want to dominate and control. They equate "having" with "controlling." Battering men gain their control through instilling fear and being intimidating. Some batterers desire control so intensely that they would rather exercise the ultimate control and kill their mates than allow them to escape their control or be influenced by anyone else. Women who live with abusive, control-seeking men are beaten down both emotionally and physically. For some, the emotional battering is even more frequent and severe than the physical abuse they endure; and their emotional scars linger long after their bruises and broken bones have healed.

The Emotional Consequences of Abuse

Considering how much emotional and physical suffering battered women endure, it is not surprising that their self-worth deteriorates. The following list is a compilation of the feelings experienced by battered women as a consequence of the abuse they receive. Some battered women experience all of these feelings, while others experience only a few.

anger	loneliness
anxiety	pain (emotional, physical,
bitterness	psychological, & spiritual)
confusion	panic
depression	post-traumatic stress syndrome
(& suicidal thoughts)	(caused by smells, sounds,
fear	touches, etc., that trigger
frustration	memories of abuse)
grief	rage
guilt	shame
helplessness	shattered confidence & self-esteem
hopelessness	sorrow
humiliation	vindictiveness
isolation	

Battered women frequently perceive themselves as having no control over their lives, and they feel powerless to change their situation. As a consequence of their misconceptions about the amount of control they really do have, battered women often develop feelings of **learned helplessness.** Typically, these feelings of learned helplessness, coupled with their poor self-esteem, become so overwhelming that battered women lose sight of the constructive choices they could make. The result: they either knowingly or unknowingly help perpetuate the cycle of abuse by becoming angry, *battering* women as well as angry, *battered* women.

Considering the Choices

Choosing whether to leave or stay with a battering mate is very hard. The degree of difficulty increases as the battered woman's self-esteem decreases. By the time a battered woman's self-esteem has been severely damaged from years of torment and abuse, the choice to leave or to stay becomes overwhelming. For those who feel extremely frightened and helpless, choosing to leave or to stay may seem next to impossible. Actually, battered women have four options. These are:

1. Stay in the abusive relationship.
   - Don't respond to the abuse, just passively absorb it. (The abuse will usually continue.)
   - Return the abuse, either passive-aggressively or aggressively. (The abuse will usually continue or intensify.)
2. Stay in the relationship and participate in therapy.
   - Attend support groups and/or therapy by yourself. (The abuse will usually continue.)
   - Don't go to therapy, but have the abuser attend by himself. (The abuse will usually continue.)
   - Attend therapy together. (The abuse may decrease or stop.)
3. Separate from the abuser.
   - Attend support groups or therapy without the abuser. (The abuse will usually resume if you return to the relationship.)
   - Have the abuser attend therapy alone. (The abuse will usually resume if you return.)
   - Stay separated except to attend therapy together. (The abuse may decrease or stop after you have had sufficient therapy, and you feel safe in the presence of your mate.)
4. Leave the batterer.

Barriers to Leaving a Battering Relationship

Ambivalence and low self-esteem. Most battered women feel very ambivalent about leaving their battering relationships, especially if their partners' abuse has eroded their self-esteem to the point where they actually believe they are unworthy of anything better than their current abusive relationship. The lower their self-esteem, the less able they are to recognize the nonabusive options available to them. Thus, the longer they remain in an abusive relationship, or the longer they go from one abusive relationship to another, the worse they feel about themselves and the harder it gets for them to break away from the abuse.

Fear. Many batterers use their anger and rage to exploit, intimidate, and manipulate their mates into doing what *they* want. When a battered woman attempts to leave the relationship, or even tries to stand up for her rights and insist that the abuse stop, quite frequently her abusive partner will try to regain control by intimidating her and threatening to kill her. If, out of fear, the battered woman returns to her dependent and submissive "victim" role, her partner's aggressive, manipulative, intimidating outbursts are reinforced and the woman's fears are intensified.

Helplessness. A lack of self-worth and confidence, along with feelings of fear, anxiety, confusion, sadness, hopelessness, and helplessness, keep many battered women believing they are "trapped" in their relationships. As long as they see themselves as helpless "victims" and remain convinced that they are unable (or that it is unnecessary for them to) accept responsibility for their behavior, they will remain perpetually "trapped" in the cycle of abuse.

Magical thinking. One of the biggest barriers to escaping the entrapment of abuse is the false sense of hope so desperately held on to by many battered women. No matter what their experiences have been, or how severe the abuse, they continue to believe that "someday the abuse will start to diminish, and eventually it will totally disappear." However, the abuse doesn't ever magically disappear. Unless both partners are willing to work hard at keeping abuse out of the relationship and to make a firm commitment to stop hurting each other, the battering is doomed to continue, and will most likely escalate into an even more abusive cycle of hurt and violence. Those women who refuse to take responsibility for their behavior, and are holding on to their belief that someday the abuse will magically disappear, are facing the biggest barrier to being free from abusive relationships.

When a battered woman is able to see her role in an abusive relationship and is able to assume at least partial responsibility for her hurtful behavior, she has taken the first and most important step toward overcoming the barriers to leaving the abusive relationship.

The next step is to start believing that she deserves to break away from the abuse and find a friend, advocate, or counselor who shares in that belief. An effective advocate is a person who can be objective yet provide the appropriate amount of sympathy, empathy, comfort, encouragement, emotional support, and truth that the battered person needs in order to start respecting herself. (See appendix E for a more detailed list of the needs of battered women and what types of assistance are helpful.) Once a battered woman's self-respect begins to grow, so will her self-esteem, self-confidence, self-knowledge, and ability to assume responsibility for her behavior. With these gains, she will find it is easier to start developing short- and long-term goals for a life free of abuse.

As long as the battered woman believes that her behavior has no influence on her mate, she continues to believe she is merely a "victim" of abuse, and her abusive mate is the only one who must change. This "victim's stance" often leads to the misconception that the woman has earned the right to express her anger in hurtful ways. In actuality, battered women have four categories of anger expression from which to choose. These are:

1. *Passive:* saying or doing nothing
2. *Aggressive:* retaliating in an obviously hurtful manner, such as yelling at or hitting the abuser (see chapter 5)
3. *Passive-aggressive:* responding in a subtly hurtful manner, such as conveniently forgetting, or pouting (see chapter 4)

4. *Assertive:* confronting in a calm, respectful, nonhurtful, nonthreatening, manner (see chapter 7)

Stopping the Cycle of Abuse

According to James Makepeace, associate professor of sociology at St. Benedictine–St. John's University in Minnesota, batterers typically come from a home where there was lots of violence, they have a low level of tolerance for stress, and they lack self-esteem. The most common triggers for abuse in a marriage are arguments over children, budgeting, or housekeeping; but over all, the main cause of violence is the batterer's poor anger-management skills.

Many battering men feel guilty (to some extent) about their abusive behavior and will often try to apologize with flowers and/or other gifts. They promise they will never be verbally or physically abusive again. However, these promises are rarely kept.

Many battered women have found temporary escape from their abusive mates by going to shelter homes. However, spending a few days or weeks in a shelter doesn't necessarily decrease the likelihood of their being battered in the future. The first step in stopping the cycle of abuse begins when *both* the man and the woman are highly motivated to get professional help and reduce their sense of isolation by keeping their commitments to participate in therapy. Additionally, both partners must be willing to:

- assume personal responsibility for their actions
- stop perceiving themselves as "victim" and "perpetrator"
- give up their mistaken belief that they have the "right" to retaliate
- recognize and respond to cues that signal the escalation of the abuse cycle
- follow through with their mutually agreed upon predetermined plans for "cooling off"

The battering male must stop seeing himself as a "helpless victim" who is unable to control his abusive behavior. For example, he must stop his irrational self-talk that may sound something like: "She made me so mad, I just had to hit her. I couldn't help it . . . she made me do it . . . it's her fault. She makes me lose control. . . . I'm a victim of my own rage."

As long as batterers believe they have no responsibility for, or control over their abusive behavior, they will remain "victims" and continue to victimize themselves and others.

One exercise that is helpful to batterers, who feel that hitting their partners is an automatic reaction they can't control, consists of asking themselves the following question: "If one of the major television networks were doing a documentary on our family, would I strike my partner the instant I felt the urge, or would I wait until the cameramen left?" The exercise is effective because the answer to that question is so obvious and indisputable. Batterers realize that they would wait, that they can control when they are abusive. This exercise helps batterers understand that they are abusive only when they *think* they can get away with it.

When the batterer lacks the necessary commitment to follow through with therapy and the corrective measures listed above, or when the battered woman's safety is habitually and/or critically endangered, she may have to choose between self-preservation and persevering with her relationship. If she chooses to leave the relationship, she must first accept the responsibility and challenge of overcoming the major barriers facing her.

Until battering men and battered women give up their hurtful, nonassertive expressions of anger, the cycle of abuse will continue. Although it may seem harsh to insist that battered women take responsibility for their behavior, it is more helpful to them in the long run to empower them with choices and responsibility than to maintain the myth that they are helpless, hopeless "victims." Abuse is never justified or deserved, but women who believe they have the right to retaliate, in either obvious or subtle ways, are helping to perpetuate the cycle of abuse. Battered women can begin to break away from abuse by breaking away from the erroneous belief that their lives are beyond their control, and replacing it with the belief that they can make a better life for themselves, free of hurt and abuse.

CHAPTER FOUR

Passive-Aggressive Anger

There are three broad categories of anger expressions: aggressive, passive-aggressive, and assertive. Both aggressive and passive-aggressive expressions are used with the intent to hurt. *Assertive* expressions of anger, on the other hand, are intended to be nonhurtful. They involve the use of nonthreatening, nonblaming, respectful "I Messages." *Aggressive* expressions include behaviors such as hitting and yelling. When people express their anger in aggressive ways (often called active-aggressive), the targeted recipients of their anger can easily see, hear, or feel the physical, mental, or emotional hurt directed at them. *Passive-aggressive* expressions of anger are also hurtful, but in either indirect or subtle, hard-to-detect ways. Pouting is typical of the observable yet subtle forms of passive-aggressive anger. Subtle expressions are often used by people who want to manipulate others, or by those who want to express their anger, hurt, or frustration, without subjecting themselves to the immediate repercussions often associated with blatant, aggressive expressions of anger. For instance, one evening about seven months after Carol and I got married, I suggested to her, in a very round-about, indirect fashion, that warm chocolate chip cookies sounded good. Carol immediately and politely responded, "If you want some, go ahead and fix them." "Good grief," I thought, "I don't want to go to all that trouble, I want *her* to fix them for me. Why can't she understand that?" Frustrated by Carol's failure to recognize that my indirect statement was actually a request for her to bake me a fresh batch of cookies, I responded by pouting (with the best "adult" pout I could muster) and it "worked." My pout induced her guilt and she immediately began to fix the cookies. Within a few months, however, she "caught on" to my passive-aggressive manipulations, and my pouts are no longer effective with her.

Procrastinating and forgetting to do something are typical examples of indirect, hard-to-detect passive-aggressive expressions of anger. For instance, when Linda was angry with her husband, Karl, she "conveniently forgot" that she had promised to call Karl's mother and invite her to dinner. Karl not only felt hurt and angry as a result of Linda's passive-aggressive behavior, he was frustrated about not being able to "prove" that Linda was angry with him.

It's often very difficult for the recipients of passive-aggressive expressions of anger to *prove* that those behaviors were intended to be hurtful, but the hurt is just as painful and destructive as the obvious damage caused by aggressive outbursts. Sometimes the people who express their anger in passive-aggressive ways aren't aware of their own hidden intentions, or they fail to notice how their passive-aggressive behaviors are subtly eroding their relationships at home and at work, until those relationships crumble. This pattern is most evident in codependent relationships where the passive-aggressive behaviors continue until one partner can no longer tolerate or cope with the hurt, and neither partner knows how to salvage or restore the relationship.

There is a fine line between some of the obvious, active-aggressive expressions of anger and some passive-aggressive behaviors. One way to distinguish between aggressive and passive-aggressive expressions of anger is by looking at their different functions. Direct, aggressive expressions of anger (such as shouting) are designed primarily for *attacking* and *eliminating* resistance to the angry person's goals. On the other hand, passive-aggressive behaviors (such as arguing) are generally used to *resist* other people and prevent them from reaching their goals.

Another distinguishing feature is the directness of the expression. Aggressive expressions of anger are very direct and there is no doubt that they are meant to hurt. By contrast, passive-aggressive expressions of anger are made indirectly or subtly, so it is often difficult for the recipient to prove whether the behavior was intentionally hurtful. For example, if someone "accidentally" bumps your favorite coffee mug and watches as it falls and shatters on the floor, that is a passive form of aggression. Actually picking up the mug and tossing it to the floor would be a deliberate, active form of aggression. In both situations, the result is the same—your mug is broken as a result of someone else's anger. The person using the passive-aggressive approach can always claim it was an "accident" and unintentional (even though it wasn't), whereas the person using the aggressive approach left no doubt about his intent to be hurtful. The more subtle the behavior (such as "reading a book" or "conveniently forgetting to do something"), the more difficult it is to prove that the person intends to be hurtful, and the less aware the person may be that he or she has hurtful intentions. Such was the case with John and Mary.

After John and Mary lashed out at each other one morning with several rounds of hurtful insults and name-calling, they departed angrily for work, and time to plan how they would respond to each other when they were back home together that evening.

Mary thought, "Am I ever furious with that son of a bitch! He had no business calling me those names. He better apologize right away. I really love him, but I sure get tired of his nasty temper. I don't want to say or do anything else that will hurt him or keep the argument going, but when I feel I can do it *calmly*, I intend to let him know how I feel when he says those kind of things to me."

Meanwhile, John was thinking, "That bitch! Sometimes she really makes me mad! Who does she think she is calling me those names? She's in for a surprise if she thinks I'm going to let her off the hook this time. She deserves the silent treatment. When I get home tonight I'm just going to lose myself in a good book." If John had made a conscious effort to be aware of his irrational, hidden, hurtful intentions, he may have noticed his secret self-talk sounding something like this: "If she tries to say anything to me, I'll just say, 'Can't you see I'm trying to read, please don't bother me now.' She won't even be able to prove I'm giving her the silent treatment. But eventually she won't be able to tolerate her overwhelming feelings of frustration, rejection, hurt, and loneliness, and she'll start feeling so guilty and anxious that she'll want to apologize."

In the preceding scenario, if Mary followed through with her plans to approach John in a calm, rational manner, she would have been expressing herself in a nonhurtful, assertive way. On the other hand, John's irrational thinking and hurtful intentions were designed to make Mary feel uncomfortable and to manipulate her into apologizing to him. John's secret intentions illustrate how a behavior that is normally regarded as socially acceptable (in this case, reading), can be transformed into a passive-aggressive way of hurting others.

Any of the three ways of expressing anger can be learned

and unlearned. No one is predestined to express anger in one particular way. For most of us, the tendency to express anger with intentionally hurtful, open, aggressive outbursts, or indirect, passive-aggressive manipulations, or nonhurtful, direct, assertive expressions, depends to a large extent on our childhood experiences and the way our parents expressed their anger. For example, children whose parents express their anger in passive-aggressive ways often develop a tendency to express their anger in passive-aggressive ways, and they often carry that tendency with them into adulthood.

The tendency to use passive-aggressive expressions of anger can also evolve out of a need to hide or deny anger. For example, when parents believe anger is sinful, or that children should not be allowed to express anger freely, their children usually develop a habit of expressing anger in less intense, more socially acceptable, passive-aggressive ways. Children raised in homes where they frequently hear admonitions such as, "Don't get angry with me, young lady [young man]. . . . Shame on you, don't you realize it's a sin to be angry?" learn to mask their anger, or gradually convince themselves that they really aren't angry. They do this by putting new, more acceptable labels on their angry feelings such as: "upset, annoyed, disturbed, troubled, hurt, confused, or frustrated."

Abuse is another common cause of people's learning to express anger in passive-aggressive ways. Battered wives and children learn quickly that while blatant, aggressive outbursts usually result in immediate retaliation and abuse, they can often "get away with" some of the less obvious, passive-aggressive expressions of anger such as: "conveniently" forgetting, feigning tiredness, acting confused, or pretending they didn't hear what was said.

There is also a cultural bias that influences how people express their anger. In spite of all the advances American women have made toward the goal of equality between the sexes, there is still the notion that "boys will be boys" and "nice girls don't quarrel." Teachers and administrators continue to be more tolerant of playground fights among boys than among girls. Girls receive much more encouragement to work things out peacefully and quietly. Even as adults, there is still a double standard in regard to the tolerance of harsh and abusive language from males and females. If a male uses strong language, society generally views him as tough and powerful. If a female uses strong language, society generally views her as a "bitch." In other words, there is more pressure put on females to avoid aggressive expressions of anger. Consequently, females often become more adept than their male counterparts at expressing their anger in passive-aggressive ways.

As you can see, there are a variety of reasons why people develop a tendency to express their anger in passive-aggressive ways. Fortunately, it is possible to overcome that tendency and learn how to express anger in nonhurtful, assertive ways. Before considering how to overcome a tendency toward passive-aggressiveness or how to cope with passive-aggressive people, let's take a look at some typical passive-aggressive expressions of anger.

Typical Passive-Aggressive Expressions

Ordinary behaviors and passive-aggressive expressions of anger are distinguished by the *intent* behind the behavior. In order for a behavior to be a passive-aggressive expression, it must be done with the intent to hurt. If you are late for a date because you got stuck in a traffic jam, you are not being passive-aggressive. If you are late for a date because you want your date to know what it feels like to be kept waiting, then you are being passive-aggressive. If the driver of your carpool responds to you with only brief nods or quick uh-huhs because he has laryngitis, he's not being passive-aggressive. However, he is expressing his anger in a passive-aggressive way if he is deliberately giving you the silent treatment because he is upset about something you said during yesterday's commute and he wants you to feel guilty about it.

The following list is included as a guide to help you recognize some of the most frequently used passive-aggressive expressions of anger. It is not a complete list, since there are as many different passive-aggressive expressions of anger as there are people. As you look over the list, you might want to see if you uncover any areas where your anger may be leaking out, or if there are certain behaviors that you associate with your loved ones, friends, or business associates. Remember, the items on this list are not necessarily passive-aggressive behaviors. In order to qualify as passive-aggressive, they must be done with the *intent to hurt*.

TYPICAL PASSIVE-AGGRESSIVE EXPRESSIONS OF ANGER

- **READING**
  ("hiding" behind a newspaper, book, etc.)

- **JOKING**
  (hiding intentionally hurtful remarks with humor and ridicule)

- **BEING TIRED**
  (feigning tiredness in order to avoid having to interact with someone)

- **USING THE SILENT TREATMENT**
  (retaliating in a quiet way, hoping the other person will feel hurt as you feel hurt)

- **ACTING CONFUSED**
  (pretending you don't understand something, or are confused by it)

- **BEING HABITUALLY LATE**
  (lacking awareness or concern for other people's needs and schedules)

- **BEING EASILY DISTRACTED**
  (acting as though anything and everything is more interesting or important than what the other person is trying to say to you)

- EXAGGERATING THE OTHER PERSON'S BAD HABITS

- PUTTING YOURSELF DOWN
(trying to win from a "one-down" position, by soliciting pity)

- BEING CONDESCENDING

- DAWDLING
(purposefully reacting with unnecessary slowness)

- AGREEING WITH EVERYTHING
(making passive comments, such as, "Sure . . . whatever")

- BEING PASSIVELY RESISTANT
(maintaining a concealed, stubborn insistence upon having your own way)

- CRYING
(seeking sympathy or trying to induce guilt, in order to get even or control the situation)

- MINIMIZING THE OTHER PERSON'S ACCOMPLISHMENTS

- NOT HEARING
(pretending you didn't hear what was said)

- ARGUING
(insisting on having your own way by refusing to cooperate, compromise, or concede)

- BEING SARCASTIC OR PESSIMISTIC
(Discrediting the other person's ideas or efforts by acting helpless or cynical)

- LAUGHING
(discounting others' feelings by laughing them off)

- POUTING
(seeking sympathy to induce guilt)

- FORGETTING
("conveniently" forgetting to do what you agreed to do)

- QUESTIONING
(subtly expressing disdain for someone by arguing or being oppositional)

- STATING YOU'RE *NOT* ANGRY
("innocently" denying you're angry, when in fact you are)

- GIVING A "DOUBLE MESSAGE"
(stating one thing while demonstrating the opposite)

- PROCRASTINATING
  (putting it off on purpose)

- DOING THINGS FAR
  BETTER THAN THEY
  NEED TO BE DONE
  (trying to make others feel
  inadequate)

- MAKING MISTAKES
  ("accidentally" doing something wrong on purpose)

- BEING INEFFICIENT
  (purposefully avoiding certain
  tasks)

- UNDER- OR OVEREATING
  (using eating as an expression
  of retaliation or anger)

- GETTING SICK
  (seeking sympathy; willing
  yourself ill out of feelings of
  bitterness, frustration, hurt,
  helplessness, and anger)

- BEING CLUMSY
  ("accidentally" breaking something on purpose)

- WALKING AWAY
  (passively withdrawing)

- GOSSIPING
  (spreading malicious rumors
  about other people)

- LYING
  (stating untruths or holding
  back certain facts, with the
  intent of hurting someone's
  character)

- OVERINVOLVEMENT
  (overextending yourself as a
  way of avoiding someone, or
  not having time to respond to
  his or her needs)

- ALLOWING SOMEONE TO
  GET HURT

Tips for Reducing Passive-Aggressiveness, and Learning How to Express Anger in Constructive, Nonhurtful Ways

If you recognized your own behavior in several of the items in the preceding list, you might be expressing your anger in passive-aggressive ways more frequently than you realized. If so, you will probably find the chapters on Self-Awareness, Letting Go, Not Taking It Personally, Self-Talk, and Adjusting Your Expectations particularly helpful.

Since each of these techniques will be described more fully in part 3, the following discussion serves mainly to clarify how each of the techniques benefits people who are looking for ways to break their passive-aggressive habits.

Self-Awareness

If you are trying to reduce your passive-aggressive behavior and learn to control your anger and express it more appropriately, one of the first things you'll want to become aware of is the *real* source of your anger. It is important to recognize whether it was the event itself, or an unpleasant memory triggered by that event, that led to your angry feelings.

Next, you'll benefit from getting in touch with your intentions. Ask yourself, "Am I doing this because I want to hurt someone or retaliate; or am I going to use this situation as an opportunity for facilitating positive change or reconciliation?" The more aware you are of when, where, and how you are hurtful, or trying to induce guilt in others, the more control you'll have over your behavior.

Another way to strengthen your personal anger control is by increasing your awareness of how you are responding to others, both verbally and nonverbally. As Harriet Lerner explains in *The Dance of Anger*, people who feel trapped and victimized in debilitating, dependent relationships are usually unaware of how their own behavior is often perpetuating the very patterns of interaction that they would like to change. Through self-awareness, you can begin to see how your response style is influencing your relationships and how your behavior might be keeping you in debilitating, dependent roles.

For example, many adults who are upset because their parents still treat them as if they were children are unaware that they are continuing to respond to their parents in childlike ways. A typical example of this type of nonproductive interchange is found in grandparents admonishing their adult children for the way they discipline, or fail to discipline, the grandchildren. Usually, neither the grandparents nor the adult children are aware of their ongoing battle or their habitual patterns of relating to one another. When adult children are talked down to by their parents, as if they were young children, they experience feelings of disrespect, hurt, frustration, and anger. Unless they are self-aware, their feelings may eventually leak out in passive-aggressive behaviors that perpetuate the ongoing cycle of ineffective interactions and keep both generations locked into their original roles of parent and child. The older parents stay in their role of "parent" and the younger parents remain in their role of "child."

Another important area of self-awareness for controlling passive-aggressive tendencies focuses on being aware of your strengths and weaknesses and your likes and dislikes. Get in touch with what really makes you feel better and what gets on your nerves. Encourage yourself to make time to do those things that are important to you. You deserve it. Besides, taking time out for yourself isn't as selfish as it may appear to you. In the long run, doing things that help you feel better about yourself actually helps make you better equipped to respond to others in nonhurtful, assertive ways.

Letting Go

People who say, "I *can't* let go" usually mean, "I *won't* let go." You can free yourself from the restrictive bonds of anger by choosing to let go of as little or as much of it as you want, at your own pace, until your anger is reduced to a manageable level. By controlling the intensity of your anger, you can control what impact it has on you. Letting go of excess or long-standing anger enables you to use the energy generated by your controlled and rational anger to help you reach your goals in positive, nonhurtful ways. People who hold on to their anger, instead of letting go of it, often stay hooked on self-destructive, dependent relationships and continue to be victimized by their own anger. When you allow yourself to let go, you not only free yourself from the burden of past hurts and anger, but you gain a new sense of power, strength, freedom, and control.

Not Taking It Personally

Traditional wisdom suggests that one way to control the impact that anger-provoking situations have on you is by not taking the provocation personally. That's often easier said than done. Some of the ways to make it easier to take provocations less personally include: emotionally disengaging from the provocation; maintaining or strengthening your self-esteem and self-confidence; and increasing your capacity to empathize with others and control your self-centeredness.

Emotionally disengaging. As you will see in chapter 30, emotionally disengaging involves separating yourself mentally, emotionally, and physically (when possible) from the provocation, so that you are controlling the degree of intensity of your emotional reaction. When you are emotionally disengaged, it is as if your emotions are in "neutral." By emotionally disengaging, you increase your objectivity and decrease your susceptibility to anger, hurt, and frustration. If you find yourself enmeshed in an anger-provoking situation, one way to emotionally disengage immediately from that situation is to imagine that you are merely observing the situation happening to a stranger instead of to yourself.

Self-centeredness. Another factor that contributes to people's ability to put anger-provoking situations into perspective and not take them personally is their degree of self-centeredness. It is important to recognize the difference between self-centeredness and self-esteem. Self-centeredness is a person's concern for self gone out of control. If you were to use physical terminology to describe the "concern for self" continuum, low self-esteem would be labeled "malnourished," positive self-esteem would be labeled "healthy," and self-centeredness would be labeled "obese." People who are self-centered aren't concerned with other people's needs or feelings. In contrast to that, people who have positive self-esteem are more inclined to be receptive to other people's needs and feelings. Generally speaking, the less self-centered and more empathic you can be about a particular provocation, the easier it will be for you to keep your anger at a manageable level, and the more control you'll have over your anger.

Self-esteem. For most people, the better they feel about themselves, the less they want to express their anger in ways that will hurt themselves or others. That is why it is so important to do whatever you can to improve your self-esteem. One way to increase your self-esteem is by associating with people who are respectful and supportive of you. It is much more important to develop and nurture a few good, healthy friendships than it is to maintain scores of superficial, uncaring relationships. Quality relationships can provide you with a genuine sense of acceptance and belonging, give you the courage to say "no" without having to fear rejection, and provide the emotional support that helps you feel better about yourself. When self-esteem increases, there's often a corresponding increase in ability and desire to express anger in more appropriate ways, and a decrease in self-defeating, hurtful expressions of anger.

Self-Talk

Some of the quickest and most effective ways to increase self-esteem and decrease passive-aggressive behavior involve self-talk. By "tuning in" to your self-talk you can be aware of any negative thoughts and immediately use the thought-stopping process to change from esteem-depleting *negative* self-talk to esteem-building *positive* self-talk.

There are many ways of structuring your private thoughts, but you'll get the most out of self-talk by transforming your internal dialogue into an "as if" format. For instance, rather than thinking: "I wish I felt strong, healthy, alert, vibrant, energetic, and enthusiastic"; transform that phrase into one that states it in the positive, "as if" it were already true: "I'm feeling strong, healthy, alert, vibrant, energetic, and enthusiastic." By repeating positive phrases to yourself over and over again, in a calm, reassuring, and assertive manner, and using the "as if" format, you dramatically increase the likelihood that the content of your self-talk will eventually become actual statements of fact.

Each of the following self-talk statements is designed to help people reduce their passive-aggressive behaviors by bolstering their self-esteem through the process of positive self-affirmation. As Robert Louis Stevenson said, "A friend is a present you give yourself." You may find the following statements helpful to you, but we encourage you to person-alize the self-talk process by creating and using your own positive, affirming self-talk statements that pertain directly to your specific situations and circumstances, and are worded in ways that feel comfortable, natural, and nurturing. (For further information about how to use self-talk to help man-age your anger see chapter 22.)

- "I like me."
- "I love who I am."
- "God always loves me."
- "I feel calm and in control of my life."
- "It's okay to win and succeed."
- "I deserve to feel happy."
- "I can say 'no' and still be accepted by my friends."
- "It's okay to make mistakes; I can learn from them."
- "It's okay to be less than perfect."
- "It's okay to play."
- "It's okay to stop taking my-self *too* seriously."
- "I can overcome challenges."
- "I'm capable of taking care of most of my needs."
- "I'm resourceful. I know how to get help when I need it."
- "I'm able to emotionally dis-engage from stressful situations and handle them appropriately."

- "I appreciate and respect me."

- "I'm proud of my accomplishments."

- "God is always with me."

- "I feel centered emotionally, spiritually, and physically."

- "I feel powerful and effective."

- "I enjoy helping others because they need my assistance, not because I need their friendship."

- "I deserve to look as good as I can."

- "I'm worthy of respect."

- "I deserve to reward myself with special treats or activities."

- "My feelings are valid."

- "It's okay to feel happy or positive even if others feel sad or negative."

- "I allow others to be responsible for their own feelings."

- "I'm not responsible for making other people happy."

- "I enjoy showing others the kindness and respect they deserve."

- "I deserve this time for myself to enjoy a favorite activity."

Adjusting Your Expectations

As you will see in chapter 28, even though you can't always control other people's behavior, or avoid anger-provoking situations, you can control your expectations. Whenever I stubbornly hold on to my irrational, unrealistic expectations that other people need to change, instead of choosing to adjust my expectations to make my own changes, I end up feeling extremely frustrated, bitter, and angry. On the other hand, whenever I get in touch with my expectations by listening to my self-talk, and adjust them so that they are more rational and realistic, my level of frustration, bitterness, and anger is greatly reduced. To see for yourself how closely your emotions are linked with your expectations, try the following experiment. The next time you feel yourself starting to get angry, tune in to your expectations by listening to your self-talk. Are you hearing phrases such as, "I wish he'd stop being so _____, and be more _____," or, "Maybe this time he'll _____." If so, your expectations may be too high or unrealistic, and you may want to adjust them until they are closer to the reality of the situation. In most situations, lowering your expectations helps lower the frequency, intensity, and duration of your anger, and increases your ability to express anger in nonhurtful, constructive, assertive ways.

Coping with Passive-Aggressive People

Perhaps you don't normally express your anger in passive-aggressive ways, but you live or work with someone who does. Just as self-awareness is essential to managing your anger, awareness is the key to coping with other people's passive-aggressive behavior. It's much easier to maintain your emotional balance when you are aware of when others may be trying to hurt you, get their own way, or coerce you into apologizing or accepting responsibility for their feelings. Passive-aggressive behaviors are designed to induce guilt, evoke sympathy, and instill or prolong feelings of anger, hurt, or frustration in others. Once you are alert to other people's passive-aggressive behaviors you can begin to protect yourself from getting drawn into their trap by emotionally disengaging and allowing them to take ownership of their feelings. You can also avoid reinforcing other people's passive-aggressive behaviors, and inadvertently increasing the likelihood that they'll repeat their manipulative passive-aggressive behaviors, by responding to them in emotionally neutral, adult to adult, assertive ways. Acting guilty, offering sympathy, or complying with their inappropriate or unreasonable requests may seem the best way to restore harmony, but in the long run it reinforces their passive-aggressive behavior. When Carol responded to my pouting by fixing the cookies I wanted, she unwittingly reinforced my behavior, and I felt encouraged to sulk again the next time I didn't get my way. After she realized what was happening, she emotionally disengaged from my passive-aggressive behavior, refused to accept ownership of my feelings of frustration, hurt, or anger, and learned to calmly but assertively deny my inappropriate or unreasonable requests without rejecting me as a person. Eventually I learned that my pouting didn't work anymore, and I gradually became less inclined to try to manipulate Carol with passive-aggressive behaviors.

In addition to following the steps for responding to angry people outlined in appendix D, "Quick Guide for Coping with Angry People," it is particularly important to remember the four *P*'s (patience, persistence, positive reinforcement, and positive regard) when responding to a passive-aggressive person.

Patience. Passive-aggressive people appreciate and benefit from those who respond to them with understanding and firmness combined with gentleness and patience. You can make interacting with passive-aggressive people more pleasant for you, as well as for them, by understanding why they choose passive-aggressive instead of aggressive or assertive behaviors; firmly resisting their efforts to knock you off your emotional balance; and patiently providing them with the time and space they need to recover their emotional composure and be able to transform their anger into rational, nonhurtful expressions. Resisting a passive-aggressive person's efforts to make you feel frustrated, angry, or guilty is *not* an aggressive or passive-aggressive action you take against anyone else. It is a gift you give yourself—the gift of allowing yourself to stay emotionally disengaged and free from having to take responsibility for someone else's feelings or behavior.

As we mentioned earlier, there are many reasons why some people prefer the protection of subtle, hard-to-detect expressions of anger, and the satisfaction of making the object of their anger suffer some type of physical, emotional, or mental discomfort. For these people, being straightforward and nonhurtful with their anger is scary and foreign, but not impossible. They can choose to work on improving their self-esteem, on accepting responsibility for their feelings and behavior, and on learning how to express themselves in appropriate, nonhurtful assertive ways. In the meantime (and it may take a long time), it will be helpful to the passive-aggressive person if you maintain patience and understanding.

Persistence. You can help passive-aggressive people develop and strengthen their ability to express their anger in nonhurtful, assertive ways by serving as a positive role model. When you persistently and consistently approach and respond to them in an appropriate, assertive manner, the passive-aggressive people with whom you interact may develop a greater sense of respect for you and choose to imitate and adopt some of your healthy, nonhurtful, assertive expressions of anger.

Positive reinforcement. Another way to help passive-aggressive people become more comfortable with expressing themselves in assertive ways is by reinforcing their attempts to be straightforward and direct. In order to increase the impact you have on their behavior, it's important to recognize and encourage what may appear to you as only slight improvements or minor positive changes in the way they express themselves. That's because what looks like an insignificant difference to you may have involved a tremendous amount of effort on their part. As someone who has a strong tendency toward behaving in passive-aggressive ways, I can verify from personal as well as professional experience that the best kinds of reinforcement for helping others to decrease their passive-aggressive behaviors and increase their assertive expressions are recognition, encouragement, and support. I attribute my progress toward replacing my passive-aggressive behaviors with assertive statements more to Carol's repeated acknowledgments and statements of appreciation of my efforts than to any other type of reinforcement, including her delicious, homemade cookies. Even though I appreciate it when Carol makes a batch just for me, I respond best to her direct acknowledgment and support of my efforts. If you feel uncomfortable stating your appreciation for someone's attempt to be more assertive, you can still be encouraging by showing your appreciation through your behavior. A positive, nonhurtful response to their efforts can be very reinforcing, as Bruce and Karen's experience illustrates.

Bruce was trying to focus on the English papers he needed to have graded by the next morning. Karen had the stereo turned up so loud that Bruce was having trouble maintaining his concentration. He felt his frustration escalating, but instead of continuing to pretend he wasn't bothered by the loud music, or of thinking of ways he could "get even" with Karen later that evening, he stated as directly and calmly as he could, "Karen, I would appreciate it if you would please turn the volume down on the stereo. I'm having difficulty getting this work done when it's so loud." Realizing that neither a sarcastic nor self-centered response would be helpful, Karen decided to avoid such hurtful, discouraging responses as, "Well, *sorrrrry*! I didn't realize you were so easily distracted," or, "Tough! That's your problem. I happen to like it this loud." Instead, Karen chose to respond in a way that would clearly demonstrate her appreciation for Bruce's assertive statement. She quickly went over to the stereo and turned it down. Through her respectful, cooperative *behavior*, Karen reinforced Bruce's effort to express his feelings in appropriate, respectful, assertive ways.

Positive regard. Because people with strong passive-aggressive tendencies often equate criticism or disagreement with rejection, it's not uncommon to feel as if you are walking on eggshells when dealing with them. Many of their passive-aggressive behaviors are triggered by their desire to protect themselves from the pain they experience when faced with criticism or disagreement. When confronting someone who frequently uses passive-aggressive behaviors, you can minimize his or her resistance and desire for retaliation by first making it clear that you value him or her as a person before commenting on the specific behavior you dislike, and concluding the confrontation with some specific things you appreciate about that person. By letting people who rely on passive-aggressive behaviors know you value them, even though you don't appreciate their specific passive-aggressive behavior, you are helping to increase their feelings of self-worth and self-esteem. Through your patience, persistence, positive reinforcement, and positive regard, you strengthen not only their self-respect but their respect for others. The better they feel about themselves, the less interested they will be in hurting others, and the more interested they will be in expressing their feelings in appropriate, nonhurtful, assertive ways.

Remember, the opposite of passive-aggressive behavior is *assertiveness*—not aggressiveness. As you will see in the next chapter, aggressive behavior may look different from passive-aggressive behavior, but the underlying *intention* between the two types of behaviors is the same: They are both designed to hurt.

CHAPTER FIVE

Aggressive Anger

Have you been taught that you should reduce your anger by "letting it all out" in some explosive way, such as hitting a pillow or screaming at the top of your lungs for two minutes? If so, you've been taught how to *increase* your anger.

Many people, including a number of professional therapists, still hold on to the myth that ventilation is the way to reduce anger. The myth persists throughout all segments of our society. Television shows and movies are filled with violence and examples of aggressive outbursts that enable the aggressors to succeed in getting what they want or controlling the situation. Instead of the media focusing on examples of creative, constructive ways to resolve conflict, they often encourage violence and promote the message that ventilating is the best way to use anger to your personal advantage. According to Rosalind Miles, author of *Love, Sex, Death, and the Making of the Male*, "the average American boy ... may have seen up to 200,000 acts of television violence by the age of sixteen, including 33,000 murders."

In their book *Creative Aggression*, authors George Bach and Herb Goldberg encourage people who are angry at work or at home to "vent their pent-up frustrations, resentments, hurt, hostilities, and rage in a full-throated, screaming outburst" or to use a cloth bat to spank the person who angered them while ". . . shouting insults and phrases of condemnation with each stroke." "Encounter bats" continue to be advertised, twenty years after their inception, as an excellent device for aggression release. There are countless toys and devices marketed as ideal for release of pent-up anger, frustration, or stress. Among them are: toys designed to tolerate however many hits you feel like giving them, and still bounce back for more; boxes full of plastic bubbles you can pop until you get tired of stomping and shouting; and toys that supposedly zap away frustrations in your car, at the office, or anywhere by imitating the sound effects of machine guns, bombs, grenades, rifles, etc.

In *I Can If I Want To*, Arnold Lazarus and Allen Fay offer their version of cathartic release of anger when they suggest, ". . . set aside a period of two minutes for a contrived fight at a fixed time each day . . . during that period of time, yell at each other, curse at each other, and go beyond anything you might say in a spontaneous fight."

The techniques that Bach and Goldberg and Lazarus and Fay promote are commonly referred to as cathartic techniques because they supposedly cleanse your body of all its anger. The theory upon which they base their techniques has two main suppositions:

1. Reacting aggressively to an anger-provoking situation will enable you to feel almost as calm as you were before you became angry.
2. Reacting aggressively toward someone who angers

you will reduce the likelihood that you'll want to act aggressively toward that person again.

Letting It Out Isn't Purging, It's Practicing

The expression of anger is a form of communication. How you express your anger is your personal way of communicating. The more successful you are in communicating in a certain manner, the more likely you'll continue to use that way of communicating.

Whatever action you associate with angry feelings becomes a habit, especially when the action appears to be immediately rewarding. If you have been reinforced for ranting and raving, or striking out at others when you are angry, because your aggressive ventilations got the immediate response you desired, then it is likely you will continue to use those same expressions of anger the next time you feel angry. The more reinforced someone has been for aggressive expressions of anger, the more habituated he or she becomes to those aggressive behaviors, and the more difficult it may be for that person to break the aggressive habit and develop new ways to express anger.

Consider the sentence: "I'm so angry I could . . . !" How would you finish it? Would you fill in the blank with a word indicative of an aggressive response to anger, such as: scream, spit, hit, or swear? Or would you say, "I'm so angry I could *relax*!" Part of the process of breaking the habit of expressing your anger in hurtful ways is learning to pair your angry feelings with pleasant, calming thoughts and nonhurtful, assertive actions.

Research[1] shows that "letting out" all of your anger in a cathartic manner often leaves you feeling more uptight, not less. Aggressive outbursts may result in fear of retaliation, or feeling guilty because you showed disrespect for a person

[1] See bibliography for specific research studies.

of authority or esteem, such as your boss or parent. Yelling at your co-worker or slapping your spouse may cause you to feel better momentarily, but it doesn't go far in reducing the likelihood that you'll react to that person in an aggressive way again. You are actually increasing the chance that you'll express your anger to that person aggressively the next time he or she angers you.

When You Let It Out Does It Stay Out?

Letting out your anger may allow you to release some of the tension you were feeling, if you aren't worried about the consequences of your outburst. But you will also increase the chance that the next time you are angry you'll let it out aggressively again. You'll grow increasingly accustomed to releasing your anger more frequently and more aggressively. For example, according to a newspaper article about two firing ranges in Marietta, Georgia, customers are able to rent submachine guns to "Ramboize" their old computer terminals, toasters, or television sets. Customers usually spend about twice as much money on second visits than they did on their first, indicating that they require more violence and aggression to achieve their initial feeling of release.

You may think you're purging yourself of your anger when you let it out in aggressive outbursts, but you are actually practicing how you will express it on future occasions, as the following example illustrates.

> Before I became Ron's staff psychologist, he had been seen by another therapist at the hospital who encouraged him to "vent" his anger by hitting a large canvas body bag like boxers use. Ron hit the rough canvas bag with his bare knuckles so frequently and so intensely that his hands became raw, requiring the staff to purchase lightweight boxing gloves for protection.

One day another youth tore the bag with a knife, rendering it unavailable for Ron's use for about three weeks. During that time, whenever Ron felt angry he would hit the walls, the furniture, other youth, or staff. After these angry outbursts Ron was put into a special discipline room to calm down, but rather than calm down, he would hit the walls or smash the windows with his bare fists, causing big, ugly gashes in his hands.

Instead of serving as a release for his anger, hitting the bag actually caused Ron's angry feelings to *increase*, and his sense of self-control and self-worth to decrease. Ron's experiences with the bag had taught him that when you are angry, you hit. It didn't matter to Ron what he hit, he just wanted to hit.

Why "Letting It All Out" Actually "Lets It All Back In"

Having other people understand and appreciate *your* needs is one of the benefits of managing your anger. When your boss refuses to give you a raise, when your spouse treats you disrespectfully, when your child refuses to do what he's been asked to do, when your neighbor backs into your hedge, or when any of these or similar things happen, you probably will feel angry. That is because your need for compensation, respect, cooperation, privacy, or special relationships has been disregarded.

It is natural to feel angry when your needs aren't being recognized. But in order to facilitate the desired understanding of your needs, it is helpful for you to recognize the needs of the other person. When you are ventilating your feelings, you aren't taking time to think about anyone else's needs or feelings. Consequently, *ventilating* your anger—letting it all hang out—actually serves to move you further from any kind of reconciliation or understanding and further from resolving your anger.

For example, when an employee ventilates his anger toward his boss because his request for a raise is denied, he usually decreases his chances that his boss will reconsider his decision. Most bosses confronted by a ranting and raving employee quickly lose interest in the employee's demands. Instead, they concentrate on their own desire for respect, low overhead, and good-natured employees. In short, ventilating to one's boss is usually counterproductive. Shouting, kicking, and/or swearing might intimidate your co-workers into getting a tool, pen, or report for you, but such aggression will also decrease the respect, rapport, and cooperation you can expect to have with your co-workers in the future. Repeatedly ventilating your anger about the garbage collector who spilled part of your trash all over your driveway five months ago won't undo the mess that he left for you to clean up, but it will keep your mind focused on your anger and frustration, and off your ability to enjoy each day to its fullest.

In tragic situations such as the murder of a close friend, the senseless death of a loved one because of a drunk driver, or your being robbed or raped, you probably are too livid with rage to care whether the perpetrator of these crimes is having his needs met. In these or similar circumstances you may feel that intense or prolonged ventilation would be beneficial. *Not so!* Continued ventilation, even though it may seem therapeutic at the time, serves no purpose other than to pollute your immediate environment with your angry feelings. It is very important to be aware of your anger and express it in constructive ways, but ventilating your anger and repeatedly expressing your vindictive thoughts keeps the hurt and anger fresh in your mind.

Let's take a closer look at some of the contrasts between aggressively ventilating your anger and resolving your anger with assertive anger management techniques by taking the imaginary train rides in the next chapter. All aboard!

CHAPTER SIX

What Will You Do with Your Anger?

As mentioned in chapter 2, whenever you are thinking angry thoughts or experiencing angry feelings, you always have three choices: how intense your anger will be; how long your anger will last; and what you will do with your anger. The third choice—what you will do with your anger—actually involves making a decision about your intentions. Do you want your expressions of anger to be hurtful or nonhurtful? Most people are capable of getting in touch with their intentions before they take *action* with their angry thoughts or feelings, and usually take less than a second to do so.

Whether you are mildly annoyed, or so steaming mad you feel as if you're going to boil over, you are the one who controls *how* your anger is expressed. The choice is yours. You can either be hurtful or nonhurtful with your anger. The two types of anger described in chapters 4 and 5, passive-aggressive and aggressive, are both ways to be *hurtful* with your anger. *Nonhurtful* expressions of anger involve "assertive" expressions of your feelings. The following description of two train trips illustrates the contrast between choosing to be hurtful versus choosing to be nonhurtful with your anger. These trips represent taking action or expressing your feelings. The first ride, aboard the Cathartic Outburst Express, illustrates the typical route that hurtful, aggressive expressions usually take. The second ride, aboard the Resolution Railway, illustrates what happens when you express your anger in nonhurtful, assertive ways.

THE CATHARTIC OUTBURST EXPRESS

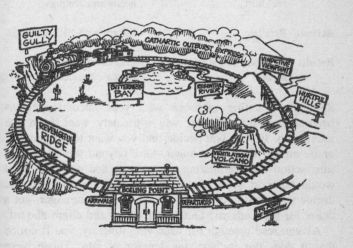

Imagine that someone or something has provoked your anger. You are so hot with anger that you are close to your "boiling point" and feel as if you could explode at any moment. Before you take *action* on your angry thoughts and feelings, you can choose to buy a ticket for the Cathartic Outburst Express or a ticket for the Resolution Railway. The easiest way to decide which ticket to purchase is by getting in touch with your intentions, to determine whether you want to be hurtful or nonhurtful with your anger. For most people, getting in touch with their intentions usually takes less than a second.

INTENTIONS

	Hurtful	Nonhurtful
Goal:	To hurt the person physically or emotionally as you feel hurt	To facilitate the understanding and appreciation of your needs and feelings
Action:	Retaliate	Inform with "I" messages
Result:	Increased anger and resentment	Decreased anger Increased understanding

Remember, getting in touch with your intentions means becoming aware of what you ultimately want from the interaction. Before you decide that you want to "get even" or be hurtful with your anger, look beyond the short-term satisfaction that ventilating may bring, and consider what would be most satisfying to you in the *long run*. If you decide you would prefer to be hurtful with your anger, get a ticket for the Cathartic Outburst Express and climb aboard.

As you read through the following itinerary, you'll notice that it does not include any lengths of stay. Those were omitted on purpose, because how long you stay at any one spot along the route, or how many times you go around the loop and complete the anger-retaliation-anger cycle, is up to you. Some people complete the trip and return to their boiling point in just a few seconds, while others seem never to get enough, and just stay on board for the rest of their lives, going around and around, time after time. You may decide to stay on it for a few minutes, hours, or days; or for several weeks, months, or years. The choice is *yours*.

Boiling Point. The trip on the Cathartic Outburst Express begins at the Boiling Point (the point at which you are boiling over with anger). This is where you get your ticket, hop on board, and ride nonstop to the Ventilation Volcano.

Ventilation Volcano. At the Ventilation Volcano, you release part of your excess energy by screaming, kicking, hitting, swearing, or indulging in any other aggressive activity you feel like doing. This "letting off steam" may seem to help you rid yourself of your overwhelming anger, but beware.

Hurtful Hills. After the Cathartic Outburst Express leaves the Ventilation Volcano, it travels up the Hurtful Hills. As you wind your way through these hills, the fleeting relief you felt when you left the Ventilation Volcano disappears as you angrily express all the hurtful remarks and spiteful names you can think of to the person with whom you are angry. These angry outbursts help you focus on the targeted person's faults and misdeeds and allow the intensity of your anger to grow as you climb higher and higher up the Hurtful Hills. The route through these hills is far from scenic. Many people find it gets quite ugly as they come face to face with hurtful remarks hurled back at them from the object of their ire.

Vindictive Viewpoint. What a spectacle awaits you here! By the time you finish climbing through the Hurtful Hills and reach the Vindictive Viewpoint, you see nothing but red! Your mind is filled not only with vivid images of the anger-provoking incident that got you to your Boiling Point in the first place, but with all of the ugly, hurtful statements and retaliatory actions taken against you along the way. Instead of the sense of satisfaction you felt as you left the Ventilation Volcano and started your climb up the Hurtful Hills, all you are aware of is the anguish you are currently feeling as a result of the other person's cruel remarks along the way, and the lack of an apology from that person for whatever he or she said or did that triggered your anger in the first place.

Resentful River. The Cathartic Outburst Express follows the course of the Resentful River as it goes from the Vindictive Viewpoint to Bitterness Bay. Not only are you resenting the other person's refusal to apologize, but the other person is resenting everything you've said along the way. The predominant self-talk for both you and the person with whom you are angry is, "I'm going to get even if it's the last thing I do."

Bitterness Bay. At this point in your journey, many unpleasant feelings are pooled together and reflected in the Bitterness Bay. Your feelings of anger, hurt, and vindictiveness are confronted by the bitter and resentful emotions that have been building up in the victim of your ventilation.

Guilty Gully. Because of all the expressions of bitterness and resentment with which you are being bombarded, you may not realize, until it is too late, that the Cathartic Outburst Express has made a sharp turn away from your desired destination—the Point of Resolution—and has headed quickly toward the Guilty Gully. Once you reach the Guilty Gully, some of the emotional outbursts fired at you along the way have had time to form a volatile mixture of anger and guilt, as well as other emotions that usually accompany anger. (Emotions that are often experienced along with anger include, but are by no means limited to: frustration, hurt, vindictiveness, fear, anxiety, depression, helplessness, irritation, hate, and rage.) You may question for a moment how appropriate your actions and reactions have been. But by now your anger is so intense that you're more focused on getting even than on apologizing.

Revengeful Ridge. This can be the most dangerous part of your journey. The Cathartic Outburst Express travels precariously along the Revengeful Ridge, because it would be easy for the victim of your ventilation to knock you off your emotional balance. Throughout your trip, you have given the recipient of your anger so many reasons to develop feelings of anger, bitterness, and resentment that the recipient is expanding his or her efforts to retaliate and get revenge. Whatever hurtful things you have said or done along the route get thrown back at you, and when this happens, it's usually with an even greater desire to be hurtful than what you originally intended.

As you ride along the Revengeful Ridge, you realize you are far from achieving any resolution of your anger. In fact, you are getting closer and closer to your original point of departure, your Boiling Point.

Boiling Point. You have come full circle, and so have your emotions. Your adventures aboard the Cathartic Outburst Express have brought you right back to your Boiling Point. The brief sense of relief you experienced at the Ventilation Volcano has been undone and reversed by the experiences you had along the rest of the journey. You have gone the long way around just to return to where you began, and your anger is far from over. In fact, the intensity of your anger is probably greater than when you boarded the Cathartic Outburst Express the first time you reached your Boiling Point. Now, in addition to your anger, you have even more emotional baggage to take with you. You have accumulated feelings of revenge, guilt, bitterness, resentment, vindictiveness, and hurtfulness. Now that you are back at your Boiling Point, you are faced with the same decision you had last time you were here. Do you want to be hurtful or nonhurtful with your anger? If you are feeling less than satisfied with the journey that lies ahead of you aboard the Cathartic Outburst Express, you can disembark and choose the Resolution Railway, the route that gets you to the point where you can resolve your anger.

RIDING THE RESOLUTION RAILWAY

The big dome and spacious windows of the dining car provide a panoramic view of your anger. Your increased awareness intensifies your desire to reach the Point of Resolution. You look at the menu, which features more than twenty constructive anger management techniques. Among your choices are: Power Relaxation; Positive Self-Talk; Not Taking Things Personally; Adjusting Your Expectations; Therapeutic Counting; Communicating with "I Messages"; Deep Breathing; Keeping an Anger Diary; and Self-Awareness. You are encouraged to choose any technique or combination of techniques from the menu and utilize them whenever you feel angry.

Anger management is a process of making choices. The difference between uncontrolled anger and successfully managed anger is *self-awareness*. The more you choose to be aware of what affects your anger, the more capable you'll be of making the choices that lead to constructive and successful resolution of your anger.

When you are aware of your anger and respond to it with constructive anger management techniques, you *resolve* rather than *recycle* your anger. Resolved anger doesn't renew itself. Unlike your journey on the Cathartic Outburst Express, the Resolution Railway doesn't circle back to your Boiling Point. Your anger may be elicited by a new provocation after you've passed the Point of Resolution, but your anger will be limited to that new provocation.

It's a Matter of Choice

Whenever you reach your Boiling Point, what you do with your anger is your choice. Remember, no matter who or what causes your anger, you always have three choices.

HOW LONG WILL YOUR ANGER LAST?

WHAT WILL YOU DO WITH YOUR ANGER?

The Cathartic Outburst Express may seem more adventuresome, and more scenic, but it can't get you to your Point of Resolution. When you want to resolve your anger, riding the Resolution Railway is the right choice.

CHAPTER SEVEN

Assertive Anger

As demonstrated by the Resolution Railway ride, you can express your anger without being aggressive or passive-aggressive. You can choose to be assertive.

The difference between being aggressive and being assertive depends on your intentions and goals. When you act aggressively, your intentions are to hurt someone physically or emotionally. The typical goals of aggressive behavior are to exploit, manipulate, wound, and/or humiliate someone else. When you choose to be assertive, your intentions are to maintain, improve, or successfully dissolve your relationship with someone. The goals of assertive behavior are to facilitate the understanding and appreciation of your needs and feelings, while respecting the needs and feelings of the other person.

Assertiveness in Action

Dr. Nash, the staff psychologist, took only a few seconds to respond to his colleague's phone call.

But Dr. Gorkum, the physician in charge of the Patient Care Team meeting, began reprimanding Dr. Nash the moment he put down the receiver. He demanded that Dr. Nash instruct his colleagues never to call him again while he was in a team meeting.

Dr. Nash's blood immediately began to boil. He felt like blurting out, "You take calls anytime you want. How dare you tell me not to take any calls from my colleagues!"

But rather than fire back at Dr. Gorkum in an aggressive and hurtful way, Dr. Nash took a slow, deep breath. He realized that in order for his response to be constructive, he would need to confront Dr. Gorkum at the right time and place, use the right tone of voice, and have the right attitude and intentions.

The next day, when and where no other people could hear their conversation, Dr. Nash said, "Dr. Gorkum, I didn't appreciate you telling me I couldn't take any more calls from my colleagues. Those calls are very important. If you didn't want me to take the call right at that moment, you could have asked the secretary to take a message. But you handed me the phone, so I thought it would be okay to take the call. What bothered me the most about yesterday's situation was your reprimanding me in front of other staff members and the patient. I can't imagine that you would appreciate such a public reprimand. Also, I was bothered by the way you spoke to me. It was more like a parent disciplining a small child than an adult talking to another adult.

"The more I think about your request, the less comfortable I feel about complying with it. I want my colleagues to appreciate you as much as I do and I don't want to say something that might lessen their respect for you. I've shared with them how competent and knowledgeable you are about medications and psychotherapeutic techniques. And I've mentioned how supportive you are when I suggest different treatment interventions. I'm afraid that if I relayed your demand to my colleagues, it might lessen their respect for you.

"Also, I don't believe we should get into the practice of censoring each other's calls. I respect your right to screen your own calls and I expect you to respect my right to do the same."

If you could have heard Dr. Nash talking to Dr. Gorkum, you would have noticed that he was speaking in a very quiet, low-key, calm voice. Dr. Nash's tone of voice, facial expressions, body gestures, and the pace of his speech all demonstrated to Dr. Gorkum that Dr. Nash had no intention of putting him down or making him feel bad. Dr. Nash's assertive response clearly indicated that his intentions were to strengthen his working relationship with Dr. Gorkum and prevent a rift from developing between them.

You may have experienced a "Dr. Gorkum" in your life. Perhaps your "Dr. Gorkum" is your boss, spouse, co-worker, or parent. You may even have more than one "Dr. Gorkum." By taking a moment to reflect, you'll be able to recall how your "Dr. Gorkum" has affected you and how you have responded to him (or them).

Anger is a natural and normal emotional reaction to a wide variety of situations and circumstances. You can express your anger in subtle, indirect ways, or by "letting it all hang out." Either way, you'll be increasing your anger and provoking anger in others. Or, you can make your anger work for you by expressing it in constructive, assertive ways. *It's your choice!*

PART TWO

Why Do People Get Angry?

CHAPTER EIGHT

What Is the Environmental Impact on Your Anger?

People become angry for a variety of reasons and express their anger in many ways, but why do some people react angrily to some things when other people don't? Why do some people seem angrier than others? Why do some people seem to have an easier time coping with angry feelings and angry people?

- What affects your emotional trigger?
- What causes you to feel angry more frequently or less frequently than other people?
- What causes you to feel your anger more intensely or less intensely than other people?
- Why do you choose to express your anger in a hurtful or a nonhurtful way?

Anger is an emotional reaction to a current provocation or the memory of a former one. That reaction is influenced by many factors. When you are aware of these factors it is easier for you to *choose* how much influence they will have on you and your anger. This chapter considers the impact one's environment can have on anger. Other factors influencing how people react to various provocations are discussed in the remaining chapters of this section.

Loud noises, crowded spaces, intense or flickering lights, extremely hot or cold rooms, excessive commotion, or other distractions can be very irritating. That is why it is important to be aware of the conditions of your surroundings. Your interactions will be least likely to provoke other people's anger when they are conducted in the most pleasant surroundings possible, or when you take the environmental conditions into consideration. If, for example, you must raise your voice in order to be heard, you may be able to avoid having the listener mistakenly assume you are angry by simply prefacing your remarks with an apology for needing to shout. Similarly, if someone is talking loudly to you, consider the surroundings. Perhaps that person isn't as angry as he or she sounds but is just speaking loudly because you are in a noisy place.

People living in remote rural areas sometimes feel frustrated and angry about their lack of access to the support and companionship of others, especially during the winter months when they are snowed in and the roads are impassable. Other people feel stressed living in big cities. They may feel that many of the conditions there, such as traffic congestion, long commutes, polluted air, and loud noises, are overstimulating and leave them feeling tense and irritable. Many people are frustrated, angry, and bitter about the high crime rates in the cities. They don't feel that the streets are safe, especially at night, and often they don't feel safe even in their homes.

Changes in one's environment can also be stressful, particularly when those changes involve noticeable changes in climate, rural or metropolitan surroundings, customs, attitudes, or socioeconomic level. People accustomed to living in a lower-middle-class neighborhood who move into an upper-middle-class neighborhood (because of marriage or job-related transfer, for example) may find it difficult and stressful to adjust to their new environment. Similarly, those who are accustomed to living a more affluent lifestyle may find it difficult and stressful to adjust to living in a lower-middle-class environment. Whether the move is up or down on the socioeconomic ladder, to a warmer or colder climate, or into or away from more populated areas, adjusting to different environmental conditions can be very stressful.

People react and respond differently to different things in their environment. What seems normal, natural, and peaceful to one person may seem very abnormal, unnatural, and disturbing to someone else. Perhaps you would not be bothered by any of the environmental factors described in this chapter, but you can think of other things in your environment that do provoke your anger.

Environmental factors should not be regarded as excuses for inappropriate expressions of anger. Certain elements in your environment may contribute to the arousal of your anger, or to the initial intensity of your anger, but regardless of your environment, you can always choose *how* you express that anger.

CHAPTER NINE

Anger As a Learned Response: The Importance of Modeling

Behaviors and attitudes are frequently acquired through modeling, a process of observing and imitating others. The effects of modeling play a significant role in determining the situations that will provoke your anger and those that won't. Modeling also plays a significant role in determining how you typically respond to anger-provoking situations. Models can be people with whom you actually interact (parents, siblings, teachers, coaches, peers, colleagues, etc.), or they can be fantasy figures.

The Role of Modeling in Your Life

Your susceptibility to the influences of modeling does not end at a certain age, but as you mature and develop your own set of values and sense of self-worth, you become more discriminating about whom you choose to model. Even young children begin to model one parent more than another. Adolescents tend to model a select group of their peers and/or their favorite TV, movie, and music personalities in preference to either parent.

Adults become even more careful about whom they model, especially if they are concerned about the possibility of any negative repercussions resulting from modeling a specific behavior. The following example serves as an illustration.

Peter Finch, as a 58-year-old emotionally distraught TV news anchorman, in a scene from the 1976 movie *Network*, appeals to TV viewers to rush to their windows and shout, "I'm mad as hell and I'm not going to take this anymore!" The next scene shows hundreds of people, with their heads sticking out of windows, responding to his plea and joining him as he shouts his phrase of rebellion.

Continuing several months after the movie's original release, thousands of people who had seen *Network* imagined what it would be like to join in the protest. Most of them, however, never went beyond ventilating their frustrations to their friends and family in the safety and privacy of their own homes and cars. Finch's protest was something that many moviegoers fantasized imitating, but in reality only a few of them acted out their fantasies. Even though the scene sparked a lot of wishful thinking, most people's internal self-talk kept them from modeling Finch's behavior.

People can acquire both desirable and undesirable behaviors and attitudes from modeling. For example, when people model classic tough guys such as Rocky or Rambo, or the characters typically portrayed in the old John Wayne movies, they respond to anger-provoking situations in destructive, aggressive ways. On the other hand, when people model characters such as Robert Young, the father in *Father Knows Best*, or Bill Cosby, the father on *The Cosby Show*, they typically respond to anger-provoking situations in constructive, assertive ways. Although children can and often do model certain fantasy figures, parents provide their children with some of the most important role models they will ever have. The following discussion explains how parents, by using the democratic discipline process with their children, can model constructive, assertive responses to anger-provoking situations. Teachers are also important models. In the next chapter we'll look at the types of models our schools are providing.

PARENTS AS MODELS: THE IMPORTANCE OF DEMOCRATIC DISCIPLINE

Children, from infancy through adolescence, are very skillful at eliciting their parents' anger and knocking them off their emotional balance. Actually, they are so adept at finding and pushing their parents' "angry buttons" that parents frequently feel they have no choice but to respond in an angry, authoritarian manner.

Fortunately, parents do have a choice. When their children misbehave and provoke their anger, they have a choice of three ways to respond. They can use the authoritarian, the permissive, or the democratic approach. It's the parents' choice, and whatever they choose, their children will model them.

The Authoritarian Approach

Parents who take the authoritarian approach typically communicate with their children in angry phrases such as, "Because I said so!" They choose this approach because they want to maintain full control of the situation and receive absolute obedience from their children. Authoritarian parents insist on setting all the rules and regulations, and they respond to infractions of those rules and regulations by using punishment.

Punishment can be in the form of inflicting physical or emotional pain. It can also include taking a privilege or possession away from the child without negotiating either before or after the child misbehaves. Authoritarian punishment usually results in the child developing feelings of resentment and a desire to retaliate. (See the charts at the end of this chapter for a description of the differences between discipline and punishment.)

The Permissive Approach

Parents who use the permissive approach typically communicate with their children in timid phrases such as: "I'm sorry you're upset, can I help?" When parents choose this approach, they are in essence relinquishing control of their children. Permissive parents assume their children will automatically choose to behave appropriately. In contrast to the harsh, domineering style of authoritarian parents, permissive parents are overly lenient and tend to pamper their children.

Pampering or overprotecting when misbehavior occurs usually increases a child's self-centeredness and/or helplessness and decreases their self-discipline and self-reliance. Thus, pampered and overprotected children are easily frustrated and angered and they frequently rely on throwing temper tantrums as a means of acquiring what they want.

The Democratic Approach

Parents who use the democratic approach typically communicate with their children using respectful phrases such as: "We need to sit down and decide on an appropriate consequence for that behavior." When parents choose the democratic approach, they are neither seeking full control of their children nor relinquishing all control. Instead, they are helping their children develop a set of inner controls including self-respect, self-control, and self-discipline. Because democratic parents believe their children need to take responsibility for their own behavior, they involve their children in the ongoing process of discipline. (See appendix A, "The Twenty Most Important Aspects of Constructive Discipline.")

Discipline involves "catching" children succeeding, striving to succeed, cooperating, or just having an enjoyable time, then giving them encouragement and positive attention. It also involves following through with logical consequences for misbehavior. Logical consequences help children develop a sense of personal accountability for their behavior. They are also an effective means of stopping some inappropriate behaviors. When used in this way, logical consequences consist of two choices given to the child when he or she misbehaves. One is maintaining a special privilege by stopping the inappropriate behavior, and the second is choosing not to stop the inappropriate behavior and losing that privilege. For example, if a child is being loud and uncooperative prior to the start of his or her favorite TV program, the parent might say, "You can have fun watching your favorite TV show if you choose to stop yelling, or you can choose not to stop yelling and go to your room and miss your favorite show. It's your choice." Depending on the severity of the misbehavior, parents may need to take immediate control of the situation, restrain their child, and then give him a choice of behaving appropriately and being freed from his restraint or refusing to cooperate and having his freedom restricted. Children are involved in the discipline process even in those situations because they still have an opportunity to make a choice.

In order for children to respond appropriately to logical consequences, however, the consequences need to be established and administered appropriately. This means they must be stated in a calm, respectful, gentle but firm, adult to adult, emotionally neutral tone of voice. When given after the misbehavior has occurred, consequences are most effective when they are negotiated and established with the child.

This should be done during a time when both parent and child are calm and relaxed and able to listen and respond to each other's needs and concerns. This does not mean, however, that the negotiation process should continue for an indefinite length of time. After informing the child that he or she will have a specified amount of time in which to suggest a consequence, the parent should decide on an appropriate consequence and follow through with it whenever the child refuses to suggest a consequence within the allotted amount of time. Thus, constructive discipline, by reinforcing the child's appropriate behaviors and involving him or her in the discipline process, encourages the child to develop a strong sense of self-respect, self-control, and self-discipline.

Responding to Children As a Responsible Model

Authoritarian parents provide an inappropriate role model by responding to their children's misbehavior with physical punishment such as spanking, slapping, or shaking. Children eventually model that behavior by expressing their angry feelings in hurtful, aggressive ways and by physically retaliating against those who provoke their anger.

Permissive parents pamper and overprotect their children from having to accept responsibility for their own feelings and behavior. Although they are typically very slow to anger, when permissive parents finally do express it they usually do so in a very passive way, or they occasionally express it in a very explosive and aggressive fashion. Thus, permissive parents provide their children with a very ineffective, inappropriate, and inconsistent model for coping with anger, and their children are apt to imitate them by responding to others in either a very helpless, dependent manner or in a very self-centered, aggressive way.

Unlike parents who model the authoritarian or the permissive approach, democratic parents provide their children with appropriate role models. When parents consistently use constructive methods of discipline, their children learn to associate nonhurtful, assertive behaviors with feelings of anger and are more likely to express their angry feelings in constructive ways.

Physical punishment is not a form of discipline, it is an act of violence used to force children into compliance. Although the words *discipline* and *punishment* are frequently used interchangeably, there is a big difference between the two. The intent of *punishment* is to hurt the person being punished. The person being punished experiences physical pain (through spanking, slapping, etc.), emotional pain (through yelling, criticizing, humiliating, unnegotiated removal or denial of privileges, etc.), or both. Punishment gives the illusion of being effective, because the pain of punishment often frightens the victim into complying with the punisher's desires. But in reality, punishment is not effective. Punishment does not result in the development of self-discipline. People who learn to respond out of fear of authority, instead of respect for others, are undeterred from inappropriate or, in some cases, criminal behavior when there is no immediate threat of punishment.

By contrast, discipline results in the development of self-discipline, self-respect, and respect for others. Discipline prepares people to exercise self-control and refrain from inappropriate behavior without the need for external deterrents such as the possibility of fines or jail sentences.

Children are great imitators. When they see parents or other adults responding to undesirable behavior in punitive and hurtful ways, they learn to lash out (verbally and/or physically) when they don't get their way. Punishment teaches "might makes right." Little wonder that so many children are attracted to the strength and power they find in gangs. Punishment builds resentment. Little wonder that so many children seek out ways to retaliate and make others experience the hurt they feel. Punishment is strictly authoritarian. Little wonder that so many children resist authority and engage in power struggles. Punishment takes very little time. Little wonder that so many children are slow to develop patience and tolerance for other people's mistakes. Punishment reacts only to undesirable behavior. Little wonder that so many children avoid accepting responsibility for their actions and are quick to blame and find fault with others.

Unlike punishment, which occurs only when a child has misbehaved, discipline is both proactive (preventative) and reactive. The proactive aspect of discipline involves "catching" children behaving appropriately and giving them positive feedback. This encourages children to develop pride in themselves. Discipline takes a long time. It is a process. This encourages children to develop patience with others and have tolerance for differences. Discipline is democratic. It is neither authoritarian nor permissive. It allows the person being disciplined to make choices and to negotiate the consequences for his or her misbehavior. This encourages children to value teamwork and to consider the rights and needs of others. Discipline builds respect. This encourages children to develop self-respect and respect for others. Discipline demonstrates that cooperation and self-control are essential to success. This encourages children to develop positive, nonhurtful ways of interacting with others and expressing their anger, and a strong sense of self-discipline that will be helpful to them throughout their lives.

The following three charts show the differences between discipline and punishment; the contrast between the democratic versus the authoritarian approach; and a description of both proactive and reactive discipline.

DIFFERENCES BETWEEN DISCIPLINE AND PUNISHMENT

Discipline	Punishment
Takes a long time.	Takes very little time.
Is *encouraging*. Reinforces desirable, cooperative behavior by "catching" the child behaving appropriately.	Is *discouraging*. Gives attention to undesirable, uncooperative behaviors and ignores the child's desirable behaviors.
Nurtures the development of *self-discipline* by teaching the child to accept responsibility for his or her behavior.	Furthers *irresponsibility* by freeing the child from the "sin" of his/her misbehavior and giving the child a clean slate each time he/she misbehaves.
Builds respect.	Builds resentment.
Fosters *cooperation* by including the child in the process of making the rules and determining the consequences for infractions of those rules	Creates *power struggles* by excluding the child from the process of making the rules and determining the consequences for infractions of those rules.

DIFFERENCES BETWEEN THE DEMOCRATIC AND THE AUTHORITARIAN APPROACH

The Democratic Approach	The Authoritarian Approach
Parents using constructive discipline follow this sequence when their child misbehaves:	Parents using authoritarian punishment follow this sequence when their child misbehaves:

The Democratic Approach	The Authoritarian Approach
If the child is misbehaving and the parent wants him to stop, the parent will:	If the child is misbehaving and the parent wants him to stop, the parent will usually:
Ask the child to stop in a calm, quiet, respectful, gentle, but firm, emotionally neutral adult-to-adult tone of voice.	1. ask nicely 2. tell firmly 3. tell harshly
If the child continues to misbehave, the parent:	If the child continues to misbehave the parent often resorts to:
Gives the child a CHOICE of maintaining his/her privilege by stopping the inappropriate behavior, or *not* stopping that behavior and losing that privilege.	1. yelling or screaming 2. threatening to pull privileges, or 3. threatening to use physical force
If the child chooses *not* to stop the inappropriate behavior, the child loses the privilege.	If the child continues to misbehave, or the parent realizes the child has misbehaved, the parent typically:
If the parent realizes (after the fact) that the child has misbehaved, the parent: follows the Reactive Discipline Sequence outlined on the next page.	1. pulls privileges without allowing any input from the child, and/or 2. uses physical force, such as slapping, spanking, or shaking

CONSTRUCTIVE DISCIPLINE
Proactive Discipline includes:

- *Catching* the other person behaving appropriately and complimenting that person about his or her appropriate behavior.
- *Teamwork*
- *Respect*

The Reactive Discipline Sequence

1. *Get calm.* Wait until you and the other person are *calm,* and you can discuss the problem in an emotionally neutral, adult-to-adult, nonhurtful, and nonblaming tone of voice.

2. *Recognize intentions.* Get in touch with your true intentions.

   Wait to approach the other person until you are sure your intentions are *nonhurtful.*

   Your self-talk (thoughts) might be: "Okay, I'm feeling calm. I'm ready to interact without being physically or emotionally hurtful. My intention is to be firm, but supportive and helpful."

3. *Inform and prepare.* Let the other person know what you want to discuss.

   "I'd like to share the feelings I had about our disagreement this morning."

4. *Appreciation statement.* State your latest appreciation of the other person.

   "Thank you for helping with . . . "

5. *"I" Messages.* Describe the problem using "I Messages." Remember, these include:

- Your *feeling* and related feelings
  ("I felt angry, hurt, and let down.")
- The other person's *behavior*
  ("You didn't wash the dishes three times this week.")
- The *reason* for your feelings
  ("I thought it was important for us to keep our commitments to each other.")

6. *Resolve with Involvement.* When appropriate, and when you can do so sincerely, ask the other person for help with the problem.

   "I'm wondering if you'd be willing to help me. I'd appreciate hearing your ideas about how we can resolve this situation."

7. *Negotiate and follow through.* Negotiate on a fair and appropriate consequence, and follow through.

   PARENT: "I appreciate your offering to wash the dishes one extra time this week as a consequence for not getting them done last night. Since I thought it should be three times, and you thought it should be one time, how about compromising at two extra times?"
   ADOLESCENT: "Yeah, sure, okay."
   PARENT: "Does that seem reasonable to you?"
   ADOLESCENT: "Yeah."

8. *Repeat appreciation.* Repeat or make a new statement of appreciation about the other person.

NOTE: Physical punishment (spanking) or verbal abuse (yelling) are *never* appropriate or beneficial. Spanking and yelling are aggressive expressions of anger, used with the intent to inflict physical or emotional pain. Recipients of these forms of punishment are *intimidated* into obeying out of *fear*. When adults spank or yell during the discipline process, they are modeling inappropriate, hurtful ways of responding to undesirable behavior.

The goal of constructive discipline is to *help* the other person understand the inappropriateness of his or her behavior and learn how to behave more appropriately in the future. Parents who use constructive discipline *encourage* their children to comply out of *respect*, and model positive, nonhurtful, assertive ways to express anger.

CHAPTER TEN

Teachers As Models: What Do Schools Provide?

Students are angry at teachers, and teachers are frustrated and angry with students. Many of our big city schools have been described as "war zones" or "schools under siege." In these schools effective discipline is decaying, and uncontrolled frustration and anger are running rampant. Why are these schools so full of violence, hate, and anger? Why are the students so out of control?

According to William Bennett, former Secretary of Education, the fault lies with the National Education Association (NEA) for blocking necessary reforms. NEA officials, on the other hand, fault the current administration for failing to help schools improve.

Disgruntled members of the community blame the schools' inadequate control over the students on groups such as the ACLU for weakening the consequences students face for misbehaving. Conversely, ACLU members blame the schools for being too harsh and restricting the civil liberties of the students.

Who is to blame? Is it the parents, teachers, administrators, superintendents, school boards, or students? Actually, they all share in this responsibility, yet many of them seem to avoid accepting personal accountability, choosing instead to place the burden on someone else. The following remarks illustrate how people from each of these groups typically project the blame onto one another.

Parents say, "Teachers should do a better job of keeping the students under control."

Teachers say, "If only parents would train their children to be a little more self-disciplined and the principal would give me some help and support with the troublemakers, then my classes would be under better control."

Principals say, "If the superintendent would agree to allow some stricter disciplinary measures, and the teachers would learn to exercise tighter control over their students, I wouldn't be plagued by so many disciplinary problems."

Superintendents say, "A good principal should be able to maintain control of his school and keep peace with the parents. If people on the school board weren't so worried about losing votes, this school district could have a lot tougher and a lot better discipline policy."

School board members say, "The superintendent should do a better job of hiring administrators who will enforce our discipline policy. If the parents weren't so overprotective of their kids, we could adopt some stricter disciplinary measures that would really work."

In order for schools to establish effective discipline, this *cycle of blame* must be stopped and replaced with each segment of the system recognizing and accepting their share of the responsibility and offering each other support and encouragement.

As discussed in the preceding chapter, parents have a significant impact on their children's lives. Except for parents, teachers are often children's most influential models. Remember, children can and do acquire desirable and undesirable behavior and attitudes from modeling other people.

When teachers interact with students in authoritarian or permissive ways students fail to learn the basics of the most important 3 Rs in education and life... *respect, responsibility,* and *relating constructively*. Teachers who consistently use the democratic approach experience relatively few disciplinary problems with students, while permissive and authoritarian teachers are often angry with their students because their students are frequently out of control.

Permissive teachers often unwittingly contribute to the escalation of students' obnoxious, hurtful, irresponsible behavior. They hope that students will respond to any leniency shown them by stopping their inappropriate behavior. However, passive responses only serve to reinforce and intensify the students' irresponsible behavior and increase the chaos in the classroom. The more chaotic the classroom, the more the teacher and serious students feel frustrated, hurt, helpless, and angry over the loss of control.

Authoritarian teachers often provoke disruptive behavior in their students by relating to them in harsh, punitive, and abusive ways and by failing to show them the respect they deserve. This often results in students feeling bitter and angry, seeking revenge, and modeling their teachers' disrespectful, authoritarian attitude by aggressively acting out in hurtful, obnoxious, and abusive ways.

When teachers relate to students in a democratic way, however, they provide their students with a constructive model. Teachers exemplify the democratic process when they:

- notice students interacting appropriately, or working on or completing their assignments, then give them sincere, heartfelt, positive reinforcement
- encourage students to participate in establishing the rules for their classroom and developing fair and appropriate consequences for infractions of those rules

- allow students to vote on decisions affecting classroom activities whenever feasible
- follow through with the agreed upon consequences in a firm, fair, and consistent manner
- encourage students to ask questions and challenge them to think, reason, and be creative
- help to create an atmosphere of respect in the classroom by communicating with the students in a calm, respectful, assertive, adult-to-adult manner, and encouraging them to relate with one another in a similar manner
- respond to students with sensitivity, compassion, warmth, kindness, and honesty
- model such characteristics as dedication, perseverance, self-motivation, enthusiasm, independence, and responsibility
- allow students freedom within a democratic structure

Students whose teachers model the democratic approach learn to respect others, develop a sense of self-discipline, and acquire skills for coping with angry feelings and angry people in constructive ways.

CHAPTER ELEVEN

How Tolerant Is Your Temperament?

You probably know some people who seem to "explode" at the slightest provocation. You probably also know people who rarely get angry, or who rarely lose their self-control even when they're enraged. Are some people just naturally more prone to anger than others?

Yes and no. Since anger is a natural reaction to anger-provoking situations, anything that affects your perception of what is or what isn't provoking has an impact on whether you become angry. Your general outlook on life, and your perception of what is and what isn't provoking, is heavily influenced by your *temperament*. But regardless of your temperament, you can choose the intensity and duration of your anger and how it is going to be expressed.

Can I Choose My Temperament?

Your temperament is your basic disposition or emotional nature. What is tolerable to one kind of temperament often

85

is intolerable to another. Although you are born with your temperament intact, you can learn to control the extent to which your temperament influences your reaction to anger-provoking situations.

The relationship between your temperament and your ability to manage your anger is similar to the relationship between your percentage of body fat and your ability to float. Those with a lower percentage of body fat are less buoyant than those with a higher percentage. But you can learn how to float no matter what your level of body fat is. Similarly, people are born with different temperaments. Some temperaments are more easily provoked and some are more tolerant. Regardless of your particular temperament, you can learn to manage your anger constructively and effectively.

There are four basic temperament types: *impulsive*, *irritable*, *temperamental*, and *calm*. Although most people's temperament usually resembles one type more than the others, most contain features from at least two of the four types. You are most likely to express your uncontrolled anger according to the temperament that yours most closely resembles. (See the charts at the end of this chapter for a comparative look at all four temperaments.)

The Impulsive Temperament

People who have an *impulsive* temperament usually are eager to please other people, optimistic, and have a tendency to do things spontaneously. If you were to ask an impulsive person if he'd like to go to a movie with you, he would probably say, "Sure," and be ready to go that instant. Impulsive people tend to be disorganized and their interest in an activity often ends as spontaneously as it begins. Consequently, they often lack the self-discipline it takes to see a project through to completion. Impulsive people are easily frustrated in situations where they must follow a preset schedule or meet specific deadlines. They are better suited for jobs that offer flexible hours rather than ones that require them to arrive and depart at set times. Impulsive people also feel more comfortable in jobs where they can socialize with their co-workers. They become very stressed when they have to work independently and be isolated from their colleagues.

People who have an impulsive temperament rarely hold grudges or keep an emotional tally sheet. They just want other people, particularly the person or persons with whom they are angry, to be aware of their anger. Thus, if you have a predominately impulsive temperament, your destructive response to anger would probably be some type of *negative attention-getting behavior*, such as slamming doors, stomping your foot, or screaming. The following chart gives anger management strategies for impulsive people and suggestions on how to avoid triggering their anger or having them provoke yours.

THE IMPULSIVE TEMPERAMENT

How to Avoid Triggering "Impulsive" People's Anger	How to Cope with "Impulsive" People So They Don't Provoke *Your* Anger	How "Impulsive" People Can Manage Their Anger
Be self-aware	Be self-aware	Be self-aware
Give positive attention for appropriate behaviors	Deep breathing	Therapeutic counting
	Rapid relaxation	Emotionally disengage
	Adjust your expectations	
Be friendly	Put things into perspective	Rapid relaxation
Make requests in a firm, gentle manner	Don't take it personally	Positive self-talk
		Self-hypnosis
Respond with "I Messages"	Consider the extenuating circumstances	Examine your thinking errors
	Humor	
	R.E.T.	

The Irritable Temperament

People who have an *irritable* temperament are often very self-sufficient, decisive, and most comfortable when they are in a position of leadership. If you were to ask an irritable person if he'd like to go to a movie with you, he would probably say, "Sure, I know a good movie we can see. I'll pick you up at six-forty."

People with an irritable temperament often set high achievement expectations for themselves. They also tend to be more sarcastic and overbearing than most people. They get very upset when other people don't keep up with their pace, especially when the slower pace results in their self-imposed deadlines not being met. People with an irritable temperament get particularly frustrated and angry when someone else is given a responsibility that was once theirs.

People with an irritable temperament think primarily in terms of *power* and *control*. Thus, if you have a predominately irritable temperament, your destructive response to anger would be to hit in order to dominate or to yell in order to intimidate. The following chart gives anger management strategies for irritable people and suggestions on how to avoid triggering their anger or having them provoke yours.

THE IRRITABLE TEMPERAMENT

How to Avoid Triggering "Irritable" People's Anger	How to Cope with "Irritable" People So They Don't Provoke *Your* Anger	How "Irritable" People Can Manage Their Anger
Be self-aware	Be self-aware	Be self-aware
Be assertive, *not* aggressive	Deep breathing	Deep breathing
Avoid power struggles	Therapeutic counting	Therapeutic counting
Don't challenge their authority or take away their responsibility	Emotionally disengage	Rapid relaxation
	Rapid relaxation	Power relaxation
	Power relaxation	Adjust your expectations
Talk in an "adult-to-adult" manner	Positive self-talk	Don't take it personally
Respond with "I Messages"	Adjust your expectations	Humor
Use humor	Put things into perspective	R.E.T.
	Reframe the situation	Examine your thinking errors
	Don't take it personally	
	Humor	
	R.E.T.	
	Let go	
	Systematic desensitization	
	Self-hypnosis	
	Examine your thinking errors	

The Temperamental Temperament

People who have a *temperamental* temperament tend to be creative, sensitive, and analytical. They also tend to be pessimistic and moody. Temperamental people get easily frustrated and angry in situations that require intuitive, spontaneous responses. However, they can be flexible if they are given enough information and time to process that information.

If you were to ask a temperamental person if he'd like to go to a movie with you, he would probably say, "What movie did you have in mind? Where is it showing? What time did you want to see it? Can we get a discount by going to the early show? Is there a co-feature? Did you want to go in my car, or would we be taking yours? Is anyone else coming with us?..."

People with a temperamental temperament often focus on *revenge*. Thus, if you have a predominately temperamental temperament, your destructive response to anger would be in the form of "getting even." This includes behaviors such as name-calling, and damaging something that is valuable to the person with whom you are angry. The following chart gives anger management strategies for temperamental people and suggestions on how to avoid triggering their anger or having them provoke yours.

THE TEMPERAMENTAL TEMPERAMENT

How to Avoid Triggering "Temperamental" People's Anger	How to Cope with "Temperamental" People So They Don't Provoke *Your* Anger	How "Temperamental" People Can Manage Their Anger
Be self-aware	Be self-aware	Be self-aware
Communicate in an "adult-to-adult" manner	Deep breathing	Deep breathing
Respond with "I Messages"	Emotionally disengage	Therapeutic counting
Show respect for their values and high standards	Rapid relaxation	Rapid relaxation
Take them seriously	Positive self-talk	Positive self-talk
Avoid power struggles	Put things into perspective	Put things into perspective
Give frequent compliments	Reframe the situation	Reframe the situation
Avoid criticism	Don't take it personally	Consider the extenuating circumstances
Confront in a gentle but firm, assertive manner	Humor	Humor
Limit your requests, give them one at a time	R.E.T.	R.E.T.
	Let go	Let go
	Favorite activity	Favorite activity
	Systematic desensitization	Systematic desensitization
	Examine your thinking errors	Examine your thinking errors

The Calm Temperament

People who have a *calm* temperament are usually quiet and dependable. They tend to be neat and orderly and are good at doing precise work, especially if they can follow a routine way of doing it. Calm people tend to be very efficient, especially when it comes to saving their own energy. However, unless they are assured of success, they would rather miss out on potentially rewarding activities or relationships than take risks or try something new.

If you were to ask a calm person if he'd like to go to a movie with you, his response would depend on whether he was used to going to movies with you, and whether he was used to going to movies on that particular night of the week. If going to movies with you on that night of the week was not something he was accustomed to doing, he would probably say, "Thanks for asking, but I can't tonight."

People with a calm temperament seem to have the strongest need to receive feedback on their performance, and they feel very uncomfortable when that feedback isn't readily available. To calm people "no news" is *not* good news: it is proof that they have done something wrong.

Calm people have such a strong desire to do things their own way (i.e., the way that has been successful for them in the past) that other people often perceive them as being very stubborn, judgmental, and overly critical.

People with a calm temperament tend to express their anger in subtle, passive-aggressive ways, which eventually result in the other person being angry. If you have a predominately calm temperament, your typical, destructive response to anger includes sulking, pouting, or using the silent treatment. However, when the other person becomes angry, you feel *helpless* or *inadequate* to do anything about their anger. In fact, most people with a calm temperament regard themselves as the helpless victim. The following chart gives anger management strategies for calm people and suggestions on how to avoid triggering their anger or having them provoke yours.

THE CALM TEMPERAMENT

How to Avoid Triggering "Calm" People's Anger	How to Cope with "Calm" People So They Don't Provoke *Your* Anger	How Calm People Can Manage Their Anger
Be self-aware	Be self-aware	Be self-aware
Make requests as far in advance as possible, avoid sense of urgency	Deep breathing	Rapid relaxation
	Therapeutic counting	Positive self-talk
Explain rationale for requests	R.E.T.	Put things into perspective
	Adjust your expectations	Reframe the situation
Minimize changes in their routine	Put things into perspective	Constructive, positive humor (avoid teasing)
Avoid capricious changes in your opinion	Don't take it personally	Favorite activity

The Importance of Being Aware of Your Temperament

It is important for you to be aware of your basic temperament so you can build upon the strengths of your temperament and overcome the weaknesses. Your temperament can have a strong effect on your general outlook on life and your perception of anger-provoking situations in particular. However, your temperament does *not* dictate how you will express your anger.

What you do with all the energy you get from your anger is your CHOICE. For example, if you are aware that you have a predominately irritable temperament, you can monitor and reevaluate your need for power and control and *choose* how you are going to meet that need even when you are angry.

TEMPERAMENTS

	Impulsive	Irritable
Characteristics	acts now—thinks later	detests detail work
	external locus of control	external locus of control
	extravert	extravert/introvert
	feeling	feeling/thinking
	people-oriented	independent
	risk-taker	intuitive
	talkative	sees the whole
	"sanguine"	"choleric"
Strengths	charming	adventuresome
	compassionate	decisive
	eager to please	hard-driving
	enthusiastic	optimistic
	flexible	persevering
	good-humored	quick and bold in
	intense	emergencies
	involved	self-confident
	likes to share	self-disciplined
	lives in present	strong leader
	optimistic	
	passionate	
	sociable	
	spontaneous	
Weaknesses	demands attention	aggressive
	disorganized	blunt
	doesn't plan ahead	doesn't anticipate
	doesn't take time	problems
	to listen	domineering
	inconsistent	frequent violent outbursts
	irresponsible	hot-tempered
	naive	ignores details
	restless	not sympathetic or
	short interest span	compassionate
	undisciplined	overly self-sufficient
		rarely apologizes
		rarely expresses approval
		thick-skinned

	Temperamental	Calm
Characteristics	internal locus of control introvert appreciates sees all the parts thinking	conservative entertains self internal locus of control introvert/extravert thinking/feeling thinks now—acts later
	"melancholic"	"phlegmatic"
Strengths	anticipates problems competent creative dependable inquiring mind loyal precise willingly gives extra effort	analyzes situation cheerful conservative consistent contented diplomatic doesn't demand attention dry sense of humor easygoing efficient good listener quiet reliable upholds tradition
Weaknesses	easily offended, hurt fearful of making mistakes frequently holds grudges indecisive moody occasional outbursts passive-aggressive perfectionistic pessimistic poor self-esteem revengeful self-doubting suspicious tense and compulsive unduly demanding unreasonable expectations	apathetic detached observer detests change dislikes being too involved inflexible lacks motivation likes to tease slow stingy stubborn

	Impulsive	Irritable
Pace	quick and light	fast and forceful
Leadership Style	too restless and weak-willed to be consistent tries to manipulate through friendliness	consistent and strong-willed controls from "one up" takes action intimidates through fear
Anger Mgmt. Style	assertive slow to anger quick to resolve	aggressive quick to violent anger usually quick to resolve
*WAR	attention	power
Provocations to Anger	unfriendliness being held accountable being ignored	lack of respect authority challenged position of leadership threatened
Stress Inducers	deadlines lack of socialization	loss of position or power having to compliment others

*Way of Acquiring Recognition

	Temperamental	**Calm**
Pace	Variable and intense	slow and steady
Leadership Style	inconsistent controls from "one down" takes the blame induces guilt	consistent, but may lack follow-through tries to avoid conflict
Anger Mgmt. Style	passive-aggressive or aggressive quick to anger slow to resolve	passive-aggressive slow to anger quick to resolve
*WAR	revenge	inadequacy
Provocations to Anger	criticism incompetence being insulted being short of perfection	pressure to perform undesirable task unexpected change in policy or routine demands for sudden decisions
Stress Inducers	making mistakes lack of positive feedback	pressure to get involved unexpected change in policy or routine

*Way of Acquiring Recognition

CHAPTER TWELVE

What's Your "Script"?

When faced with a new or difficult task, do you usually say to yourself with firm determination, "I *will* do it!" Or do you generally say to yourself, with only a hint of confidence and conviction, "I'll *try* to do it"? If you normally respond to the challenges of life with a "can do" attitude, you tend to have positive self-esteem (or, as it is called in Transactional Analysis terminology, a *winner's script*). If you normally regard the unavoidable and unexpected challenges of life as insurmountable hurdles, and respond to them with a "can't do" attitude, you tend to have a more negative self-esteem (or, in Transactional Analysis terms, a *loser's script*).

Your self-esteem, or life script, is the value you place on your self-worth. The core of your life script is established by early childhood experiences, but it is not a fixed measurement. Depending on the experiences you have throughout your life, your script can be modified at any age.

Children tend to evaluate their self-esteem *primarily* in terms of how well their basic needs are being met, espe-

WHERE'S YOUR FOCUS?

LOSER'S SCRIPT   **WINNER'S SCRIPT**

cially the need for a sense of belonging, affection, and respect. The *need to belong* is so basic that babies have died because they didn't receive the cuddling and individualized attention necessary for the development of their early sense of belonging. Thus, the more positive attention, love, and respect you received from your parents during your first five years of life, the more likely you were to develop a sense of belonging, and consequently a positive self-esteem, or winner's script, as illustrated by the following diagram.

WINNER'S SCRIPT

Likewise, children who are disrespected and receive negative attention in the form of abuse and/or neglect from their parents during the first five years of life tend to develop negative self-esteem, or loser's script, as illustrated in the following diagram.

LOSER'S SCRIPT

Fortunately, this can be changed. If you developed a loser's script originally, you can develop a sense of belonging and acquire a winner's script through relationships you have with relatives, friends, co-workers, supervisors, organizations, or other supportive individuals. The script that is established during your first five years of life (your core script) never completely disappears, but the more positive experiences you have, the more you will think, feel, and act like a winner.

ACQUIRED SCRIPTS

The extent to which life experiences influence the development of an *acquired winner's script* depends on how much those experiences result in positive changes in (1) your personal evaluation of your abilities and performance, and (2) your perception of other people's evaluation of your worth. The impact that other people's evaluations have on your self-esteem is moderated by the degree to which you accept or reject their evaluations of you and by the extent to which you value their opinions.

For example, the movie *Good Morning Vietnam* was an overwhelming success, and audiences cheered Robin Williams for his performance in that film. Yet, all the positive reaction he received from the movie audiences, with whom he had no personal sense of affiliation, couldn't override his personal evaluation of his self-worth. As he put it, "I'm happy about the movie. But right now I'm moving through my personal life like a hemophiliac in a razor factory."[1]

On the other hand, a high school basketball player usually feels a sense of community and affiliation with his audiences, so their cheers often *do* contribute to his level of self-esteem. For instance, when a high school basketball star shoots the winning shot in the state championship game, his self-esteem begins to soar. Contributing to the rise in his self-esteem are his own evaluation of his performance, or his positive self-talk, and the praise and cheers from his coaches, teammates, classmates, parents, and other spectators, which reinforce his self-evaluation.

Generally speaking, the stronger your winner's script, the more capable you are of recognizing the validity of other people's evaluations and putting their evaluations into the proper perspective. On the other hand, those with a loser's script tend to focus on the negative evaluations and opinions of others, often accepting them as *fact* even when they are unsubstantiated or exaggerated.

Acquiring a winner's script and maintaining positive self-esteem is an important part of anger management. When you feel good about yourself and are confident that people respect and appreciate you, it is easier to respond constructively to anger-provoking situations. Those with winner's scripts are more willing to accept responsibility for and the consequences of their behavior. That is because "winners" are usually aware of their angry feelings and generally accept full responsibility for the choices they make regarding the duration, intensity, and expression of their anger.

When your self-esteem is low, however, even minor disappointments or slight provocations can trigger your anger. Those with loser's scripts fail to assume responsibility for their behavior, choosing instead to blame others or make excuses for their inappropriate behaviors. Consequently, "losers" rarely care about who or what gets hurt by their hurtful, aggressive expressions of anger.

Remarks made by a patient who was hospitalized because of his uncontrolled anger illustrate how difficult it can be to express anger in positive ways when you have negative self-esteem:

I'm so *angry* I could kill him. I hate his guts. For as far back as I can remember, my father abused me. I get angry just thinking about how he used to beat me. He was always telling me how rotten I was. After a while I began to figure he was right.

After all, my real mother gave me away when I was a baby. I guess she didn't believe in abortions, so when she accidentally got pregnant she just waited until I was born, then gave me away.

How do I feel about myself? That's easy. I feel like a scummy bastard. I have no idea who my natural parents are, or how or where I *belong*. My mother obviously didn't want me and I was raised by a father who hated me and abused me. I can't begin to describe how much anger, hate, and resentment I feel.

Sure, I've tried to do something about all of this anger that I'm always feeling. But not all of it is directed at my father. I get angry at lots of things and with lots of different people. I've been through three series of anger management training sessions here at the hospital. Each session lasted eight weeks. After twenty-four weeks of intense anger management training, you'd think I'd have my anger under control. But I don't.

I understand all of the techniques and how to use them, but I can't put them into practice. Until I learn to like myself—I don't care how angrily I behave, because I AM ANGRY!

I don't care what I do with my anger. Hell, I don't want to control my anger. Sometimes I *want* to hurt others, because I feel hurt.

I feel as if I need to feel better about myself before I'll have any real use for anger management. As long as I feel like I'm worthless, it doesn't make any difference to me how I express my anger.

When I don't even like myself, why should I give a damn about managing my anger? Why don't the therapists put their energy into helping me learn how to *like* myself, before they spend so much time trying to get me to *control* myself? Maybe if I felt that *I* had some value, I could begin to see the value of managing my anger.

Although the patient incorrectly identified positive self-esteem as a prerequisite to constructive anger management, he was correct in recognizing that a relationship exists between people's self-esteem and the ease with which they can manage their anger. In reality, however, this particular patient might never see the value in managing his anger, no matter how good he felt about himself, because of his severe Self-Serving personality (see chapters 19 and 40) and his refusal to accept responsibility for his misguided thinking and actions.

Those with a loser's script and low self-esteem are more likely to express anger toward themselves and others in negative, hurtful ways. That's why it is so important for you to be *aware* of your life script and take the necessary steps to raise your self-esteem. Regardless of whether you have a winner's script or a loser's script, you can always choose how you are going to respond to anger-provoking situations and what you are going to do with your angry feelings. Constructive expressions of anger are the result of your deliberate *choices*, not your life script.

Taking responsibility for your angry feelings and angry behavior can be a tremendous challenge, particularly if you have a loser's script. However, by taking it one step at a time and increasing your self-awareness and self-esteem, you *can* do it!

CHAPTER THIRTEEN

External and Internal Forces: Where's the Control?

Do you feel you can usually control what happens to you? Or do you feel other people usually have that control? Where do you think the power to control what happens to you is located? Is it inside or outside you? Your answers to these questions are an indication of your "locus of control."

Locus of control is your *perception* of who has the power to control what happens to you. (The word *locus* means "*location*.")

Two high school students with equal athletic ability consider trying out for the team. Athlete 1 thinks to himself, "I don't know why I should even go through the motions of trying out. I bet the coach already has his mind made up about who he wants on the team before tryouts even start." Athlete 2 thinks to himself, "I've worked hard all year to get ready for tryouts. The coach will be able to see right away how much I've improved. I intend to make the team this year."

Even though these two students have an equal opportunity

for making the team, they have opposite expectations. Why? Because they have different *perceptions* of their ability to control what happens to them. One of them has an *external locus of control* and the other has an *internal locus of control*.

As far as Athlete 1 is concerned, making the team is beyond his control. He thinks there is nothing he can do to improve his chances for making the team. Athlete 1 typifies people who feel they can't control what happens to them. They believe control of the situation is in someone else's hands, or the outcome is simply a matter of chance, luck, or fate. Because people such as Athlete 1 believe that control over what happens to them is located in someone or something else, these people are said to have an *external* locus of control.

On the other hand, as far as Athlete 2 is concerned, he believes he can influence the coach's decision by working hard and demonstrating his athletic ability. Athlete 2 typifies people who believe they can control what happens to them through their own personal effort. Because people such as Athlete 2 believe the control for what happens to them is located within themselves, they are said to have an *internal* locus of control.

David Hartman, former co-host of the ABC morning news program *Good Morning America*, concluded each morning's broadcast with the phrase, "*Make* it a good day." This unconventional farewell communicated to his listeners that they had the power to control what type of day they were going to have . . . internal control. By contrast, the standard phrase "Have a nice day!" communicates to its recipients that they are powerless to control what type of day they have, and that the quality of their day is determined by such uncontrollable factors as chance, luck, or fate . . . external control.

Most people tend to have either a predominately internal - predominately external locus of control, but rarely does anyone have totally one or the other. In fact, people who usually have an external locus of control may have an internal locus of control in situations where previous experience has shown that they can have an impact on the outcome. Likewise, people who usually have an internal locus of control may have an external locus of control in those situations where previous experience has shown that the outcome is unrelated to the quality or quantity of their personal effort.

Your tendency to be more internally or externally oriented is initially established in childhood by modeling your parents. However, it is possible to change your orientation, depending on the experiences you have with significant others such as your classmates, teachers, peers, people at work, your friends, or your spouse.

Children usually acquire the same locus of control their parents have. Parents with an internal locus of control pass along to their children the attitude, "I can make things happen through my own effort." They do this by being a positive role model and by encouraging their children to be curious, inquisitive, imaginative, and resourceful. These parents, by example, are teaching their children that they have sufficient internal resources to validate their own self-worth. Parents help children develop an internal locus of control when they provide them with:

- a positive, warm, nurturing, supportive (but not overly protective) environment that allows them to experience success
- consistent, positive, democratic discipline, including logical consequences for inappropriate behavior

Children who receive this kind of parenting learn to recognize the value of their own efforts. They rely on their own evaluation of their performance and reward themselves with complimentary self-talk, such as, "Good job" or, "I really accomplished a lot today!'' They also learn to accept responsibility for their own behavior and to develop positive self-esteem, self-confidence, and self-discipline.

Parents who have an *external* locus of control, however, tend to be negative, inconsistent, and emotionally detached. They usually vacillate between:

- being overly permissive (due to their lack of emotional involvement)
- being overly authoritarian

Children whose parents have an external locus of control often model their parents' chronic pessimism, and their feelings of powerlessness, helplessness, and ineffectiveness. They learn to depend on *others* for validation of their worth. They either passively wait for or aggressively seek out external sources of reinforcement, since they regard the absence of feedback as confirmation of their negative self-worth. Children of these parents also acquire their parents' habit of using *thinking errors*, such as blaming, justifying, and excuse-making.

Constructive anger management is difficult for people who have a predominately external locus of control. There are two reasons for this: their tendency to blame others, and their difficulty in understanding the relationship between their behavior in anger-provoking situations and the outcome of those situations. If your locus of control tends to be more external than internal, you can increase your feelings of self-control and personal effectiveness by increasing your positive self-talk and using the techniques for improving your self-esteem described in part 3.

CHAPTER FOURTEEN

Thinking or Feeling: Where's Your Base of Operations?

There are frequent reminders throughout this book that, "How you think is how you feel, how you feel is how you think, and how you think and feel is how you behave." Although thoughts and feelings are formed in your head, emotions are typically thought of as coming from your heart. People who seem to be guided more by their thoughts and the dictates of their heads are referred to as *thinking people*. People who seem to be guided more by their emotions and ruled by their hearts are referred to as *feeling people*.

How "Thinking People" Operate

Thinking people tend to evaluate situations from an objective, analytical, logical, and cognitive perspective. They are reluctant to let others see their anger even though they may be feeling it intensely. When they do express their anger they usually do so without considering the impact their outburst may have on others. Consequently, thinking people often appear to be impersonal, uncaring, and insensitive to other people's feelings.

How "Feeling People" Operate

Feeling people tend to evaluate situations from a more subjective, sympathetic, personal, emotional, and sometimes illogical perspective. They express their anger openly and freely whenever they feel they have been slighted or mistreated, but they are also sensitive to other people's feelings and values. Consequently, feeling people appear to be more caring and empathic.

Is It Better to Rule with Your Head or Your Heart?

Both the thinking and feeling perspectives have built-in strengths and weaknesses. Thinking people tend to remain cool and calm under pressure, but they also remain emotionally cold and aloof even when emotional involvement would be appropriate. Feeling people are emotionally warm and caring, but they tend to get emotionally overheated under pressure. Fortunately, most people are a blend of the two, and not one extreme or the other. Once you recognize where you are on the thinking/feeling continuum, you can make a conscious effort to draw from the strengths of both perspectives, thereby improving your ability to maintain your emotional balance.

Thinking/Feeling Quiz

The answers you give to the following questions provide some indications as to whether you have more thinking or more feeling tendencies.

NOTE: This scale indicates only your basic tendencies. You may fluctuate between being more "thinking" and being more "feeling" depending on the specific circumstances and the specific people with whom you are interacting.

DIRECTIONS: On a separate sheet of paper, write down your choice of either "a" or "b" for each of the following ten questions. Then compare your responses with the answers at the end of this quiz to determine whether you tend to be more thinking or more feeling.

1. When a co-worker appears upset, you are more likely to:
   a. feel rather uncomfortable and not say anything about it
   b. be concerned about the co-worker's mood and inquire about his or her feelings
2. When there appears to be some kind of dissension between two of your co-workers, you:
   a. try to help resolve the conflict
   b. continue working on your project, without being bothered by the disharmony
3. When someone you supervise needs to be told his or her work is not up to department standards, you prefer to
   a. tell the person yourself
   b. ask someone else to tell him or her
4. When a policy needs to be enforced, you usually pay more attention to:
   a. the demands of the policy
   b. the needs of the people affected by the policy
5. When you are listening to someone, you usually
   a. concentrate in a sympathetic manner to *how* it is being said
   b. concentrate in a firm-minded manner to *what* is being said
6. You prefer to have your supervisor
   a. occasionally express his appreciation for you in a warm and friendly manner

     b. evaluate you in an unemotional, but fair, manner

7. When you are asked to give your opinion of a situation, you tend to:
   a. give an objective analysis based on your observation of the facts
   b. give a personal opinion based on your careful consideration of the emotional impact which that situation will have on others

8. When you become frustrated or angry with your co-workers, you:
   a. usually consider how your expression of anger will affect your co-workers' feelings
   b. tend to express your anger without worrying about how it may affect your co-workers' feelings

9. In telling someone about a movie you've seen, you usually:
   a. give a factual account of the technical aspects of the movie, such as the plot, location, photography, special effects, etc.
   b. describe the characters and the emotional impact the movie had on you

10. When a co-worker explodes with rage, you tend to:
    a. focus on and respond to the specific issues raised by your co-worker without attending to his or her feelings
    b. show concern for your co-worker by focusing and reflecting on his or her angry feelings

How to score yourself:

Compare your answers with the following guide. If the majority of your answers match with the **thinking** scale, then you probably tend to be more thinking. If the majority of your answers match with the **feeling scale,** then you probably tend to be more feeling. Remember, however, that you are probably a blend of both.

Answers for Thinking/Feeling Quiz:

Thinking tendencies: 1a, 2b, 3a, 4a, 5b, 6b, 7a, 8b, 9a, 10a

Feeling tendencies: 1b, 2a, 3b, 4b, 5a, 6a, 7b, 8a, 9b, 10b

CHAPTER FIFTEEN

Introvert or Extravert: How Do You "Recharge" Your Battery?

Another way in which people differ from one another is the extent to which they tend to be *introverted* or *extraverted*. You can get a general idea of what your introvert/extravert tendencies are by looking at how you cope with stress. When you become emotionally drained and feel a need to "recharge your batteries" before you can face another stressful situation, what do you do? If you long for some quiet time in order to recharge yourself, you probably tend to be more of an *introvert*. If you feel more energized after being involved in a group activity, then you're probably more of an *extravert*.

Characteristics of the Introvert

Introverts usually don't initiate social interactions. They tend to be bashful, reserved, aloof, withdrawn, cautious, conservative, timid, emotionally disengaged, deliberate, and shy. They feel perfectly content being alone, quietly reflecting on their own thoughts and feelings. In fact, social situations are often overly stimulating and anxiety-provoking to introverts. Because introverts are so easily stressed by spontaneous social interactions and emotional confrontations, they strive to maintain their self-control in anger-provoking situations by expressing their anger in passive ways, such as pouting or giving others the "silent treatment."

Characteristics of the Extravert

Extraverts enjoy being around other people and being involved in lively, spontaneous group activities. They desire the stimulation provided by social interactions and actually seek out companionship when they are stressed or anxious. Extraverts appear to be natural leaders and communicators because they are so outgoing, sociable, active, and adventuresome. On the other hand, extraverts are also known for their impatience, impulsiveness, and sudden, aggressive expressions of anger.

It is important for you to recognize whether you tend to be more of an introvert or an extravert. When you know what your tendencies are, you can be more successful at finding effective ways to revitalize yourself and reduce your stress. Remember, by keeping your stress at a manageable level it will be easier for you to manage your anger.

Extravert/Introvert Quiz

The answers you give to the following questions provide some indications as to whether you have more extravert or more introvert tendencies.

NOTE: This scale indicates only your basic tendencies. You may fluctuate between being an extravert and an introvert depending on the specific circumstances and the specific people with whom you are interacting.

DIRECTIONS: On a separate sheet of paper, write down your choice of either "a" or "b" for each of the following ten questions. Then compare your responses with the answers at the end of this quiz to determine whether you tend to be more of an introvert or more of an extravert.

1. You prefer parties where you can:
   a. mingle with lots of different people
   b. talk quietly with a few people
2. When you have some paperwork to do, you:
   a. prefer to do the work where you can see other people while you are working
   b. prefer to do the work in a place where you can be alone
3. When you've had a busy morning, you:
   a. prefer to have a quiet lunch by yourself
   b. prefer to have lunch with some of your co-workers
4. While working on a lengthy project, you:
   a. tend to be patient, thorough, and attend closely to details
   b. try to get the job done as quickly as possible
5. When you are learning a new skill, you:
   a. prefer to start as soon as you have a general idea of how to do it
   b. prefer to start after you have had time to carefully review all of the instructions
6. You prefer jobs that usually allow you to:
   a. follow a routine
   b. perform a variety of tasks
7. You usually think of telephone calls as:
   a. acceptable interruptions
   b. distracting, undesirable interruptions
8. Generally speaking, you find that you:
   a. have difficulty remembering other people's names
   b. are good at remembering other people's names

9. When you are unexpectedly confronted by someone's anger, you:
   a. tend to feel anxious and distressed
   b. tend to take it in stride
10. In planning, developing, and implementing a project, you:
   a. prefer to work independently on planning and developing the ideas for the project
   b. prefer to work with others on implementing the plan and completing the project

How to score yourself:

Compare your answers with the following guide. If the majority of your answers match with the **introvert** scale, then you probably tend to be more of an introvert. If the majority of your answers match with the **extravert** scale, then you probably tend to be more of an extravert. Remember, however, you are probably a blend of both.

Answers for Extravert/Introvert Quiz:

Extravert tendencies: 1a, 2a, 3b, 4b, 5a, 6b, 7a, 8b, 9b, 10b

Introvert tendencies: 1b, 2b, 3a, 4a, 5b, 6a, 7b, 8a, 9a, 10a

CHAPTER SIXTEEN

Anger: Are You "Misbehaving" for Recognition?

For the past twenty-five years I have been asking my students, workshop participants, colleagues, friends, and family members, "Why do people misbehave?" Some of the typical responses I receive are: "For the heck of it." "For some kind of payoff." "Because they have some kind of character disorder." But the most frequent response has been: *"Because they are frustrated and angry."*

Why Do People Express Their Anger by Misbehaving?

People are social beings with a need to experience a sense of belonging and feeling of affiliation with others. The quality of that affiliation is measured by the quality and quantity of attention they receive from others. The *need for attention* is so basic that most people would rather have negative attention than no attention at all. When their positive efforts to gain attention are unsuccessful, people often become frustrated and angry and begin to use a variety of inappropriate behaviors to get attention and validate their self-worth. In 1933, Rudolph Dreikurs, author of *Children: The Challenge*, identified Attention, Power, Revenge, and Inadequacy as the four broad categories of inappropriate behavior that children use to gain attention and demonstrate their importance as individuals.

Although these four categories of misbehavior emerge during early childhood, people continue to use them at any age. These four ways of acquiring recognition frequently develop into patterns of misbehavior and negative thinking, which are easily triggered throughout a person's lifetime by feelings of frustration and anger.

Children validate their self-esteem through receiving attention from their parents, so not getting that attention can be devastating. Some children will seek attention by trying to be special; they might strive to be overly cooperative or helpful or excessively diligent about completing their homework.

Parents of children who use these constructive methods of getting attention may be content to have "model" children, but these children usually are very unhappy. They feel they always have to be the "best" in order to be accepted at all. When the pressure to stay #1 becomes too great, or they don't receive adequate attention for their positive pursuits, they become frustrated and angry and begin using negative attention-getting behaviors.

Negative Attention

Negative attention-getting behavior usually results in the child getting negative, rather than positive, attention. But when faced with a choice between *no attention* (which children interpret as, "My parents don't really care about me, I'm not important, I don't belong") and *negative attention* (which they interpret as, "I must really be important, look at how much attention I'm getting, I belong"), children will seek negative attention.

Power

Another way children feel that they are important is by judging how much *power* they have over others. They may equate being the boss with being worthwhile. Thus, they will go to great lengths to ensure that they win, no matter what the cost. Some children will try to exercise their control over others through aggressive behaviors, such as shouting, arguing, or demanding. Others may use passive behaviors such as taking an excessive amount of time to complete a nonappealing task.

Revenge

Sometimes children feel as if no one really cares about them and they have no control over others. When this happens, they may feel that the only way to get any attention or sympathy from their parents is by making them hurt as they feel hurt. In seeking *revenge*, children often resort to name-calling or damaging or destroying their parents' belongings.

Inadequacy

Children who have been unsuccessful at achieving a sense of belonging and who have been unable to get attention, no matter what they do, may feel their only recourse is to give up. Children who are in this state of mind mistakenly believe that by behaving in a totally helpless and inadequate manner they'll protect themselves from further defeat. They also believe that in order to get attention it is necessary to get people to do things for them. Behaviors that are commonly associated with *inadequacy* include: refusing to try new activities, sulking, pouting, and showing a lack of initiative to do even routine tasks.

Responding to the Need for Recognition

When someone confronts you with one of these patterns of misbehavior, you can respond in destructive or constructive ways. Constructive responses help you: decrease the annoying person's negative attention-getting behavior, effectively withdraw from and/or avoid power struggles, reduce the confronting person's desire for revenge, and constructively confront his or her mistaken concept of inadequacy. Constructive responses involve:

- ignoring the misbehavior or refraining from arguments, choosing instead to wait until you are calm and can make positive responses to the person's appropriate behaviors
- doing the unexpected . . . surprising the person by doing something positive (Avoid hurtful or punitive responses.)
- redirecting the inappropriate behavior into something constructive.

As you can see in the chart on pages 126–127, each of the four *Ways of Acquiring Recognition* (W.A.R.) has its own characteristic pattern of self-talk, misbehavior, and communicating with others. You can easily determine which pattern of misbehavior people are using by listening to what they're saying and being aware of your emotional reactions to their comments and behavior.

Once you are aware of the typical behaviors and reactions associated with each of these patterns of misbehavior and negative thinking, it is easier to:

- break away from any destructive patterns you may be using and manage your anger by using positive self-talk and constructive anger management techniques
- respond to *others* in ways that decease *their* anger even when they are using these patterns of misbehavior

Why Do Certain Misbehaviors Seem to Occur Almost Automatically Whenever You Are Angry?

It is only natural and expected during infancy and early childhood that children are extremely self-centered, caring only about having someone fulfill their needs. When their needs aren't met, children become angry and fuss until they are. They have little or no concern for other people's needs or feelings.

As people mature, however, they usually develop an awareness of other people's feelings and a concern for helping others meet their needs. Yet, even as adults, we may find ourselves occasionally reverting to early childhood patterns of self-centered, self-serving behavior. Why? The reason is this: children are not the only ones who get angry when their needs are not being met—adults do too. Remember, *adults, as well as children, gauge their sense of self-worth according to the quality and quantity of attention they receive from others.*

How you think is how you feel. How you feel is how you think. And how you think and feel is how you behave. As a child, the more often you succeeded in getting attention, by using a certain type of misbehavior, the more reinforcing it was for you to use that behavior. Thus, either consciously or unconsciously you began to associate using that type of misbehavior whenever you were angry and wanted attention. For some people, expressing anger by "misbehaving" eventually develops into a *habit*.

Sometimes people become so habituated to using these patterns of misbehavior when they're angry that they use them in an increasingly wide variety of situations. For instance, they may respond with their pattern of misbehavior to one person even though they're angry with someone else. Or they may find that just visualizing an anger-provoking situation is enough to trigger one of these misbehaviors.

Older children and adults often strengthen and perpetuate

their ways of acquiring recognition, or habits of misbehavior, by using certain patterns of self-talk, known as *thinking errors*. For instance, the Power habit is perpetuated by several thinking errors, one of which is the "closed channel." The closed channel thinking style is characterized by disdainfully ignoring or selfishly rejecting the opinions of others, yet insisting they listen to and respect yours. The underlying theme of Closed Channel self-talk—"*My* opinion is the only one that counts"—reinforces and strengthens the belief from the person's established Power habit: "I only count when you're doing what I want you to do."

The twenty most common thinking errors are described in detail in the next chapter, but you can begin to see the relationship between thinking errors and the four ways of acquiring recognition by looking at the chart on page 128.

WAYS OF ACQUIRING RECOGNITION (W.A.R.)

	Negative Attention Getting	Power	Revenge	Inadequacy
Misbehaving Person's Typical Self-Talk	"I only count when I am being noticed or served."	"I only count when I'm dominating, when you're doing what I want you to do."	"I don't have any power, but I can prove my importance by making you hurt as I feel hurt."	"I can't do anything right, so I won't try to do anything at all. I'm no good."
Typical Misbehavior	Teasing, interrupting, making frequent complaints and requests for assistance	Arguing, demanding	Name-calling, destroying property, physically hurting others	Sulking, pouting, acting helpless
Typical Statement	"I know you're busy, but I've just got to tell you a couple more things!"	"I still say, my way is the best way!"	"You're such a stupid jerk!"	"I can't do it.... it's too hard!"

Other Person's				
Reaction	Feels annoyed, bothered	Feels angry, provoked, challenged	Feels furious, hurt, betrayed	Feels helpless
Destructive Response	"Not now... I'm really busy!"	"I refuse to discuss this anymore, so stop arguing!"	"Don't you ever talk to me that way!"	"We've discussed this before, so stop complaining."
Misbehaving Person's Reaction to Reprimand	Temporarily stops annoying behavior after receiving attention	Intensifies desire to dominate	Puts energies into "getting even," making self even more disliked	Feels there's no use in trying
Other Person's Constructive Response	"I appreciate your wanting to share, but I can't visit anymore right now... could we meet for lunch?	"I'm sorry if it seems unfair to you, but we need to do it this way."	"You're obviously angry with me. When you're calmed down and through name-calling, let's talk about it."	"I realize it seems very difficult to you, but I know you can do it."

THINKING ERRORS ASSOCIATED WITH EACH OF THE FOUR WAYS OF ACQUIRING RECOGNITION

Attention	Power	Revenge	Inadequacy
anger	anger	anger	anger
fragmentation	blaming	blaming	blaming
instancy	closed channel	failure to act responsibly	excuse-making
lack of empathy	fragmentation	instancy	fragmentation
super-optimism	I can't	lack of empathy	I can't
uniqueness	lack of trust	lying	suggestibility
	lying	minimizing	victim stance
	minimizing	ownership	zero state
	power	vagueness	
	vagueness		

CHAPTER SEVENTEEN

"Thinking Errors": How Are Your Misconceptions Contributing to Your Anger?

Thinking errors[1] are "flaws" in our sense of self-worth that can become rigid patterns of self-talk. These flaws or thinking errors arise from assuming that our needs and desires should take priority over anyone else's. (See the chart at the end of this chapter for a description of twenty most commonly used thinking errors.) The three characteristics common to each of the thinking errors can easily be remembered by using the acronym SIN, which stands for:

S = self-centeredness
I = irresponsible behavior
N = nonempathic feelings

Most people use at least some of these errors from time to time. Do you know of anyone who has *never* told a lie, or

---

[1]The concept of "thinking errors" described in this chapter is based on the description of "thinking errors" in Yochelson, Samuel, and Stanton E. Samenow. *The Criminal Personality, Volume 1: A Profile for Change*. New York: Jason Aronson, 1976.

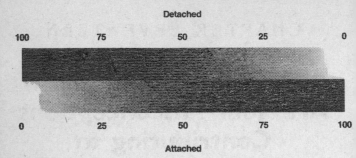

Detached

| 100 | 75 | 50 | 25 | 0 |

| 0 | 25 | 50 | 75 | 100 |

Attached

ATTACHED-DETACHED CONTINUUM

never tried to put the blame on someone else? Depending on the extent of our self-centeredness, and the degree to which we are emotionally detached from or attached to others, we use thinking and behaving errors with greater or lesser frequency. Those who behave in an extremely self-centered manner, without regard for the impact their behavior has on others, may rely on these patterns of self-talk to justify their self-centered, irresponsible behavior. Those who are very empathic toward others generally use fewer thinking errors. All of us fit somewhere along the attached - detached continuum, but no one is ever 100 percent attached or 100 percent detached.

People who are at the "attached" end of the continuum honor their commitments, enjoy maintaining strong emotional attachments to others, and use relatively few thinking errors. Their self-talk usually consists of positive statements which reflect realistic expectations of themselves and others, and their behavior is usually selfless, responsible, and empathic.

On the other hand, people who are at the "detached" end of the continuum are emotionally detached from others and refuse to make any long-term commitments. Their self-talk is dominated by thinking errors and angry statements that reflect their unrealistic expectations of themselves and others. There are some individuals whose behaviors are extremely self-centered, irresponsible, and nonempathic. These people are so detached and hurtful that they are frequently confined to penal or mental health institutions.

Anger is a natural, normal reaction to anger-provoking situations, but, as we've already seen, *how* you express your anger is a matter of *choice*. When your self-talk is filled with thinking errors, it is easy to get into the habit of destructively expressing your anger in aggressive or passive-aggressive ways. The more your self-talk consists of thinking errors, the harder it is to break that destructive habit and replace it with habits of positive self-talk and constructive expressions of anger.

Are You Rehearsing Your Anger Habit?

Earlier we saw that the more you rehearse something the more intense it becomes. Thinking errors are a way of rehearsing self-centeredness, irresponsible behavior, and nonempathic feelings. Remember: How you think is how you behave, and how you behave is how you think. Thus, each time you use one of the thinking errors, you are reinforcing and intensifying your self-centeredness, irresponsible behavior, and nonempathic feelings for others.

The extent to which you rehearse and reinforce your anger habit by using these errors either decreases or increases your willingness to take control of your anger. The more you repeat self-centered, error-filled self-talk in your mind, the more you perpetuate your self-centeredness. The more self-centered you are, the more resistant you will be to breaking away from your destructive anger habit and replacing it with appropriate self-talk and constructive anger management skills.

As long as you continue to insist that it is your right not only to *get* angry but to *stay* angry, you will continue to *be* angry. As long as you continue using your anger to hurt others because you feel hurt, you will continue to intensify and perpetuate your anger habit. When you become willing to let go of your desire to hurt others when you feel hurt, you'll find it is easier to break out of your destructive anger cycle, behave responsibly, and discover a sense of personal power. When you are willing to stop using your anger as a way of manipulating or intimidating others into giving you what you want, you will begin to experience the benefits that come from expressing your anger in constructive, assertive ways.

Most young children have noble intentions to cooperate and stay out of trouble. Yet, most young children get reprimanded occasionally for either not doing what they were asked to do or for behaving inappropriately. The problem usually exists not with their intentions but with their sense of responsibility (which is not yet formed) and their empathy for others (which has not yet developed).

As an adult, you may have the best of intentions to learn how to manage your anger. But if you have been in the habit of using several of the thinking and behavior errors, you will probably be too self-centered, too irresponsible, and too lacking in empathy to be willing to manage your anger successfully.

The key to decreasing your self-centeredness, and increasing your sense of responsibility and empathy for others, is to reduce the frequency with which you fill your self-talk with thinking errors. If your thinking error habit is not too strong, you can reduce the frequency of your thinking errors by listening to your self-talk, identifying your thinking errors, and replacing them with appropriate self-talk. People who have severe thinking error habits may need professional help to manage their anger, reduce their thinking errors, and increase their responsible behavior. (Professionally managed treatment interventions for severely self-centered people are discussed in chapter 42.)

The following chart describes the characteristics of each of the twenty most commonly used thinking errors.

TWENTY COMMONLY USED THINKING ERRORS

Thinking Error	Definition	Self-Talk	Hidden Message
Anger	Responding emotionally to manipulate and control others in order to fulfill your own needs	"I'm so angry I could . . ."	"If I don't get what I want, I'll use my anger to get it. Either I'll use some form of passive anger (such as pouting) to manipulate others into giving me what I want, or I'll use some aggressive expression of anger (such as shouting) to force others into giving me what I want."
Blaming	Placing the responsibility for your irresponsible behavior on others in order to avoid accepting the responsibility yourself	"They made me do it, it was their fault."	"I can probably get away with this if I refuse to admit it is *my* fault."

Thinking Error	Definition	Self-Talk	Hidden Message
Closed Channel	Disdainfully ignoring or selfishly rejecting other people's opinions while insisting that they listen and respect yours	"I don't want to hear what you have to say, but you better listen to *me!*"	"*My* opinion is the only one that counts."
Excuse Making	Justifying irresponsible behavior	"I had a perfectly good reason for doing that."	"As long as I can come up with an excuse, I can't be accused of irresponsible behavior."
Failure to Assume Responsibility	Failure to accept personal responsibility for your irresponsible behavior	"This assignment is boring and I don't see what I can get out of it anyway."	"I'm not going to do something that doesn't seem fun or exciting."
Fragmentation	A pattern of enthusiastically embracing a new relationship or task, then dropping it as soon as it becomes boring or no longer meets *your* needs	"I can't seem to finish anything I start. Oh well. I guess I didn't really want to do it after all."	"It's my right to break my commitments whenever I feel like it."

I Can't	A stubborn, passive-aggressive way of saying, "I won't; controlling others from a position of helplessress, gaining attention, and eliciting help from others by making yourself appear inadequate	"I can't do that." "I don't want to do it, and I *won't* do it."
Instancy	An immature, self-centered insistence upon the immediate gratification of your own needs without regard for others	"To heck with it, I'm not waiting for anyone." "I want what I want, when I want it . . . not just when it's convenient for someone else."
Lack of Empathy	A failure to consider the impact your irresponsible behavior has on others	"So what if he got hurt, it didn't hurt me." "I don't care about anybody, and nobody really cares about me."

Thinking Error	Definition	Self-Talk	Hidden Message
Lack of Trust	Demanding that others place their trust in you, even though your lack of respect for others prevents you from trusting them	"He should just take my word for it!"	"You have to trust *me*, but you can't make me trust you."
Lying	Attempting to deceive oneself or others in order to satisfy your own desires	"I didn't do it."	"The important thing is to get what I want. If I have to lie to get it then I'll lie. Lying is no big deal."
Minimizing	Purposely discounting the hurtfulness of your irresponsible actions	"Why the big fuss? What I did wasn't all that bad."	"If I can minimize the severity of my actions, I won't get in as much trouble."
Ownership	The perception that other people and their possessions exist for meeting your own needs and desires	"Why shouldn't I take it? It's what I wanted and it was right there."	"It's my right to have whatever I want."

Power	The excessive desire for power, control, and dominance over others	"I refuse to do it his dumb way."	"I don't care if I have to manipulate or intimidate them, it's going to be done *my* way!"
Suggestibility	Noted for being quickly and easily led into irresponsible behavior	"Sure I'll do that with you, it sounds fun!"	"To heck with what I should be doing!"
Superoptimism	Having an unrealistic evaluation of your own capabilities	"Of course I can do it, I can do anything I want to, once I put my mind to it."	"No one can stop me from doing what I want to do."
Uniqueness	Adhering to the mistaken notion of specialness based on an unfounded, self-serving distinction between yourself and others	"So what if this is a 25 mph zone . . . I'm in a hurry."	"I'm special, so the rules that everyone else has to follow don't apply to me."
Vagueness	Giving nonspecific responses to avoid the consequences of your irresponsible behavior	"Probably . . . more or less . . . I guess so . . . I'm not sure."	"If I withhold certain bits of information, I won't get in trouble."

Thinking Error	Definition	Self-Talk	Hidden Message
Victim Stance	Avoiding accountability for your actions by portraying yourself as a helpless victim of circumstances beyond your control	"It wasn't my fault, he started it. Don't blame me. I didn't have any other choice."	"As long as I can put the responsibility on someone else, I won't be held accountable."
Zero State	Having an unrealistic, negative perception of yourself as a total failure whenever you aren't recognized as an unqualified success	"I'm no good, it's no use, I can't do anything right."	"My worth is validated in being #1. If I'm not #1, then I'm a failure."

CHAPTER EIGHTEEN

T.A. at a Glance: Communicating Effectively

Do some people tend to "get your goat," or get under your skin, no matter what they say? Or do people sometimes get so angry with you that they refuse to listen to what you are trying to say?

Advertisers would have you believe that you'll have a captive audience if you just use the right mouthwash, perfume, or cologne, or if you chew the right gum or eat the right breath mint. But in reality, no matter how good you smell, or how attractive you may appear, it takes more than saying "E.F. Hutton says" to get people to listen to you, especially when you're angry. Many people don't realize that *how* they say what they say can be more infuriating than *what* they say. What is there about the *way* in which people communicate that seems to be more anger-provoking than *what* they are actually saying?

Transactional Analysis

Transactional Analysis (T.A.), developed by Eric Berne, is a system for understanding human behavior and analyzing the basic types of communications or transactions people have with one another. According to Berne's system of Transactional Analysis, there are three basic ways people can relate to their environment or interact with others. Berne labeled these the *Parent, Adult,* and *Child* . . . **not** because people use these styles when they are a specific age, but because those terms are descriptive of the attitude represented by each style. (A simplified description of each of these styles is provided at the end of this chapter.)

Characteristics of the "Parent" Style of Communication

Your communication is said to be coming from the Parent style when you are modeling how your parents or parent substitutes communicated with you when you were a small child. Most parents relate to their children either as an authority figure or as a nurturing care-giver. Thus, the Parent style of communication includes words and behaviors that are critical, domineering, judgmental, demanding, and demeaning, as well as those that are caring, supportive, and compassionate.

Typical Parent-type messages would be, "You'd better get this d—— report out by ten o'clock sharp! Do you hear me? If you f—— up, you can just start looking for a new job!" or, "I think we should sit over here where the sun won't be in your eyes. You should have the chef salad for lunch today, it will be good for you and it won't make you so sleepy after you eat."

Characteristics of the "Adult" Style of Communication

Your communication is said to be coming from the Adult when you are focusing on the current situation, and you are gathering and evaluating all the pertinent facts in an objective, unemotional manner. Thus, the Adult style of communication includes words and behaviors that are specific, factual, inquisitive, confident, and informative.

Typical Adult messages would be, "This needs to go out in the ten o'clock mail today, please take care of it," or, "Where would you prefer to sit, by the window or by the fireplace? I understand they have a good chef salad here, have you ever tried it?"

Characteristics of the "Child" Style of Communication

Your communication is said to be coming from the Child style when it mimics the feelings and actions you had as a young child. Thus, the Child style of communication includes words and behaviors that are creative, impulsive, fun-loving, playful, and spontaneous, as well as highly emotional, self-centered, rebellious, and aggressive.

Typical Child messages would be, "Gee whiz, I need this stupid report mailed by ten o'clock. Which one of you guys would be willing to do me a teensy weensy little favor and drop it in the mail lickety-split?" or, "Come on, guys, let's sit next to the window. I get a charge out of 'people-watching' while I eat my lunch! What do you say we all take a break from our nutrition kick and have a big, fat, juicy hotdog and hot fudge sundae with *all* the trimmings!"

So, Who Is the Most Effective Communicator?

Each of the three styles of communicating and interacting contributes to your relationships with others in many positive ways. However, each style also has features that can be very anger-provoking, depending on the time and situation. For instance, you may appreciate the Parent message, "Watch out!" if you aren't aware that the car driving in the lane next to you is starting to swerve into your lane. In this situation the Parent statement might protect you from harm. However, further Parent statements such as, "You should learn to drive defensively," or, "You're the worst driver I've ever seen," may provoke your anger, especially if the comments seem critical and judgmental.

The lack of emotion and spontaneity that make rational, logical, practical Adult statements ideal in situations that call for problem-solving also make this style of communicating very frustrating to people who are sad and seeking sympathy, or happy and looking for a playful companion. Similarly, the carefree, impulsive nature of Child statements can be very enjoyable and uplifting under the right circumstances. Their irresponsible, highly emotional nature, however, can be very exasperating to deal with—especially when you have serious matters to discuss or important decisions to make.

Any of the three styles of communication can be appropriate, given the right circumstances. But in terms of coping with angry feelings and angry people, communicating in a straightforward Adult-to-Adult manner is the most effective style. When you communicate from your Adult directly to the other person's Adult, you are least likely to elicit or intensify that person's anger.

When you communicate from your Parent to someone's Child it is easy for that person to feel as if you are trying to control him or her from a "one up" position. When you communicate from your Child to someone's Parent it is easy for that person to feel as if you are trying to manipulate him or her from a "one down" position. But when you communicate from your Adult to the other person's Adult (and use "I Messages" as described in chapter 36), your statements will usually be well received even if you aren't wearing any special perfume or cologne.

ADULT-TO-ADULT TRANSACTION

Sender   Responder

PARENT-TO-CHILD TRANSACTION

Sender   Responder

PARENT, ADULT, AND CHILD AT A GLANCE

	Parent	Adult	Child
Characteristics	Authoritarian, critical, nurturing, supportive	Unemotional, confident, informative, factual	Emotional, spontaneous, impulsive, self-centered, rebellious
Functions	Instill values in children. Make quick decisions.	Gather and study data. Make logical decisions	Have fun. Experience life to its fullest.
Tone of voice	Harsh, demanding, or sympathetic	firm, calm, unemotional	Exuberant, playful, or aggressive
Key words	"Should," "ought," "don't worry"	"How," "when," "according to"	"I want," "let's play"
Body language	Pointing an accusing finger	Attentive, alert, good eye contact	Demonstrative or dejected

CHAPTER NINETEEN

Personality: How Do You Characteristically Respond to Life and Cope with Anger?

Stress is one of the biggest obstacles to constructive anger management. Most people find it difficult to cope with angry feelings and angry people when they are stressed, and the higher the level of stress, the more difficult coping becomes. By reducing the unnecessary stress in your life you can increase your interest in constructive anger management and reduce the likelihood that you'll use destructive expressions of anger in the future.

Being aware of the source of your stress is the key to controlling the amount of stress you experience. And being aware of your basic personality type(s) is the key to understanding what things are stressful or anger-provoking to you. Remember, what is stressful or anger-provoking for one person may not necessarily be stressful or anger-provoking to someone else. Different personality types have different ways of perceiving and reacting to various situations.

The term *personality* refers to the complex mixture of desirable and undesirable psychological traits that are manifested by our distinctive and habitual method of relating to others and coping with our emotions, thoughts, and perceptions. Our personalities reflect not only the basic temperament with which we were born, but the impact of our life experiences and what we learn by modeling others. Our personalities also reflect our life script, locus of control, introversion/extraversion preference, ways of acquiring recognition, thinking errors, and styles of communication we use.

Personality types become personality "disorders" only when the person develops a tendency to display the undesirable characteristics associated with a specific personality type much more frequently and consistently than he or she displays the desirable characteristics of that personality. When the person reflects the undesirable characteristics to the extent that he or she become dysfunctional and is unable to think or behave rationally or in a socially appropriate manner, that person may be diagnosed as having a personality disorder. Just because you identify with or feel you have some of the undesirable characteristics of a particular personality type does not necessarily mean that you have a personality disorder. Only a mental-health professional with sufficient training is qualified to give anyone a personality "disorder" diagnosis. The predominance and severity of undesirable traits must significantly outweigh the desirable ones before anyone is considered as having a dysfunctional personality.

Each person consists of a unique blend of characteristics from different personality types. A person's personality is rarely, if ever, limited to characteristics from just one type. People usually have one predominant personality type or another, with additional qualities and characteristics from at least one or more of the other personality types. How a person reacts to a particular situation depends on some of the related factors such as: how that person is currently feeling about himself (his self-esteem at the time); his degree of self-confidence; his present level of stress and the extent of his coping abilities; his temperament; and his personality type. An individual's pattern of behavior, which can be observed day after day, is shaped by his personality. For example, when we commute to work during the morning, some people drive over the speed limit, weaving in and out of traffic; some stay in one lane, adhering strictly to the posted speed; others drive slower than the posted speed and allow ample time each morning for unexpected delays. These driving patterns usually remain fairly consistent week after week. Yet, under stressful circumstances (i.e., poor driving conditions, the alarm clock didn't go off, or an earlier-than-usual appointment) these same people may demonstrate a much different driving pattern. This does not mean that their personalities have changed or that they have "multiple personalities." It simply demonstrates that everyone's personality consists of characteristics that influence how we react to both *stressful* and *calm* situations. This conglomeration of characteristics are what blend together to make each of us a special and unique being.

As previously indicated, identifying the intricate details of your specific personality is a complicated process requiring the help of a trained professional. However, by comparing yourself to the following descriptions of ten basic personality types, you can obtain a general awareness of your predominant personality type, and your most likely patterns for coping with angry feelings and angry people. Look at the characteristics under the desirable and undesirable traits of all ten personalities. Each personality type has its own set of desirable and undesirable characteristics. Since no one is "perfect," everyone has at least some undesirable characteristics within the composition of his or her personality.

Some people might claim to have every characteristic, but you should limit your selection to those characteristics that are descriptive of you *most* of the time (either under calm or stressful situations). For example, you may be "charming" when you are sober or in nonstressful situations, but "obnoxious" when intoxicated or in stressful situations. Or, you could be either obnoxious or charming in both stressful and nonstressful situations. Therefore, it is up to you to decide whether you are more charming or obnoxious *most* of the time. The more understanding, acceptance, and insight you have about yourself, the more accurately and easily you'll be able to pinpoint the blend of characteristics that comprises your particular personality. Although we all have characteristics from more than one personality type, we often tend to have a predominant number of characteristics from just a few of the ten personalities described in this chapter. For example, if someone found that a large percentage of the characteristics listed under the Dramatic personality were quite descriptive of him, but a few of the characteristics mentioned under the Dependent and Oppositional personality types fits him also, he would describe himself as having a personality blend that was predominantly Dramatic, with certain features of the Dependent and Oppositional types.

The charts located at the end of this chapter provide some anger management techniques and ways to avoid triggering the anger of each of these personalities. They also suggest how to cope with each personality type so that they don't provoke your anger.

Knowing what types of things are stressful to you and/or likely to trigger your anger makes it easier for you to:

- prepare yourself for and cope with certain unavoidable situations
- reduce the amount of undesirable stress in your life
- increase your willingness to respond constructively to anger-provoking situations

It also helps to be aware of the personality type(s) of others. When you are aware of their personality types you can choose whether you add to or help reduce their stress. As long as you help keep their stress levels high, either by interfering with their special ways of recharging their batteries, or behaving in ways that trigger their stress, you are contributing to their anger management problems. However, when you help others reduce their stress, by respecting their need to do what is relaxing to them, you increase the likelihood that in the future they'll choose to respond constructively to anger- or stress-provoking situations.

The Actively Withdrawn Personality

People with an Actively Withdrawn (AW) personality tend to be very creative and perceptive. Outwardly they appear calm, quiet, and pleasant, but inwardly they are trying to avoid further rejection by keeping themselves emotionally distant from others. Because of their fear of rejection, most AWs want a guarantee that a relationship will last before they are willing to enter into it. As a result, AWs have very few friends. AWs want others to like them and accept them, but their self-doubt, low self-esteem, shyness, and strong mistrust of others often make them appear emotionally cold and uncomfortable in social situations. Consequently, they tend to push others away.

Rather than risk possible rejection by confronting others directly with their anger, AWs tend to express their anger in passive-aggressive ways, such as giving people the silent treatment, pouting, expressing doubt by rolling their eyes, smirking, acting confused, procrastinating, or conveniently forgetting to follow through with a request.

The Ambivalent Personality

People with an Ambivalent personality (AB) usually make a very favorable first impression because of their charming, charismatic, and friendly manner. Other people are quickly drawn to them because of their warmth and intensity. ABs are fun to be around because of their intelligence, creativity, spontaneity, and colorful demeanor, yet their relationships are often stormy, unstable, and unsatisfying. ABs' difficulties with their relationships stem from their own conflicting feelings, which vacillate dramatically from feeling confident and good about themselves to feelings of self-disgust, insecurity, and fear of being rejected by others. As a result of their difficulty in sustaining close and personally satisfying relationships, they frequently experience feelings of loneliness, emptiness, insecurity, anxiety, irritability, anger, and self-hatred. The "cycle of loneliness" often experienced by ABs is triggered because their attempts at drawing someone close to them conflicts with their fear of intimacy. After they've used their warmth and charm to attract someone, they begin to feel they don't deserve a satisfying relationship, and they worry about that person abandoning them. These fears lead ABs into "testing" the other person's commitment to the relationship. They sabotage their relationships by switching off their charm and replacing it with demanding, obnoxious, repulsive, abusive (and sometimes self-destructive) behaviors. ABs may resort to engaging in binges—overindulging in alcohol, food, or sex, for example— then suffer from feelings of guilt, worthlessness, and inner rage, which last until they eventually push the other person away and are back to feeling abandoned and lonely. Thus, the cycle of loneliness usually includes the following components:

- feelings of loneliness
- use of charm and warmth to attract others
- sabotaging of the relationship through obnoxious behavior
- engaging in binges
- guilt
- feelings of worthlessness
- self-inflicted punishment (not always)

- anger
- Pushing others away
- renewed feelings of loneliness

ABs have an intense inner conflict of feeling both independent and dependent. They fear abandonment, so they
cling dependently to others, while at the same time they
detest being too intimate and emotionally close, due to their
fear of being engulfed and controlled ("owned") by others.
They seem driven by their inner conflict to push others
away.

ABs are intolerant of criticism because they equate it with
being rejected. They are constantly on guard against rejection. If their charm doesn't earn them the attention they
desire, they may quickly switch to manipulative behaviors,
such as sulking, sobbing, or suicidal gesturing, until they
get their needs met. ABs' expressions of anger are frequently inappropriate and intense, and they find it particularly difficult to disengage emotionally and look at things in
a calm, rational way.

Life for ABs seems to be a series of distressing contradic-
tions. They continually move in and out of entangled relationships, and they frequently vacillate between feeling
underwhelmed and overwhelmed, and from feeling lonely
and rejected to feeling engulfed by intimacy. ABs' expressions of anger are very unpredictable. They may vacillate
quickly between passive-aggressive expressions (i.e., sulking,
being sarcastic, or giving double messages) and explosive,
aggressive expressions (such as being intrusive, hostile,
rageful, or physically assaultive).

The Compulsive Personality

People with a Compulsive (CO) personality are generally
dependable, neat, orderly, meticulous, and punctual. They
maintain high standards and dedicate themselves to hard

work and compulsive attention to detail in their attempts to achieve perfection. Unable to reach many of the goals they set for themselves, COs often feel inadequate and dissatisfied with their achievements.

They have a strong need to feel in control. Although they usually don't express their feelings openly or directly, COs often feel angry when their performance or authority is criticized or challenged. This is especially true if that criticism comes from people they admire or respect.

The Dependent Personality

People with a Dependent (DE) personality are usually friendly, loyal, generous, easygoing, and agreeable. They typically have a generous nature and a strong need for acceptance. Since DEs already reject themselves, one of their biggest fears is of being rejected by others. In order to cope with their overwhelming fear of rejection, DEs eagerly strive to keep harmony and please others, and they frequently yield to the demands and desires of others. The more fearful they are, the more dependent, indecisive, passive, submissive, and self-sacrificing they are. The more dependent they are, the more they are susceptible to and tolerant of abusive relationships.

Even when they are angry, most DEs would rather suffer in silence than risk further rejection. Consequently, they tend to express their anger in very passive ways that do little to resolve their anger.

The Dramatic Personality

People with a Dramatic (DA) personality are socially outgoing and can be quite charming, adventuresome, amusing, and friendly. Even though they can usually make friends easily, DAs' self-centeredness and lack of empathy make it difficult for them to sustain close and satisfying personal relationships.

DAs seem to have an insatiable need for attention, reassurance, approval, and praise. They're easily angered when those needs aren't met, and they usually express their anger in loud and aggressive ways. Although their outward expressions of anger and other emotions are often very dramatic, DAs' feelings may dissipate or change quickly from one emotion to another.

The Egotistical Personality

People with an Egotistical (EG) personality are generally quite self-reliant, ambitious, hardworking, and proud of their achievements. Although they appear self-confident, their self-esteem tends to be very fragile. EGs are envious of other people and often overrate their own abilities and accomplishments in order to make a good impression on others.

EGs view themselves as special and unique. Consequently they often expect and demand special treatment without considering the hardships and inconveniences their self-centered needs may be placing on others.

When EGs are angry they typically try to hide their feelings by pretending to be calm and unemotional. If they are criticized or don't get their own way, however, they may become enraged and react with brief but very aggressive outbursts of anger.

The Mistrustful Personality

People with a Mistrustful (MI) personality are usually energetic, ambitious, and serious-minded. They are capable of being objective and rational; however, they also tend to be argumentative and critical of others. MIs often have difficulty accepting responsibility for their own shortcomings, yet they tend to be overly critical of other people's mistakes.

MIs tend to be suspicious and to feel unappreciated. They

also tend to avoid intimacy and appear to lack tender feelings. Perhaps as a result of experiencing the trauma of childhood abuse or neglect, most MIs continue to expect others to exploit them.

MIs often appear pessimistic and seem to have a poor sense of humor. MIs are very sensitive to criticism and are easily offended, frustrated, and angered. Once their anger is provoked, MIs usually harbor a grudge for a long time and seek revenge against whoever provoked their anger.

The Oppositional Personality

People with an Oppositional (OP) personality are usually very loyal individuals and strong advocates for justice. They usually have a good sense of humor and are capable of showing tender feelings toward others. However, OPs tend to withhold their feelings except from a few close friends, because they frequently feel so misunderstood and unappreciated.

OPs tend to be emotionally sensitive, erratically moody, habitually discontent, impatient, impulsive, and irritable. OPS are particularly vulnerable to stress because of their constant vacillation between feeling dependent on others and wanting to be independent. Consequently, OPs become frustrated, angry, and resentful quite easily, then hold on to these feelings for a long time. Sometimes OPs express their anger aggressively in loud, obnoxious outbursts, but usually they express their anger indirectly by giving others the silent treatment, procrastinating, conveniently forgetting to do what they were asked, sulking, arguing, or making snide, cutting remarks.

The Passively Withdrawn Personality

People with a Passively Withdrawn (PW) personality typically feel content to work quietly and independently.

Their preference for solitary pursuits often makes them appear emotionally cold and aloof. PWs often immerse themselves in activities such as playing video games or tinkering with electronic or mechanical gadgets. To PWs, activities such as these are relaxing, refreshing, and revitalizing.

PWs tend to be disinterested in forming social relationships and often lack the desire to express warm, tender feelings. They are often criticized and ridiculed by others because of their dull, boring, unemotional dispositions. They react to this criticism and ridicule by having even greater needs for the comfort of isolation and solitary activities.

PWs are calm, peaceful individuals who have a limited range of emotions. They rarely experience emotional extremes such as elation or rage. When they do feel angry they may occasionally flare up with brief outbursts of verbal aggression, but much more often they respond by passively withdrawing from the provocation or by giving people the silent treatment.

The Self-Serving Personality

On the surface, people with a Self-Serving (SS) personality seem quite friendly, outgoing, relaxed, carefree, and self-confident. They are often the center of attention at parties and other social gatherings, charming other people with their sense of humor and quick wit. Underneath their superficial charm, however, they are habitually angry, emotionally detached, extremely self-centered, immature, irresponsible, and nonempathic.

SSs are easily frustrated and angered. They often express anger in hostile and aggressive ways that intimidate others into complying with their demands. For example, SSs are intolerant of criticism, so they often exaggerate their anger to intimidate their critics from making further criticisms. SSs are also adept at using manipulative passive-aggressive expressions of anger to control others and get their own way.

Identifying Your Personality

If you're having difficulty identifying your particular personality type, don't be discouraged. The preceding descriptions give only a broad overview of ten of the most common personality types. And remember, your personality is probably a blend of at least two or more types.

The following charts can be used to help identify your predominant personality type and provide a general indication of the personality type(s) of others. They also contain some anger management strategies for each personality type and suggestions for decreasing the likelihood that other people will provoke your anger. Most of the techniques described here may be used with any personality type. However, the appropriateness of these techniques varies from one personality to the next. Consequently, each of the following charts lists only those techniques that are most appropriate for the particular personality being described.

The more insight you have into your and other people's personalities, the easier it is to cope with your or someone else's anger. Being aware of another's personality can help you avoid triggering his or her anger and avoid having that person provoke your anger. The more aware you are of your personality's characteristics, the more aware you will be of what is stressful to you and what situations are most likely to trigger your anger. That awareness can help you avoid many stressful or anger-provoking situations and enable you to choose the anger management techniques most effective for you.

THE ACTIVELY WITHDRAWN PERSONALITY

Desirable Traits	Undesirable Traits	
Acutely perceptive observers	Appear emotionally cold and uncomfortable in social situations	Low self-esteem
Creative	Apprehensive	Masks inward anxiety with evasiveness
Gentle	Easily hurt by criticism, ridicule	Mistrustful of others
Imaginative	Exaggerates potential difficulties	Overly sensitive to potential rejection, continuously anticipates being slighted
Outwardly calm	Excessive self-analyzing	
Pleasant	Few close friends	Self-defeating coping mechanisms
Quiet	Inflexible	Timid and withdrawn in spite of desire for affection and acceptance
	Inwardly anxious and ill at ease	
	Irrational thinking	

THE ACTIVELY WITHDRAWN PERSONALITY

To Avoid Triggering Anger In Persons With This Personality Type	To Cope With This Personality Type so They Don't Provoke *Your* Anger	Anger Management Strategies For This Personality Type
Be Self-Aware	Be Self-Aware	Be Self-Aware
Avoid excessive friendliness or complimenting too frequently	Deep Breathing	Positive Self-Talk
Build trust gently and slowly	Therapeutic Counting	Adjust your expectations
Extend an impartial, sincere respect	Emotionally Disengage	Put things into perspective
Avoid sympathizing	Rapid Relaxation	R.E.T.
Respect their need for distance between themselves and others	Power Relaxation	Let Go
Avoid criticizing, blaming, or reminding them of past mistakes	Positive Self-Talk	Favorite Activity
Give feedback in a non-threatening, non-judgmental manner	Adjust your expectations	
Make positive comments in a sincere, emotionally neutral, matter of fact manner	Put things into perspective	
	Don't take it personally	
	R.E.T.	
	Let Go	

The Ambivalent Personality

Desirable Traits	Undesirable Traits	
Active	Abandonment fears	Intolerance of solitude
Adventurous	Aggressive	Intrusive
Appealing	Ambivalent/undecided	Irritable
Articulate	Angry/rageful	Lack of empathy
Artistic	Argumentative	Low self-esteem
Assertive	Arrogant	Manipulative
Charming	Assaultive	Mood swings (severe) (from euphoria to depression)
Colorful	Belligerent	
Creative	Bitter	Moody
Exciting	Blaming	Pessimistic
Friendly	Bored easily	

Desirable Traits	Undesirable Traits	
Fun	Demanding	Sarcastic
Humorous	Easily discouraged, distracted, and frustrated	Self-centered
Intelligent		Self-defeating
Inspiring	Feelings of emptiness	Self-destructive
Intense	Hostile	Self-hatred
Intuitive	Identity confusion	Stormy, unsatisfying relationships
Outgoing	Impulsive	Stubborn
Persuasive	Incongruent	Suspicious
Spontaneous	Inconsistent	Suicidal thoughts and threats
Stimulating	Independent/dependent conflict	Talkative
Vivacious		Unpredictable
Warm	Insecure	

THE AMBIVALENT PERSONALITY

To Avoid Triggering Anger In Persons With This Personality Type	To Cope With This Personality Type So They Don't Provoke Your Anger	Anger Management Strategies For This Personality Type
Be self-aware	Be self-aware	Be self-aware
Use the "S.E.T. System" (Support, Empathy, & Truth) originated by the staff at St. John's Mercy Medical Center in St. Louis. (Support them by showing concern; Empathize by acknowledging their feelings; and respond with emotionally neutral, nonthreatening, nonjudgmental Truth statements, indicating they're responsible for their own problems)	Deep breathing	Deep breathing
	Therapeutic counting	Therapeutic counting
	Emotionally disengage	Power relaxation
	Rapid relaxation	Positive self-talk
	Power relaxation	Put things in perspective
	Positive self-talk	Don't take it personally
	Adjust your expectations	Humor
Be friendly, but avoid overinvolvement by keeping a safe emotional distance	Put things in perspective	Keep an anger diary
	Reframe the situation	Examine your thinking errors
Listen attentively, and communicate with "I Messages"	Don't take it personally	R.E.T.
	Humor	Let go
Avoid power struggles and entanglements	R.E.T.	Favorite activity

To Avoid Triggering Anger In Persons With This Personality Type	To Cope With This Personality Type So They Don't Provoke *Your* Anger	Anger Management Strategies For This Personality Type
Give frequent compliments, avoid criticizing, blaming, reminding of past mistakes, or being deliberately hurtful	Let go	
	Favorite activity	
Give *specific* suggestions for improvement	Systematic desensitization	
Redirect away from ventilation of anger	Self-hypnosis	
React calmly to their ambivalence and changeability	Role-play	
Avoid kidding, teasing, or mocking		
Communicate in straightforward manner, avoid contradictions or ambivalence		

THE COMPULSIVE PERSONALITY

Desirable Traits	Undesirable Traits	
Accurate	Compulsive preoccupation with details	Masks anxiety with compulsiveness
Dependable		Perfectionistic
Gives attention to detail	Difficulty discarding unnecessary objects	Poor self-image
Hardworking	Difficulty expressing tender feelings	Reluctant to give time, money, or gifts
Meticulous		
Neat	Empathy inhibited by compulsive behaviors	Reluctant to try new things or make changes
Orderly	Expresses anger indirectly (passively)	Rigid insistence on doing things their way
Persevering		
Polite	Indecisive (fearful of disapproval, making mistakes)	Skeptical
Precise		Workaholic
Predictable	Inflexible	
Punctual		
Scrupulous		
Thorough		

THE COMPULSIVE PERSONALITY

To Avoid Triggering Anger In Persons With This Personality Type	To Cope With This Personality Type So They Don't Provoke *Your* Anger	Anger Management Strategies For This Personality Type
Be Self-Aware	Be Self-Aware	Be Self-Aware
Show respect for their values and high standards	Deep Breathing	Deep Breathing
Take them seriously	Therapeutic Counting	Therapeutic Counting
Don't pressure them to express tender feelings	Emotionally Disengage	Power Relaxation
Establish realistic time limits when making requests	Rapid Relaxation	Positive, calming Self-Talk
Avoid requests for sudden changes or decisions	Positive Self-Talk	Adjust your expectations
Limit your requests	Adjust your expectations	Put things into perspective
Give frequent compliments, avoid criticism	Put things into perspective	Reframe the situation
Explain rationale for requests, include them in decision-making	Reframe the situation	Consider the extenuating circumstances
Respond with "I Messages"	Don't take it personally	Humor
	R.E.T.	R.E.T.
	Let Go	Favorite Activity

THE DEPENDENT PERSONALITY

Desirable Traits	Undesirable Traits	
Agreeable	Allows others to make decisions	Inappropriately optimistic
Caring	Avoids self-assertion	Indecisive
Eager to please others	Dependent	Passive and submissive
Easy going	Difficulty coping with social tension, interpersonal conflicts	Perceives self as: weak, inadequate, and stupid
Enthusiastic		
Flexible	Fears abandonment	Self-sacrificing
Friendly	Feels helpless, especially when alone	Susceptible to and tolerant of abusive relationships
Generous (likes to share)		
Good intentions	Gullible, easily exploited, exposes fears and weaknesses	Timid
Good sense of humor		Weak-willed
Kind	Hurt easily by criticism	
Loyal		
Pleasant		
Positive		
Sociable		
Supportive		
Tender		
Warm		

THE DEPENDENT PERSONALITY

To Avoid Triggering Anger In Persons With This Personality Type	To Cope With This Personality Type So They Don't Provoke Your Anger	Anger Management Strategies For This Personality Type
Be Self-Aware	Be Self-Aware	Be Self-Aware
Recognize their appropriate behavior by giving frequent positive attention	Deep Breathing	Therapeutic Counting
	Emotionally Disengage	Emotionally Disengage
Be friendly	Rapid Relaxation	Rapid Relaxation
Provide encouragement	Positive Self-Talk	Positive Self-Talk
Avoid criticizing	Adjust your expectations	Adjust your expectations
Confront them in a gentle, warm, caring, firm, Adult-to-Adult way	Put things into perspective	Put things into perspective
Don't pressure with undesirable or multiple tasks	Don't take it personally	Humor
	Consider the extenuating circumstances	R.E.T.
Respond with "I Messages"	Humor	Let Go
Comply with their appropriate requests	R.E.T.	Favorite Activity
	Role-play	Systematic Desensitization
Be non-authoritarian		Self-Hypnosis
Include them in decision-making		Role-play

THE DRAMATIC PERSONALITY

Desirable Traits	Undesirable Traits	
Adventurous	Craves reassurance, approval, praise	Overly reliant on others
Amusing	Easily distracted, frustrated, and influenced	Persistent attention-seeking (insatiable need for attention)
Appealing	Fearful of rejection	Prone to exaggeration
Charming	Frequent tantrums	Seeks immediate gratification
Creative	Hysterical	Self-centered
Friendly	Inconsiderate in quest for attention	Shallow
Generous with praise	Inconsistent	Stormy, unsatisfying, superficial relationships
Imaginative	Intense expression of emotions	Unable to sustain close relationships
Lively	Lacks genuineness	Vain (excessive concern with personal attractiveness)
Makes friends easily	Manipulative with emotions	
Socially outgoing	Overly dramatic	

THE DRAMATIC PERSONALITY

To Avoid Triggering Anger In Persons With This Personality Type	To Cope With This Personality Type So They Don't Provoke *Your* Anger	Anger Management Strategies For This Personality Type
Be Self-Aware	Be Self-Aware	Be Self-Aware
Be assertive, NOT aggressive or passive	Deep Breathing	Deep Breathing
Give frequent recognition for appropriate behavior	Therapeutic Counting	Therapeutic Counting
Don't make demands (especially for tasks requiring high level intellectual or analytical skill)	Emotionally Disengage	Rapid Relaxation
Avoid power struggles	Rapid Relaxation	Positive, calming Self-Talk
Listen attentively, communicate with "I Messages"	Positive Self-Talk	Put things into perspective
Respect and respond to appropriate quests for attention	Adjust your expectations	Favorite Activity
Redirect conversation to non-anger provoking topics., don't encourage negative ventilation of angry feelings	Put things into perspective	Examine your thinking errors
Be friendly, but keep an emo-	Reframe the situation	
	R.E.T.	

THE EGOTISTICAL PERSONALITY

Desirable Traits	Undesirable Traits	
Ambitious	Conceals weaknesses	Passive
Assertive	Conceited	Presumptuous, overrates abilities, expects special favors
Creative	Criticism elicits indifference or rage	Self-Centered
Entertaining	Demands attention	Self-Indulgent
Hard-working	Envious of others	Selfish
Independent	Fragile self-esteem	Superficial
Optimistic	Independent	Vacillates between glorifying and disregarding others
Self-assured	Non-empathic	Vain
Self-confident	Non-maliciously arrogant	
Self-reliant		
Takes pride in achievements		
Theatrical		

THE EGOTISTICAL PERSONALITY

To Avoid Triggering Anger In Persons With This Personality Type	To Cope With This Personality Type So They Don't Provoke Your Anger	Anger Management Strategies For This Personality Type
Be Self-Aware	Be Self-Aware	Be Self-Aware
Be assertive, NOT aggressive	Deep Breathing	Deep Breathing
Respond with "I Messages"	Therapeutic Counting	Therapeutic Counting
Focus on desirable behavior	Emotionally Disengage	Rapid Relaxation
Don't complain, make demands, or criticize them in public	Rapid Relaxation	Power Relaxation
Show respect, communicate in a gentle, firm, fair, Adult-to-Adult manner	Power Relaxation	Positive Self-Talk
	Positive Self-Talk	Adjust your expectations
Give feedback privately in objective, non-judgmental, unemotional ways, accurately reflect their concerns	Adjust your expectations	Don't take it personally
	Put things into perspective	R.E.T.
	Don't take it personally	Let Go
Be attentive and patient		
Avoid power struggles		
Don't challenge their authority		
Include them in the decision-		

THE MISTRUSTFUL PERSONALITY

Desirable Traits	Undesirable Traits	
Ambitious	Argumentative	High-strung
Energetic	Avoids intimacy	Impatient and impulsive
Keen observer	Blames others	Indecisive, ambivalent
Inquiring mind	Defensive	Irritable
Objective	Difficulty relaxing, letting down their guard	Jealous (especially of those in power)
Persevering	Easily angered, frustrated, offended	Lacks motivation
Self-sufficient	Emotionally cold, lacks tender feelings	Mistrustful of people's loyalty and intentions
Vigilant	Expresses anger indirectly; procrastinates, acts confused, stubborn, forgetful	Overly critical and pessimistic
	Feels unappreciated	Poor sense of humor
	Harbors grudges	Rigid
		Spiteful
		Sullen and contrary

THE MISTRUSTFUL PERSONALITY

To Avoid Triggering Anger In Persons With This Personality Type	To Cope With This Personality Type So They Don't Provoke *Your* Anger	Anger Management Strategies For This Personality Type
Be Self-Aware	Be Self-Aware	Be Self-Aware
Avoid power struggles	Deep Breathing	Deep Breathing
Respect their need for distance and independence	Therapeutic Counting	Therapeutic Counting
Build trust slowly	Emotionally Disengage	Power Relaxation
Avoid excessive friendliness	Rapid Relaxation	Positive Self-Talk
Don't question their opinions	Power Relaxation	Put things into perspective
Allow them to proceed at their own pace	Positive Self-Talk	Don't take it personally
Don't sympathize with them	Adjust your expectations	Humor
Include them in the decision-making	Put things into perspective	R.E.T.
Request politely, don't demand	R.E.T.	Examine your thinking errors
Don't criticize, blame, or remind them of their past mistakes	Let Go	
Give feedback in an objective, non-threatening, non-judg-mental Adult-to-Adult way	Systematic Desensitization	
	Self-Hypnosis	

THE OPPOSITIONAL PERSONALITY

Desirable Traits	Undesirable Traits	
Advocate for justice	Critical	Lacks motivation, self-discipline
Analytical	Easily frustrated, angered	Pessimistic
Anticipates problems	Emotional ambivalence (love/hate)	Resentful
Capable of showing tender feelings	Erratically moody	Spiteful
Creative	Feels misunderstood, unappreciated	Stubborn
Gives attention to detail	Habitually discontent	Typically expresses anger indirectly (silent treatment, forgetting, procrastinating, sulking)
Loyal	Impatient	Unpredictable
Persevering	Impulsive	Vacillates between being cooperative and defiantly resistive
Sense of humor	Indecisive	Vacillates between dependency and independency
	Irritable	

THE OPPOSITIONAL PERSONALITY

To Avoid Triggering Anger In Persons With This Personality Type	To Cope With This Personality Type So They Don't Provoke *Your* Anger	Anger Management Strategies For This Personality Type
Be Self-Aware	Be Self-Aware	Be Self-Aware
Be assertive, NOT aggressive	Deep Breathing	Deep Breathing
Communicate with "I Messages"	Emotionally Disengage	Therapeutic Counting
Show respect, talk Adult-to-Adult	Rapid Relaxation	Emotionally Disengage
	Power Relaxation	Power Relaxation
Give encouragement and infrequent, short, concise, sincere compliments	Adjust your expectations	Adjust your expectations
	Put things into perspective	Put things into perspective
	Reframe the situation	Reframe the situation
	Don't take it personally	Don't take it personally
	R.E.T.	Humor

THE OPPOSITIONAL PERSONALITY

To Avoid Triggering Anger In Persons With This Personality Type	To Cope With This Personality Type So They Don't Provoke *Your* Anger	Anger Management Strategies For This Personality Type
Don't complain, make demands, or criticize	Let Go	R.E.T.
Avoid power struggles		Let Go
Don't encourage negative ventilation of angry feelings; redirect conversations to non-anger-provoking topics if possible		Favorite Activity
		Examine your thinking errors
Give feedback privately, calmly, and in an Adult-to-Adult manner		Positive Self-Talk
Limit your request and avoid a sense of urgency		
Allow them to participate in decision-making		

THE PASSIVELY WITHDRAWN PERSONALITY

Desirable Traits	Undesirable Traits	
Calm	Apathetic	Lacks initiative
Enjoys hobbies	Boring	Unable to sense other people's feelings
Gentle	Doesn't make feelings known	Unintentionally aloof and indifferent
Not easily angered	Emotionally bland	Unintentionally unkind and under-responsive to others
Peaceful	Lacks enthusiasm, energy, and spontaneity	
Self-sufficient		
Works quietly and independently		
Untroubled		

THE PASSIVELY WITHDRAWN PERSONALITY

To Avoid Triggering Anger In Persons With This Personality Type	To Cope With This Personality Type So They Don't Provoke *Your* Anger	Anger Management Strategies For This Personality Type
Be Self-Aware	Be Self-Aware	Be Self-Aware
Avoid excessive friendliness	Deep Breathing	Positive Self-Talk
Build trust slowly	Therapeutic Counting	Humor
Allow them to proceed at their own pace	Emotionally Disengage	R.E.T.
Respect their wish for distance between themselves and others	Rapid Relaxation	Favorite Activity
Remain emotionally disengaged	Power Relaxation	
Respect their preference for remaining socially withdrawn and independent	Positive Self-Talk	
Avoid making demands	Adjust your expectations	
Gently encourage their occasional participation in non-threatening social activities	Put things into perspective	
	Don't take it personally	
	Humor	
	Let Go	

THE SELF-SERVING PERSONALITY

Desirable Traits	Undesirable Traits	
Active	Aggressive	Insufficient feelings of guilt
Adventurous	Angry	Intimidating
Bold	Arrogant	Irresponsible
Courageous	Blaming	Irritable, moody
Eloquent	Cynical	Manipulative, exploitive
Energetic	Demanding, domineering	Nonempathic
Enthusiastic	Disdainful of authority	Poor judgment
Generous (occasionally)	Dissatisfied	Rarely apologizes
Good sense of humor	Distrustful	Rarely profits from past experience
Intelligent	Emotionally detached	Self-centered, selfish
Outgoing	Hostile	Shallow relationships
Persuasive	Hurtful	Superficially charming
Playful	Immature	Thrill seeking
Self-confident	Impatient, easily frustrated	Untrustworthy
Straightforward	Impulsive	Vindictive
Tough	Independent	

THE SELF-SERVING PERSONALITY

To Avoid Triggering Anger In Persons With This Personality Type	To Cope With This Personality Type So They Don't Provoke *Your* Anger	Anger Management Strategies For This Personality Type
Be Self-Aware	Be Self-Aware	Be Self-Aware
Be assertive, NOT aggressive or passive	Deep Breathing	Deep Breathing
Respond with ''I Messages''	Therapeutic Counting	Therapeutic Counting
Show respect, talk Adult-to-Adult	Emotionally Disengage	Power Relaxation
Give encouragement, make suggestions, don't complain or make demands	Rapid Relaxation	Positive Self-Talk
	Power Relaxation	Put things into perspective
Avoid critical remarks	Positive Self-Talk	Don't take it personally
	Adjust your expectations	Humor
Give feedback privately, in a straightforward, non-judgmental, firm, fair, non-emotional manner	Put things into perspective	Keep an anger diary
	Reframe the situation	Examine your thinking errors
	Don't take it personally	

THE SELF-SERVING PERSONALITY

To Avoid Triggering Anger In Persons With This Personality Type	To Cope With This Personality Type So They Don't Provoke *Your* Anger	Anger Management Strategies For This Personality Type
Be objective	Humor	
Accurately reflect their concerns	R.E.T.	
Avoid sarcasm	Let Go	
Don't challenge their authority or get into power struggles	Favorite Activity	
Include them in decision-making	Systematic Desensitization	
	Self-Hypnosis	

PERSONALITIES AT A GLANCE

	Actively Withdrawn	Ambivalent
Temperaments	Temperamental, Calm	Impulsive, Irritable, Temperamental
Ways of Acquiring Recognition (WAR)	Revenge, Inadequacy	Attention, Power, Revenge, Inadequacy
Locus of Control	External	External
Thinking Errors	Excuse Making, I Can't, Lack of Trust, Vagueness, Victim Stance, Zero State	Anger, Blaming, Closed Channel, Excuse Making, Failure to Assume Responsibility, Fragmentation, "I Can't," Instancy, Lack of Empathy, Lack of Trust, Lying, Minimizing, Power, Suggestibility, Superoptimism, Vagueness, Victim Stance, Zero State
DSM-III-R Designation	Avoidant	Borderline

PERSONALITIES AT A GLANCE

	Compulsive	Dependent
Temperaments	Temperamental, Calm	Calm, Impulsive
Ways of Acquiring Recognition (WAR)	Revenge, Inadequacy	Inadequacy, Attention
Locus of Control	Internal	External
Thinking Errors	Anger, Closed Channel, Excuse Making, Instancy, Lack of Empathy, Lack of Trust	I Can't, Suggestibility, Vagueness, Victim Stance, Zero State
DSM-III-R Designation	Compulsive	Dependent

PERSONALITIES AT A GLANCE

	Dramatic	Egotistical
Temperaments	Impulsive, Temperamental	Irritable
Ways of Acquiring Recognition (WAR)	Attention, Power, Revenge, Inadequacy	Power, Attention
Locus of Control	External	External
Thinking Errors	Anger, Blaming, Fragmentation, Instancy, Lack of Empathy, Power, Suggestibility, Superoptimism, Uniqueness, Victim Stance, Zero State	Anger, Blaming, Closed Channel, Excuse Making, Instancy, Justification, Lack of Empathy, Lying, Ownership, Power, Superoptimism, Uniqueness, Zero State
DSM-III-R Designation	Histrionic	Narcissistic

PERSONALITIES AT A GLANCE

	Mistrustful	Oppositional
Temperaments	Temperamental, Calm	Temperamental, Calm
Ways of Acquiring Recognition (WAR)	Revenge, Power, Inadequacy	Revenge, Inadequacy
Locus of Control	External	Vacillates between Internal/External
Thinking Errors	Anger, Blaming, Closed Channel, Excuse Making, Failure to Assume Responsibility, I Can't, Justification, Lack of Empathy, Lack of Trust, Victim Stance	Anger, Blaming, Excuse Making, Failure to Assume Responsibility, I Can't, Instancy, Lack of Empathy, Lying, Minimizing, Ownership, Suggestibility, Vagueness, Victim Stance, Zero State
DSM-III-R Designation	Paranoid	Passive-Aggressive

PERSONALITIES AT A GLANCE

	Passively Withdrawn	Self-Serving
Temperaments	Calm	Impulsive, Irritable
Ways of Acquiring Recognition (WAR)	Inadequacy	Attention, Power, Revenge, Inadequacy
Locus of Control	Internal	External
Thinking Errors	Lack of Trust, Vagueness	Anger, Blaming, Closed Channel, Excuse Making, Failure to Assume Responsibility, Fragmentation, I Can't, Instancy, Lack of Empathy, Lack of Trust, Lying, Minimizing, Ownership, Power, Suggestibility, Superoptimism, Uniqueness, Vagueness, Victim Stance, Zero State
DSM-III-R Designation	Schizoid	Antisocial

CHAPTER TWENTY

Intentions: Are Your Expressions of Anger Designed to Hurt or Help?

While some expressions of anger result in an escalation of tension and an intensified feeling of anger, other expressions of anger "clear the air" and actually reduce the level of tension and anger. Why do the consequences of expressing anger vary so much from one instance to another? They differ because people's *intentions* differ.

> An *intention* is the ultimate result that you want from an interaction, your purpose. Intentions can be either negative or positive.

The Consequences of Negative Intentions

Sometimes when people express anger, their intentions are negative and destructive. Their intentions are to hurt others as they feel hurt—to make them feel sad, or guilty. For example, parents often spank because they want to inflict some physical pain on their children in return for the emotional pain that their misbehavior caused them, and they want to force their children to respond immediately to their authority and control. Spankings can result in feelings of bitterness and resentment, especially when they are administered in order to relieve the parent of his or her feelings of anger and frustration, rather than to help the child develop self-discipline. Eventually, parents must turn to other methods of controlling their children as the children grow bigger and stronger. As one trainer at Sea World exclaimed, "We can't lay a 12-thousand-pound killer whale across our knee and spank him, so we're forced to find alternative methods of discipline when he misbehaves."

Similarly, any expression of anger made when the person has negative intentions will usually *increase* the feelings of tension and animosity between the people involved. This is true whether it is from a boss to an employee, one co-worker to another, a teacher to a student, or whomever.

The Consequences of Positive Intentions

At other times, people have positive, constructive intentions behind their expressions of anger. Their intentions are to make their needs known and improve the quality of their relationships with the people who provoked their anger. Consequently, when they express their anger they *decrease* the feelings of tension and animosity between themselves and the people who provoked their anger, and increase the feelings of understanding, empathy, and reconciliation.

Becoming Aware of Your Intentions

If you are unaware of your intentions, you may be letting your anger leak out in subtle yet hurtful ways, without even realizing what you are doing. You may be making little snide comments here and there, exaggerating the extent of the other person's mistakes, or giving the person a mean, disrespectful look.

Becoming aware of your intentions requires listening to your self-talk. Does it reflect negative, destructive intentions?

> "I wish I could make him at least half as miserable as he makes me."

> "I'm so angry I could scream, but I won't give him the satisfaction. I'll just clam up and make him feel sorry for treating me this way. I hope he gets to feeling so guilty he'll start to hurt as badly as I do."

Or does your self-talk reflect positive, constructive intentions?

> "Even though I'm angry with him right now, I don't want to make him angry with me. I just want him to stop that annoying behavior. I love him, and I'm going to do my best to let him know what's bugging me without hurting him too much."

> "I hope I confront her in such a way that she'll be able to sense how much love and respect I have for her. I want her to know that I'm angry, but I don't want her to be hurt."

Becoming aware of your intentions is an important part of constructive anger management. When you are aware of your intentions you can share them with the person who provoked your anger. You can do this by prefacing your expression of anger with remarks such as: "I don't want to hurt you," or, "I don't want to make you feel bad. However, I need to tell you how I'm feeling."

Intentions

	Hurtful	Nonhurtful
Goal:	To hurt the person physically or emotionally as you feel hurt	To facilitate the understanding and appreciation of your needs and feelings
Action:	Retaliate	Inform with "I Messages"
Result:	Increased anger and resentment	Decreased anger Increased understanding

When you express your anger in constructive, assertive ways using a nonjudgmental, adult-to-adult tone of voice *after* you have clarified your intentions, your expressions of anger are much more likely to lead to constructive dialogue and reconciliation, rather than to destructive arguments and retaliation.

Remember, you can always choose what you are going to do with your anger. When you are unaware of your intentions, you may unwittingly be expressing your anger in ways which are hurtful and destructive. When you are aware of your intentions, however, you are more likely to express your anger in constructive, nonhurtful ways that result in strengthened relationships and constructive resolution of your conflict.

PART THREE

Techniques for Coping with Angry Feelings and Angry People

CHAPTER TWENTY-ONE

Self-Awareness:
The Fishbowl Technique

Anger management is *not* the process of avoiding or eliminating anger; rather, it is the process of using your self-
awareness to make your anger work for you rather than
against you. Constructive anger management requires self-
awareness, especially in these three areas:

1. what emotion or emotions you are feeling and why
   you are feeling that way
2. what your intentions are in expressing your feelings
3. how you are expressing your feelings

Trying to manage your anger *without* self-awareness is as
difficult as trying to train a bear to leap like a kangaroo, or a
kangaroo to fly like an eagle. It's impossible. When you
aren't aware that you are angry, you become a "slave" to
your anger; but when you *are* aware of your anger, you have
the power to control your anger and stop it from controlling
you. The more self-aware you are, the harder it is to get

knocked off your emotional balance, and the easier it is for you to put your anger into perspective and use it constructively. Self-awareness works as an electronic burglar alarm protecting your self-control. When your self-awareness is on alert, it becomes more difficult for anyone to sneak in your back door, push your emotional buttons, and knock you off your emotional balance. As long as your emotional balance is intact, you will be able to maintain your self-control and make your anger work for you.

Managing your anger is like crossing a busy intersection— *awareness* is the key to success.

SELF-AWARENESS

The Fishbowl Technique

Learning to be self-aware is easy when you use the fishbowl technique. Because it requires no special equipment or time away from whatever you are doing, you can use the fishbowl technique at work, at home, at school, or while shopping, driving, or playing.

As the illustration depicts, the fishbowl technique enables you to step back and observe yourself and the entire interaction you are having with another person from an *objective viewpoint*. By putting the interaction into your fishbowl you are able to emotionally disengage and mentally extract yourself from the interaction to the extent that you are able to observe *yourself* in an objective manner. While you are actively involved in the interaction occurring in the fishbowl, you are also outside the fishbowl, objectively looking and listening to yourself with the eye and ear of your creative imagination, which you normally use for seeing and hearing past events. For example, when asked to think about the Fourth of July, you probably can "see" the colorful fireworks displays and "hear" the sound of the fireworks. The fishbowl technique expands the usefulness of your creative imagination by enabling you to hear and see your interactions *as* they occur.

Observing your external communication. The fishbowl technique allows you to listen to *your* part of the interaction and become more aware of how you may be contributing to the other person's anger. It does this by helping you become aware of the following elements of your voice:

- volume
- force
- pace
- pitch
- tone

Using your fishbowl to observe your external communications helps you be aware of the volume of your voice and notice whether it is loud and aggressive, quiet and passive, or moderate and assertive. You can also hear the force of your voice and the pace of your speech. You can evaluate whether it is unusually rapid or slow by listening to the pauses in your speech and the words you are emphasizing. By listening to the pitch of your voice you can be aware of whether your voice is unusually high or low and how much variety you have in your voice. Listening to the tone of your voice helps you monitor what type of transaction you are initiating. Do you sound as if you are a "parent" (talking *down* to the other person), an "adult" (talking *with* the other person), or a "child" (talking in a *childlike* manner to the other person)? Thus, the fishbowl technique enables you to hear *what* you are saying and *how* you are saying it.

WHAT IS UNDERNEATH YOUR ANGER?

WHAT IS COVERING YOUR ANGER?

Observing your internal communications. The fishbowl technique also enables you to hear your internal dialogue—your private self-talk. Listening to your self-talk is one of the easiest ways to become aware of your feelings, intentions, and thinking errors.

Anger can be aroused by anger-provoking situations, or it can evolve from other emotions you are experiencing such as frustration, hurt, or helplessness. Anger may be the only emotion you are experiencing, or it may be the covering or core of several layers of emotion. If you believe it's not right to feel angry, you may intentionally or unintentionally mask your anger with other, more personally acceptable emotions. Anger can be compared to the layers of an onion. Sometimes anger is the outer layer covering other emotions, and sometimes it is one of the inner layers covered by other emotions, as you can see in the preceding illustrations.

By placing your emotions into the fishbowl and peeling them back one layer at a time, you can discover what emotions may be accompanying your anger. Although the specific sequence of emotions is unique for each person and each situation, the layers may resemble the following sequence.

1. initial anger
2. hurt
3. vindictiveness (because of your hurt)
4. guilt (because of your vindictive feelings)
5. frustration
6. depression
7. helplessness
8. anger

The fishbowl technique enables you to peel away the extra layers of emotion, discover what emotions you are really feeling, and gain insight and knowledge that can help you utilize your emotions in constructive ways. Feelings of helplessness are emotionally and physically draining. When you become angry about feeling helpless, your anger can generate the energy it takes to renew your sense of personal power, overcome your helplessness, and resolve your original anger.

Observing your nonverbal communications. Your communication with others consists of more than just your external and internal verbalizations. It also involves your nonverbal communications and changes in your facial expressions. By putting your interaction into the fishbowl you can see how you are presenting yourself. For example, you can see when your lips are pursed tight, your eyebrows are knitted, your eyes are rolling, or your hands are making angry gestures.

Becoming self-aware is easy when you use the fishbowl technique. You can obtain information about yourself with the fishbowl just as spontaneously as you learn about a friend by observing him. For example, you don't use a mental checklist to observe your friend's tone of voice, facial and bodily gestures, or other aspects of his communication style, do you? Probably not. You are simply aware of them because your ears and eyes observe those things almost automatically. Similarly, by putting yourself into your fishbowl you can use the ear and eye of your imagination, as well as your physical senses, to observe your participation in an interaction.

The following example illustrates how I used the fishbowl technique to help manage my anger on an occasion when I was playing racquetball.

I had mixed emotions when John asked me to play. On one hand I was eager to play racquetball, but on the other hand I was still upset with him for declaring himself the winner of the last game we had played. I had understood we were playing a 15-point game, but he declared himself the winner as soon as he scored the short-game limit of 11.

The way John emphasized that this game would be to 15, I thought he might be trying to apologize for his conduct earlier that evening, so even though I was reluctant, I agreed to play another game with him.

I got ahead of him 11 to 3, but not without paying a painful price. He kept hitting me in the back with his powerful cross-court shots. When one of his shots hit me in the head so hard that it knocked me off my feet, I became enraged. Realizing the intensity of my anger and the need to regain control of my emotions, I decided to put our interaction into my fishbowl.

While I could hear John swearing and yelling, "Wake up and play racquetball," I could also hear my self-talk, "This time I'm going to stay in complete control. I am not going to argue with him. I'm going to take a slow, deep breath, and use my energy to stay focused on the game. I'm not going to allow him to intimidate me or make me lose control. I can respond to him without putting him down. I can win if I stay focused."

Because I was using my fishbowl, I could "see" myself standing there looking at John. I had an undisturbed, matter-of-fact expression on my face. After listening to my self-talk, I realized my intention was to get John to play fairly so he'd be more fun to play with, not to criticize him so he'd be angry with me and less fun. I knew John would resent it if I talked down to him as an angry parent would to a naughty child, so I listened closely to my tone of voice and made sure I was talking to him in an assertive, adult-to-adult manner. I said, "John, I have the right to hold center court as long as I give you room to make your shot." Then I "saw" the pleasant, nonjudgmental expression on my face (as reflected in a slight hint of a smile) and heard myself say without any bitterness in my voice, "John, you hold center court about as well as anyone, and no one complains. Holding center courts is just good racquetball." We finished the game, and I won 15 to 4.

John was so angry at himself for losing that

game, he smashed his racquet against a concrete wall and began swearing at himself. He apparently appreciated the fact that I didn't retaliate against him during our game, because he's never deliberately hit me with the ball again. By using the fishbowl technique to increase my self-awareness, I was able to stay in control of my anger and make *my* anger work *for* me.

Self-awareness is the key to staying in control of your anger, maintaining your emotional balance, refraining from responding impulsively to other people's anger, and breaking the destructive cycle of mismanaged anger. Regardless of whether you use the other anger management techniques described in this book independently or in various combinations, their effectiveness depends on your being self-aware.

CHAPTER TWENTY-TWO

Positive Self-Talk

Self-talk consists of the words and ideas you think to yourself. And, since how you think influences how you feel and how you behave, being aware of your self-talk is an essential component of the anger management process.

How can you tune in to your self-talk? Initially, you can train the ear of your imagination to listen to your self-talk by closing your eyes, ignoring all the external sounds around you, and focusing your attention on the talk that is going on inside your mind. The more you allow yourself to focus on your self-talk, the more of it you will hear. Once you become skillful at tuning in to your self-talk in this manner, you'll be able to hear it without having to close your eyes, and be able to benefit from the self-talk process wherever you are.

Your self-talk is very informative. By listening to it, you become aware of your feelings, your goals and intentions, your expectations, your beliefs, and your thinking errors—all of which have a tremendous impact on your anger. When you are *aware* that you are becoming angry, you can use your self-talk to help you control the intensity and duration of your anger and put the situation into a more objective perspective. Listening to your self-talk is helpful before, during, and after anger-provoking situations.

Before a Possible Anger-Provoking Situation

Sometimes you know in advance that you will be in a situation that might provoke your anger, such as heavy traffic, meeting with a demanding boss, or having to confront an incompetent co-worker. Listening to your self-talk gives you the opportunity to adjust your *attitude* and *expectations* so the situation will be *less* anger-provoking. The following phrases illustrate the type of self-talk you can do *before* the provocation to lessen your anger:

- I will refuse to take the provocation personally.
- No matter how difficult the situation may get, I know I'll be able to stay in control of my emotions. I believe in myself and my abilities.
- I will be able to remain calm and in control.
- If I start to become upset, I will be able to take a few deep breaths and stay relaxed and in control of my emotions.
- I am creative and will be able to find a way to handle the situation.
- If I feel myself getting angry, I'll be able to shift my focus to something pleasant.
- If I become irritated with his poor performance again today, I'll lower my expectations, disengage myself emotionally, and remain calm and in control of my emotions.

During an Anger-Provoking Situation

Sometimes it's not possible to anticipate or foresee anger-provoking situations, so you can't always prepare yourself with positive self-talk. However, you can always use self-talk *during* a provocation. Here are a few examples:

- I don't have to allow this situation to "get my goat."
- It feels terrific to stay calm and in control of my emotions.
- I feel my muscles starting to tense. Now they are relaxing as I take a few deep breaths.
- Letting my anger get out of control will *not* help. I can resolve this situation by remaining calm and in control of my emotions.
- It feels so good to keep my emotions under control and not give this person the satisfaction of making me angry or seeing me behave in an irrational manner.
- Because I'm keeping myself calm and in control, no one can knock me off my emotional balance.
- I feel so good about myself. I'm really handling this situation well.
- Focusing on something pleasant is more enjoyable than focusing on this negative situation.
- Obviously he isn't living up to my expectations. From now on I won't expect him to be able to . . .

After the Anger-Provoking Situation

After the anger-provoking situation is resolved, it is helpful to use positive self-talk to reward yourself for having used good anger management skills. Such reinforcement helps to increase your self-esteem and self-concept and strengthen your winner's script. After the anger-provoking situation is resolved, making positive self-talk statements also helps to reaffirm your belief that indeed you *are* capable of controlling your anger. Following are examples of appropriate self-talk statements you can use *after* the provocation is resolved.

- I did it!
- I'm really developing and improving my skills as an anger manager.
- I made it through the whole event without getting angry!
- I'm so proud of myself for managing my anger constructively! I knew I could do it.
- Shifting my focus away from the provocation really helped me stay in control of my emotions.
- Lowering my expectations really helped to reduce my anger.

Self-talk can be a very effective tool for managing your anger. Listening to your self-talk helps you increase your self-awareness. And using positive self-talk before, during, and after anger-provoking situations helps you maintain the self-control you need to manage your anger in a constructive and effective manner.

CHAPTER TWENTY-THREE

Breathe Deeply

The more capable you are of utilizing self-control when your anger has been provoked, the easier it will be for you to manage your anger. Controlled deep breathing is one of the quickest ways to strengthen your self-control so that you can reduce the intensity of your anger to a manageable level. Deep breathing is the type of breathing you do naturally while you are asleep.

Deep breathing involves pushing your stomach out as you inhale, and leaving your chest and shoulders relaxed. Hold your first two deep breaths for two seconds each, then exhale with a sigh, freeing your body from any unwanted tension.

There are four ways deep breathing helps you manage your anger:

1. Deep breathing helps relax your muscles by increasing the amount of oxygen in your blood. When your muscles are relaxed, it is difficult to feel angry.

2. When you focus on your breathing, your attention shifts from the source of your anger to your breathing. Thus, your breathing becomes a pleasant and positive diversion from your anger.

3. When you take time to breathe slow, deep, rhythmic breaths, you take time away from your angry feelings, and this "buys you time" to put the provoking situation into a new perspective and reduce it to manageable proportions.

4. As you inhale slowly and deeply, you feel more and more in control of yourself, physically, mentally, and emotionally. The more self-control you have, the easier it is to control your anger.

Breathing is something that you already do, but it's *how* you breathe and *what you do* while your are breathing that converts this natural function into a powerful anger management technique.

CHAPTER TWENTY-FOUR

The Rapid Relaxation Response

Many people benefit from relaxation procedures, but there are some who feel uncomfortable with traditional relaxation methods. The rapid relaxation response can be used effectively by almost anyone because it avoids the common barriers to relaxation. It allows you to stay in full control and be as active as you choose. You can use rapid relaxation so quickly that you can benefit from it even while you are participating in such activities as working, driving, or conversing.

The rapid relaxation response consists of only four steps. **Refocus, relax, reevaluate,** and **refresh.**

Refocusing is the process of directing your focus away from the provocation and toward a resolution of the conflict. You can do this by mentally rehearsing a positive resolution to your situation and visualizing that positive outcome occurring. For example, if someone is yelling at you, you can imagine that person listening to you while you are explaining your point in a calm, assertive manner.

Relaxing is achieved by focusing on your relaxing and calming self-talk. Listen to your positive, supportive, and encouraging self-talk. Focus on how calm, relaxed, in control, and powerful you feel.

Reevaluating is done by putting the situation into perspective and evaluating its importance to you. You have a right to be angry. You may feel irritated or you may feel enraged. But when you put the situation into perspective and reduce your anger to a manageable level, you can utilize the energy from your anger to manage your anger effectively.

You can put the provocation into perspective by asking yourself: Is this provoking incident worth losing my life, a treasured relationship, my job, my mental, emotional, or physical health, or my reputation? Then compare your situation to the broader picture. For instance, is your situation as important as nuclear disarmament?

Refreshing yourself results from being aware of your mental, physical, and emotional power. Notice the surge of energy flowing throughout your mind and body. Your mind is focused, and you experience a feeling of increased self-control and personal power.

When you feel yourself beginning to tense up, or needing some extra energy to cope with an anticipated or actual anger-provoking situation, use the rapid relaxation response. You'll find that using the rapid relaxation response makes it easier for you to maintain self-awareness and self-control and to cope constructively with angry feelings and angry people.

CHAPTER TWENTY-FIVE

Power Relaxation

The power relaxation technique allows you to feel more energetic, more in control, and more powerful over your anger by enabling you to let go of your unnecessary tension. You can experience the benefits of the power relaxation technique by following these seven steps:

1. *Get comfortable.* Begin by choosing a comfortable place to sit and allowing your body to feel totally supported. Once you are comfortable you will begin to experience the complete control you have of your mind and body.

2. *Refocus.* As your eyes close, you can control your thinking by focusing your attention inward to your thoughts, feelings, and bodily sensations. You may wish to recall pleasant memories from experiences you have had while enjoying a favorite activity.

3. *Breathe.* Inhale a slow, consciously controlled deep breath (a breath that leaves your chest relaxed and

pushes your stomach out as you inhale) and hold it for five seconds. Release it with a sigh, as you say to yourself, "Relax. Let go." Letting go of your mental, emotional, and physical tension strengthens your self-control.

4. *Scan*. While you continue your slow, rhythmic, consciously controlled deep breathing, locate your tension by mentally scanning your mind and body.

5. *Release*. Take one more slow, deep breath and hold it for five seconds. As you release this breath, you are freeing your mind and body of all unnecessary tension. Notice your feeling of inner peace and self-control.

6. *Relax*. Allow yourself to enjoy a few moments of relaxation and experience a feeling of inner strength and peaceful alertness. Your mind focuses on pleasant thoughts of a peaceful, tranquil place and imagines the smell of cool, crisp, clean air such as you'd find in a mountain forest after a rainfall. As you take this time to restore your vitality, you feel warm, secure, and in control. Your muscles feel relaxed and heavy, momentarily free from any desire to move. As you continue to breathe slowly and rhythmically, you feel more centered and more in control. Remember, you are in full control of the pace and duration of your relaxation.

7. *Energize*. After taking a few moments to relax, you notice a surge of energy flowing throughout your body. You feel energized in your head, neck, shoulders, arms, hands, and fingers; energized in your chest, abdomen, back, and buttocks; in your hips, thighs, calves, ankles, feet, and toes. When you feel ready, begin to count from one to five, saying a number each time you exhale. As you count, your eyes begin to open and your muscles begin to feel lighter and lighter. You gradually feel more and more energetic. By the time you reach five, you are completely alert and have the power, self-confidence, and determination to return energetically to your activities with an open-minded, positive attitude.

CHAPTER TWENTY-SIX

Keep on Counting

What can you do when people provoke your anger by being demanding, overbearing, and self-centered? And what can you do when people provoke your anger by acting helpless or obnoxiously passive? Count them out! Count silently in a calm, even rhythm.

The soft, soothing, rhythmic sounds of internal counting modify your mood and help offset the emotional impact of other people's anger-provoking behavior. Taking time to count to twenty or higher helps decrease your anger to a manageable level and enables you to control your response so that you won't elicit or increase the anger of the person whose behavior angered you.

The Process of Therapeutic Counting

Therapeutic counting is something you do *internally*. While listening well enough to get the "jist" of what the other person is saying, concentrate on counting silently to yourself with a calm, even rhythm. In order for your counting to be effective, you need to use your fishbowl so that you are aware of *all* your nonverbal communications. You need to be particularly aware that you are *not* moving your lips or the muscles in your throat. By practicing in front of a mirror, you can improve your ability to maintain good eye contact with others while counting to yourself, to the point where your counting is *invisible* to others. When you keep your counting to *yourself* you avoid provoking others.

The Benefits of Therapeutic Counting

Counting buys you time to get in touch with your intentions and avoid the negative consequences of responding impulsively. When you are aware of your intentions, you can respond to whomever angered you without trying to hurt that person in return. The steady rhythm of your counting helps to stabilize your emotions so that you can make your anger work *for* you. Your counting serves as a private reminder that you don't have to let this person drain your emotional energy. With each number you count, you help yourself feel more calm, more in control of your anger, and more capable of responding in a firm, assertive, constructive manner.

CHAPTER TWENTY-SEVEN

Gain Control by Letting Go

During Tom Nelson's eligibility interview for a college scholarship, his mother frequently interrupted with complaints about how miserable her life had been since Tom's father divorced her. Concerned about the intensity of Mrs. Nelson's anger, Tom's counselor attempted to offer some words of encouragement. "I'm sorry about your recent divorce," he said. "Just remember, time is a great healer of most wounds." But Mrs. Nelson was not to be appeased. "Time?" she shouted at the counselor. "I've been divorced for sixteen years and I'm still angry at the SOB. He ruined my life. I'm physically, mentally, and emotionally drained and it's all *his* fault. The longer I think about it, the *angrier* I get!"

When you keep rehearsing your anger over and over again in your mind, as Mrs. Nelson was doing, your anger stays fresh and intense. But when you *let go* of your anger, it gradually becomes nothing more than a faded memory.

Try the following exercise:

Make a tight fist. (If you have long fingernails, make your grip such that your fingernails aren't digging into your hand.) Keep your fist tight while you count out sixty seconds. Once you reach forty, intensify your squeeze with each count. Even though your hand aches and the pain keeps getting stronger, hold your fist tighter and tighter until you finish the count to sixty. The physical pain you feel represents the mental and emotional pain that accompanies your anger. Now *slowly* begin to relax your grip. Take about fifteen seconds to open your hand, then let it return to a relaxed position in your lap. As you gently let go of your tight grip, notice the pleasant sensation of the tenseness and pain melting away. You are freeing your hand of its discomfort, enabling it to return to its maximum usefulness. Similarly, when you let go of your anger you free yourself of mental and emotional pain and enable yourself to experience life to its fullest.

Mismanaged anger is as restrictive and useless as an emerging butterfly's cocoon. Just as the cocoon keeps the butterfly from utilizing its new wings, mismanaged anger keeps you from realizing the positive potential you have deep inside. Just as the butterfly sheds his cocoon and flies away, you can let go of your anger and move forward with a fresh outlook on life.

When you hear people say, "I *can't* let go," they are really saying, "I *won't* let go." They are clinging to anger for dear life, but actually their lives would be much richer if they would let go.

When your anger is provoked by something as inconsequential as your spouse disagreeing with you, or a co-worker parking in your favorite parking space, you may be able to resolve your anger by forgiving the person who provoked you. Occasionally, however, you may encounter some provocations that are beyond your capability to forgive. Each person has his or her own comfort level, but most people feel uncomfortable forgiving those who rob, rape, or murder. Few have been able to forgive Hitler for his atrocities against the Jewish people.

Regardless of where your comfort level lies, when you encounter situations that are beyond your comfort level to forgive, you can choose between allowing your anger to dominate your life or freeing yourself from its restrictive bonds by letting go. Continually holding on to anger can be emotionally and physically draining, but allowing yourself to let go can be very energizing. No matter how angry you feel, or how unforgivable the situation, letting go is a gift of healing you can give yourself.

The process of letting go is different for each person. You might imagine your anger is inside a backpack, weighing down every step you take. As you lighten your load, by letting go of your anger little by little, the weight of your backpack no longer remains a hindrance to your journey. You can use your imagination to develop the visual image that is most meaningful to you. It doesn't matter what mental picture you create for yourself in order to let go of your anger. The important thing is that you choose the image of letting go that is comfortable for you, and then *let go!*

CHAPTER TWENTY-EIGHT

The Flexibility Factor: Adjusting Your Expectations

One way you can reduce the frequency, intensity, and duration of your anger is by reducing your expectations. If you insist on rigidly adhering to your expectations, and do nothing to close the gap between your expectations and reality, your anger will develop readily and intensely and last for a long time.

Murphy's Law, "If something can go wrong, it will," takes the idea of lowering your expectations to a humorous extreme. But it illustrates how you can adjust your expectations to avoid leaving room for disappointment and frustration.

I am *not* advocating that you get your anger under control by lowering your standards. Quite the contrary! High standards are commendable. What you need to adjust are your *expectations*. When you are able to expect that people, including you, will make an occasional mistake, then you'll be more tolerant of, and less angered by, those mistakes.

For example, a person who is responsible for the selection and supervision of employees can lower his expectations about absences without altering his standards. Even if he now expects that an employee will occasionally miss more than one day of work per month, his absentee policy (his standard) remains unchanged. Sometimes he may even decide he needs to dismiss an employee who is habitually absent.

KNOW YOUR EXPECTATIONS

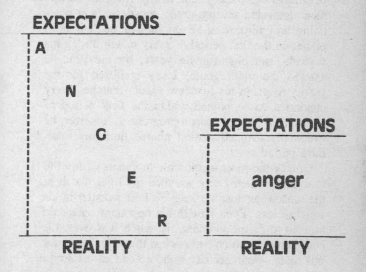

Parents also set standards and expectations for their children. Parents who maintain their standards but adjust their expectations according to the abilities and temperament of each child will experience less frustration and anger toward their children. For example, a parent of a learning-disabled child can adjust her expectations of that child's ultimate academic achievements without lowering her standard that all of her children use their full potential.

The closer your expectations (your goals) are to reality (your achievements), the less frustration and anger you'll experience and the better you'll feel about yourself. It is good to strive for improvement and to set new goals for yourself, but keep in mind your abilities and monitor your achievements in relation to *your* past endeavors, not the achievements of others.

When I was the coach for a junior high school wrestling team, Larry, one of my least skilled but most dedicated seventh-grade wrestlers, kept practicing and improving. Even though he had been pinned in the first period of every match during his seventh- and eighth-grade years, by the time he entered the ninth grade, Larry qualified for the varsity team. In his first few varsity matches Larry continued to be pinned within the first period of each match. As the season progressed, however, he eventually avoided getting pinned until the final, third period.

One of the most memorable moments of my life took place when Larry wrestled his final match of the season, against the league's best wrestler in his weight class. Even though his opponent outscored him 10 to 5, the moment his match was over, the entire crowd, which had packed the gymnasium for this meet, spontaneously stood up and gave Larry a thunderous ovation.

No, Larry hadn't won the match, but he *had succeeded* at something far more significant. Because he had refused to quit, Larry had finally succeeded at reaching his personal goal of making it through an entire match without getting pinned. His family and friends, who had faithfully watched Larry wrestle for three years, cried tears of joy. His teammates, many with tears in their eyes, were so proud of Larry that they rushed out and carried him off the mat on their shoulders in celebration of his "victory." Larry had set his goals in relationship to his past achievements and he had succeeded. The crowd, his friends, his family, his teammates, and I were extremely proud of Larry, but most important of all, Larry was proud of himself.

You don't have to be a professional superstar or winner of a world championship to experience the thrill of personal success. You can have that experience by setting *your* goals and expectations in accordance with *your* abilities.

You can't always control other people's behavior, nor can you always avoid anger-provoking situations. You do, however, have control over your expectations. The more willing you are to adjust your expectations, and lower them when it is appropriate to do so, the easier it will be for you to control the frequency, intensity, and duration of your anger.

CHAPTER TWENTY-NINE

Reframing

Reframing is the process of looking at a situation from a different perspective so that you can cope with it in a constructive manner. When you use reframing as an anger management technique, you are adjusting your expectations so they are more appropriate for the actual situation.

A psychologist friend of mine, Dan, was co-leading group therapy sessions with his co-therapist, Rick. Dan was angry and exasperated with Rick for not providing any help with the leadership of the group. After the third frustrating session, Dan explained to Rick in a calm and assertive manner exactly what he expected from him as a co-therapist. But Rick remained apathetic and unsupportive.

Dan came to me feeling frustrated and helpless. "What am I going to do?" he asked. "I might as well not even have a co-therapist! I really like him as a friend, but I can't stand the way he just sits there as if he were one of the group." His description of the problem unveiled the solution. I pointed out to him that his anger was a result of the enormous gap between his expectations and his co-therapist's actual performance.

Dan decided to adjust his expectations by reframing his co-therapist as a "member of the group." His expectations changed from expecting his co-therapist to provide therapeutic assistance, to expecting his co-therapist to need therapeutic intervention.

A week later Dan returned to thank me. By lowering his expectations, so they were closer to his co-therapist's abilities, Dan had decreased his frustration and anger. Consequently, his friendship was strengthened and he increased his appreciation for his co-therapist's abilities in other areas.

You can use reframing to help manage your anger by following these three steps.

1. Be aware of your anger by using your fishbowl.
2. Be aware of your expectations and the perspective you have of the situation by listening to your self-talk.
3. Adjust your perspective and expectations to fit the situation, in order to reduce your anger to a manageable level.

As the following examples illustrate, reframing is helpful in a wide variety of situations.

You can think of driving to work as a time when you have to battle traffic and wait through long lights, or you can reframe it as a golden opportunity to listen to music no one else in your family likes, or a time to further your education by listening to self-help tapes.

Former United States national doubles and singles handball champion Irving Simon refuses to think of the people with whom he is playing handball as his opponents. Instead, he *reframes* them into his "associates." He thinks of them as people who share his goal of making the game as fun and challenging as possible.

A friend of ours, who had been talking on the phone for an hour, started to get frequent interruptions from her toddler. She could have looked at the situation as her time for adult conversation, maintained her expectation that *no one* should interrupt her while she was on the phone, and felt frustrated and angry when her child started fussing for something to eat. Instead, she kept her frustrations to a minimum by *reframing* the situation as interaction time she had interrupted by talking on the phone.

Sometimes you may find yourself using reframing in order to cope with an anger-provoking situation until you can get away from that situation or make permanent changes in it. That's what the therapist cited earlier in this chapter did when he reframed his co-therapist as a "member of the group." (Needless to say, once the series of therapy sessions was completed, Dan did not ask Rick to be his co-therapist again.)

You can also use reframing to help you cope with situations having no apparent end in sight. For example, Ted Kennedy, Jr., whose right leg was amputated because he had bone cancer, works diligently to help other people who are angered by their physical handicaps. Even though many of these people will be confined for the rest of their lives to wheelchairs, he helps them reframe their "disabilities" as "physical challenges."

The reframing process is also valuable in helping you

prevent the escalation of anger in unavoidable situations. For instance, you can reframe situations that involve an irritating boss, co-worker, upset child, or spouse. You can also use reframing to make situations such as traffic jams or long lines at checkout counters more tolerable.

Even though you may not have any control over your particular anger-provoking situation, you can always control your expectations. When you reframe your situation and look at it from a different perspective, you're adjusting your expectations so that they are closer to what the situation actually warrants. By making those adjustments, you minimize your opportunities for frustration and reduce your anger to a manageable level.

CHAPTER THIRTY

Don't Take It Personally

"You stupid idiot! You make me sick! You can't do anything right!" If remarks such as these were directed at you, would you take them personally, and to what extent would they elicit your anger? The answer depends on how you determine your self-worth and how you feel about yourself. It also depends on how you feel about the person who made those statements and what the person's intentions were.

The more emotionally invested you are in a situation, the more difficult it is for you to respond in a rational, logical manner and the easier it is for you to feel angry. For instance, you don't become angry about every robbery that occurs in this country each day, but if you are the victim of a particular robbery, or know the victim of a robbery, you do get angry about that crime. Unless you want a specific parking space, you aren't angered by someone else parking in it. Unless you have a personal involvement with a particular team, you don't become angry whenever that team loses a game. But when you are personally involved, it is easier to feel angry. That is why knowing how *not* to take the situation personally can help you manage your anger. When you don't take the provocation personally, you're able to look at it from an objective viewpoint and maintain the emotional distance that constructive anger management requires.

If you find yourself taking situations personally, you can learn *not* to by:

- emotionally disengaging yourself from the provocation
- improving your self-esteem
- reducing your self-centeredness

Emotionally Disengaging

You can emotionally disengage yourself from anger provoking situations by using the following procedure.

First, use the fishbowl technique to be *aware* of your feelings. *Recognize* that you are angry.

Second, *evaluate* your expectations. Notice the gap between your expectations and the reality of the situation.

Third, put the situation into *perspective*. It's important to have self-respect and take yourself seriously. However, taking yourself too seriously can increase the intensity of your anger and reduce your ability to put things into perspective. When you are uncertain about the value of confronting someone, it helps to ask yourself, "Will pursuing this issue result in an improvement in the person's attitude or behavior, or will it more likely result in that person becoming even angrier or more disagreeable?"

Fourth, mentally *separate* yourself from the source of your anger. Using the fishbowl technique, imagine yourself gathering up your pride, positive self-esteem, and self-control, then calmly and assertively walking away from the person with whom you are angry. Then imagine the person with whom you are angry all alone to carry on as he or she desires.

Sometimes reminding yourself that "this too shall pass" helps to make the separation process easier. When you distance yourself from the situation and look at it more objectively, it might not seem as serious as it originally did. Mentally distancing yourself from the person provoking your anger frees you from the emotional impact which he or she might otherwise have.

Maintaining your self-awareness helps you control your emotions and choose how much emotional distance exists between yourself and others. When you are in control of your emotions, you can be emotionally disengaged or emotionally involved whenever you choose.

Improving Your Self-Esteem

As we saw earlier, your self-esteem plays an important role in determining what triggers your anger and how you express it. Remember, how you think affects how you feel. How you feel affects how you think. How you think and feel affects how you behave. And how you behave affects how you think and feel. So the better you treat yourself, the better you'll feel about yourself. Even the scriptural message that we must love our neighbor as ourselves points out how important our self-concept is. It is easier to care about others when you feel good about yourself.

One way to feel good about yourself emotionally is by improving how you feel physically. Try treating yourself to regular aerobic exercise, such as walking, jogging, swimming, or bicycling. The boost in your circulation and metabolism will boost your self-esteem by helping you feel more vibrant, more alert, and more self-confident. The better you feel about yourself, the less you'll take things personally and the less angry you'll feel. The better your self-esteem, the more interest you'll have in managing your anger.

Your self-esteem is your *personal* evaluation of yourself,

so only *you* can improve it. But you can give it a boost by surrounding yourself with the right kind of people. Instead of being around overly critical people, choose to associate with people who will compliment you and recognize and appreciate your good points.

When evaluating yourself, focus on your strengths rather than your weaknesses. Distinguish between losing and being a loser. Even people regarded as successful have had their share of failures. Remember Babe Ruth, the longtime world-record holder for hitting the most home runs? He also held the record for the most strike-outs. You deserve to focus on your successes and positive qualities and put your "failures" in their proper perspective.

Decreasing the gap between your expectations and reality is another way to increase your self-esteem. Look at the size of the gap between what you expect out of life and what you really get out of life. Do you expect it is your right to *have* a good day and find that your day often falls short of your expectations? Or do you expect it is your choice to *make* it a good day and find that your day often meets your expectations?

You can increase your self-esteem by choosing to accept responsibility for your happiness. The more often you choose to take charge of your life, and make the choices that result in positive outcomes, the more positive you'll feel about yourself.

You can also increase your self-esteem by paying attention to your self-talk. Your mind is constantly sending and receiving messages. Listen to them, and notice whether you are mentally patting yourself on the back or kicking yourself in the rear. When you increase your positive self-talk, your self-esteem will increase accordingly.

Reducing Your Self-Centeredness

Reducing your self-centeredness is another way you can reduce the anger that results from taking things personally.

It's not easy to do, however, because reducing your self-centeredness requires the courage to:

- become aware of your self-centered thoughts and behavior
- develop and show more respect and empathy for others
- consider the other person's perspective
- be more willing to meet the needs and desires of others and be less concerned about constantly gratifying your own

Listen to your self-talk. Is it filled with comments such as, "Why does it have to rain on *my* day off?" "Why did they have to interrupt *my* favorite TV show with that ———— news report?" "Who cares what *they* think . . . I know *I'm* right!" "They'd better do it *my* way, or else!" "They can just wait for *me*!" "He'd better give that to me *now*!" Notice how the focus of these thoughts includes no consideration for the needs or desires of others. Instead, they focus exclusively on your own.

The more you are willing to consider the needs and requests of others, the less self-centered you'll be. The less self-centered you are in a particular situation, and the more objective you can be about it, the easier it will be for you to keep your anger at a manageable level. The more objective you are, the more control you'll have over your emotional reactions.

CHAPTER THIRTY-ONE

Put Things into Perspective

Putting the situation into perspective and evaluating it in relation to your personal sense of priorities makes it easier to regain your emotional balance and self-control. Putting things into perspective involves asking yourself questions such as:

- Is the person who provoked my anger emotionally significant to me, or is it someone I hardly know?
- Is this person economically important to me, such as my boss or a co-worker, or is it someone I can probably avoid in the future?
- To what extent did that person intend to hurt me?

When someone says something that angers you, and that person is not significant to you, you can refrain from taking the provocation personally by dismissing those comments as insignificant and unimportant to you. When the person is significant, you still can put the situation into its proper perspective by taking that person's intentions into account. Intentionally hurtful comments usually contain very little truth or are gross exaggerations, so you should not take them personally. You can spot statements that are made with the intention of hurting by paying attention to the speaker's *tone of voice* and listening for certain cue words such as, "you *never* . . . ; you *always* . . . ; you couldn't do it even if you tried . . . ; you're nothing but a ————."

There also are times when you can keep from taking the provocation personally by evaluating it in terms of your personal priorities. A personal story serves as an example.

I first met my wife, Carol, when she had a summer job at an off-campus cafe. One day, she put the coffee filter into the coffeemaker, then put the carefully measured coffee grounds into the filter. Observing this, the cook became outraged, saying, "What are you doing? Don't you know we always put the coffee into the filter and *then* put the filled filter into the coffeemaker? We have a system here and you'd better learn to follow it! Don't you know anything?"

Carol avoided taking that outburst personally by evaluating the situation in terms of her priorities. On a scale of one to ten (ten representing something of significant value to *her* life), learning to duplicate the exact methods of her co-workers at that cafe rated about a two. She also put the situation into perspective by remembering that she wasn't going to be there forever and that her value as a person was not dependent on when and how she filled the coffee filter. Although she was always careful after that to fill the filter in the prescribed manner, Carol knew that in the long run it was relatively unimportant whether the coffee filter was filled before or after it was placed in the coffeemaker.

Indeed, ten year later, my wife and I took our daughter to that cafe to show her where we had met, and discovered the cafe had been converted into a parking lot.

When you put things into perspective, it helps to do it both in terms of your personal perspective and in terms of a more global perspective. For example, as John McKay, former USC coach, reportedly said to his dejected team after they had lost an important postseason game, "Men, even though we lost, I know each one of you played your best and I'm proud of your effort. It was a tough loss all right, but I want you to remember, there are 600 million Chinese who don't even know we played the game."

CHAPTER THIRTY-TWO

Consider the Extenuating Circumstances

Another way you can control your anger arousal is by taking into account the extenuating circumstances surrounding the anger-provoking situation. The judicial system does this when it considers what the appropriate sentences should be for various crimes. Premeditated crimes often receive stiffer sentences than crimes committed in the heat of passion.

You can diffuse your anger and reduce your desire for retribution by considering the intent of the person who provoked your anger and the extenuating circumstances at the time of provocation. Did the person intend to step on your toe, or was he pushed into you by someone else? Did your wife intend to keep you waiting in the rain for twenty minutes, or was she caught in a traffic jam? Did your son mean to track mud through the house, or was he sick and just trying to get to the bathroom as fast as he could? Did the person intend to anger you, or was the provoking incident the result of circumstances beyond the provoker's control?

The following example illustrates the significant effect that extenuating circumstances can have on determining the intensity and duration of your anger.

> We had pulled into the service station to fill the tank with gas. When the driver of the car in line ahead of us started her car it immediately went into reverse and smashed the front of our brand new car. I was furious. I quickly got out of our car to talk with this inconsiderate, incompetent driver. I couldn't understand how anyone could be so blatantly careless and irresponsible.
>
> The moment I saw the driver, however, my feelings changed from anger to empathy because the driver didn't meet my expectations at all. Rather than finding an irresponsible, drunk, self-centered teenage boy, I found a very frightened, responsible-looking, middle-aged lady. The driver apologized profusely, then explained that her car had had a manufacturing defect that caused it to slip automatically into reverse and lunge backward no matter what gear it was in, but she had been assured the problem had been corrected and wouldn't happen again.

Even though the front end of our new car was badly damaged, my feelings of anger toward the driver turned into feelings of concern and compassion, because I recognized the extenuating circumstances surrounding the accident.

Not all situations result in such a dramatic change in emotions as occurred in this example, but in your search for the reasons behind the provocation, you may discover information that allows you to decrease the intensity of your anger. When your attitude is "there may be some logical explanation for this," rather than, "he's just trying to make me angry," you are less likely to react in an impulsive and/or aggressive manner.

Not all anger-provoking situations can be resolved by discovering some extenuating circumstance. Sometimes anger is the *intended* result of a person's behavior, so there are no extenuating circumstances. But in those situations where someone has angered you unintentionally, taking the extenuating circumstances into account helps you put the situation into perspective, decrease your desire for retaliation, and adjust the intensity of your anger so it is at a manageable level.

CHAPTER THIRTY-THREE

Rational Emotive Therapy

Rational Emotive Therapy (R.E.T.), developed by Albert Ellis, demonstrates how self-awareness and self-talk can be combined to form a constructive anger management technique. According to the R.E.T. model, your anger is a consequence of your *interpretation* of a given situation, rather than of the situation itself, so you can control your anger by changing your thoughts. R.E.T. focuses on disputing your destructive, *irrational* thoughts about a situation and substituting those thoughts with constructive, *rational* ones.

R.E.T. is built on these ABCs.

A: the *activating experience* (anger-provoking situation)
B: your *beliefs* (self-talk) about the activating experience
C: the emotional *consequences* of your beliefs (how you feel about the activating experience)

The following examples illustrate how the *consequences* (C) of any anger-provoking situation are determined more by one's *beliefs (B)* than by the actual *activating experience (A)*.

From Bob's Perspective

As far as Bob was concerned, his life was as aggravating as the five o'clock traffic he was stuck in. He had just suffered through another frustrating day at work and wasn't expecting the situation at home to be any better. As he fought his way through the congestion, he began thinking to himself:

> "What am I doing? Every day I face this same rat race, and for what? I'm stuck in a business that's almost bankrupt. I'm stuck in a lousy marriage. I'm stuck with two unruly kids. And I'm stuck in this damn traffic!
>
> "Here I am, forty-three-years old, and I'm nothing but a loser. I feel so frustrated and depressed. My business just keeps sinking farther and farther into debt, and I'm getting to be more and more like my dad, yelling and screaming at Betty and the kids. I promised myself I'd never do that. But Betty makes me so f—— mad!"

A: Bob's business is failing, his marriage is lousy, and his children are unruly.

B: Bob believes that winners have successful businesses, marriages, and children. Since his business, marriage, and children are plagued with problems, he thinks, "I must be a loser."

C: Bob feels frustrated and depressed because he believes he's a loser.

> "If only she'd just shut up and stop her constant nagging. She's always nagging at me or the kids.

I'm sick of it! When she starts her nagging tonight, I'm just going to ignore her. It's time she stopped nagging and started showing me some respect."

A: Betty nags Bob.
B: Bob believes, "Betty nags me because she thinks I'm a loser."
C: Bob feels hurt and angry about Betty's nagging, and retaliates by yelling at her and the children.

"I know she thinks I'm no good. Maybe I am a horrible husband. She's been seeing a marriage counselor. Now she wants me to go with her. Why should I? I don't need some smart a—— telling me how to run my life. What I need is a drink."

A: Bob's wife is seeing a marriage counselor.
B: Bob believes, "People go to marriage counselors because they think their spouse isn't any good, or isn't worthy of respect."
C: Bob feels angry because he thinks he's not appreciated or respected.

From Betty's Perspective

As soon as Betty got home from the community college where she teaches chemistry, she started her nightly routine of fixing dinner, doing some laundry, and straightening up around the house. While she was bustling around she was thinking:

"I gave such a great explanation of chemosynthesis today. And who cares? Certainly not Bob! He's the one who should care the most, but all he cares about is himself. If it's not related to his work or his bowling, it's not important to him. He wouldn't even give up one night of bowling last year to see me get my certificate of recognition at the awards banquet. So I know he couldn't care less how well my class went today. That self-centered S.O.B. I don't know why I married him.''

A: Bob went bowling instead of to Betty's awards banquet.
B: Betty believes, "A caring husband would show ar interest in his wife's career. My husband is so self-centered, he cares more about his business and his bowling than he does about me and my career.''
C: Betty feels sad and angry about being married to ar uncaring husband.

''I'm sick of his constant grumbling about his work. He's always bitching about his employees, his customers, his overhead, and his bad location. Why doesn't he just sell his business and go to work for his uncle? He'd be happier and easier to live with.''

A: Bob makes frequent complaints about his problems a' work.
B: Betty believes, "Life around home wouldn't be so miserable if Bob would sell his business.''
C: Betty feels resentful and bitter about the interest and commitment Bob has to his business instead of to her.

''I wish I could just walk away. I've had it! He never helps out with the work around the house, or with disciplining the kids. His idea of discipline is to yell at them or hit them. It's no wonder that the kids have so little respect for him. It hurts to think they probably don't have much respect for me anymore either, especially after all the times they've seen their father put me down.''

A: Bob criticizes Betty and puts her down in front of the children.

B: Betty believes, "The children have lost their respect for me because they're always seeing Bob treat me with total disrespect."

C: Betty feels hurt, rejected, and angry.

"I feel so hurt and rejected. It's been so long since he's held me, cuddled me, or even kissed me. He used to be so loving. But now he has more interest in his booze than he has in me. I just can't seem to please him anymore. I must be a lousy wife. I don't know what to do. I feel so *trapped*. I'm so frustrated. I feel so helpless around that S.O.B."

A: Bob seldom shows Betty any affection, but he frequently criticizes her, and he drinks to excess.

B: Betty believes, "If I were a good wife, he would be interested in me, not his booze. I must be a lousy wife."

C: Betty feels frustrated, angry, and helplessly trapped in an unsatisfying marriage.

What a Difference a "D" Makes

In the preceding examples, neither Bob nor Betty utilized the "D" of R.E.T. They didn't *dispute* their irrational beliefs. In the following examples, you can see how the emotional *consequences* (C) of the *activating experiences* (A) change as a result of Bob and Betty *disputing (D)* their irrational beliefs with rational beliefs. First, we'll look at Bob disputing some of his irrational beliefs.

A: Bob's business is failing, his marriage is lousy, and his children are unruly.

D: "Sure my life seems like one big mess right now. But am I really a loser? No . . . I just keep thinking I am. True, my business isn't going as well as I had thought it would by now . . . but a loser couldn't have gotten it off the ground and kept it going as long as I have. Besides, I'm tired of struggling with something I don't really like in the first place. I'd lots rather manage my uncle's business than have all the headaches that come with owning my own. Dammit, I just can't seem to cope. I've been so wrapped up in my business, the rest of my life is starting to come unglued. I feel like such a loser. Wait a minute, there I go with that negative self-talk again. I need to think positive thoughts, relax, and stay calm. After all, if I started putting some of the time and energy I've been spending on my business back into my relationship with Betty and the kids, things would start to improve at home. Hell, I know I'm not perfect, but I'm no loser. I've survived bad times before. . . . I can get back in control again. Like Betty's counselor says, when I keep thinking all those negative, irrational thoughts like I was doing, I must make my life seem worse than it actually is. I'm going to start thinking of myself as a winner!"

C: "I guess I'm the one who is making it so hard on myself. When I'm in a positive frame of mind, it seems as if I have more options. I feel less frustrated and depressed, realizing I'm not really a failure after all."

The following example shows Betty disputing some of her irrational beliefs:

A: Bob seldom shows Betty any affection, but he frequently criticizes her, and he drinks to excess.

D: "I wish I weren't such a lousy wife. Hey, wait a minute! Why am I letting myself get carried away with a bunch of negative, irrational thoughts? Who says I'm a lousy wife? How about that weekend I helped Bob paint his office. We laughed at the mess we made of everything, and Bob seemed to have a great time with me. He even started inviting me to go bowling with him on Sunday afternoons. That was a fun activity while it lasted. Where did I fail? Why am I such a rotten wife now? Stop, stop, stop! There I go again. Just like my counselor said, I'm using negative, irrational self-talk. I need to stop blaming myself for everything, and start thinking more rationally. Maybe I'm not the perfect wife (who is?), but maybe not all our problems are my fault. Besides, I've already taken the first step toward improving my marriage by seeing that marriage counselor. As my counselor said, it took a while for Bob and me to drift apart, so it will probably take us a while to get closer together again. Maybe things would seem better if I stopped thinking so negatively of myself and being so critical of Bob. I'm a very capable person, a great teacher, and I can be a very supportive wife. It's just going to take more time, patience, and positive self-talk.''

C: Betty feels hopeful and confident that she can make her marriage more satisfying.

Using the ABCs of R.E.T. to Help You Manage Your Anger

You can apply R.E.T. to your situations by using your fishbowl and being aware of your self-talk. You can hear your rational and irrational beliefs by listening to your self-talk. Remember, you want to dispute your irrational beliefs with rational beliefs. So, the first step is to be *aware* of your irrational beliefs.

How can you determine whether your beliefs are rational

or irrational? You can do it by listening for certain words in your self-talk. Are you saying to yourself, "It's terrible," "It's awful," "It shouldn't be," "Obviously I'm totally worthless"? Those phrases indicate that you have an *irrational belief* that everything and everybody *should* be perfect, and/or fair to you all the time, and if something doesn't go according to your expectations, it is *disastrous*. (A rational belief would be: you *wish* everything would go smoothly and/or be fair to you, but if it doesn't, it's *disappointing*, not disastrous).

You may find some of your irrational beliefs represented in the following list. If you do, I encourage you to read the corresponding rational beliefs and practice using them to *dispute* your irrational ones. Before you can dispute your irrational beliefs you need to be aware of them. When you listen to your self-talk and identify your destructive, irrational beliefs, you can dispute them and convert them into constructive, rational beliefs.

Irrational Belief	Rational Belief
1. "I must be loved by everyone, and all of my actions and ideas must be liked, or I am no good."	"I like for people to love me and like my ideas and actions, but I'm a worthwhile person even if people disagree with me."
2. "I must do everything perfectly, or I am a failure."	"I want to do things well, but I'm a valuable human being even when I make mistakes."
3. "If that situation doesn't happen the way I want it to, it will be horrible. I should be able to have things go my way."	"If that situation doesn't happen the way I want it to, I'll be disappointed, but I realize life is not always fair or pleasant."

4. "I can't help feeling angry, that's the way he [she] makes me feel."

"Other people can make me angry, but I can choose how intense and how long my anger will be, and what I'm going to do with my anger."

5. "I must find the one and only right solution to this problem, or it will be catastrophic."

"I will benefit from looking at various solutions to this problem and selecting the best one. I know there is usually more than one way to solve a problem."

6. "If he [she] won't help me with this, I'll be a failure, and nobody likes a failure."

"I'll try this on my own, or I may ask for assistance. If I don't succeed, at least I'll know I tried."

7. "If it can't be done the way it used to be, it will be awful."

"I can't expect everything to stay the same, because change is an inevitable part of life."

Although the complete Rational Emotive Therapy process requires the skills of a professional therapist, you can use the few modified concepts adapted from R.E.T. presented above to help you cope with the mismanaged anger of others, and to help you control your own anger. It is easier to maintain your emotional distance and not take other people's angry outbursts personally when you realize that their outbursts are often the result of destructive, irrational beliefs. And knowing how to replace your irrational beliefs with rational beliefs helps you reduce your negative, angry feelings and increase your feelings of self-control and positive self-worth.

CHAPTER THIRTY-FOUR

Make a Place for Humor

Laughter provides relief from your anger because it is very difficult, if not impossible, to laugh and feel angry at the same time. When your attention is directed to the humor in a situation, you cannot focus on your anger. It is like watching TV. The set is capable of receiving a variety of channels, but you can view only one channel at a time. Similarly, you are capable of looking at a situation from a variety of viewpoints, but you can see it from only one vantage point at a time. You cannot be focusing on the irritating aspects of a situation when you are focusing on its humorous ones.

It is also physically impossible to maintain your angry tension when you laugh, because your body becomes relaxed immediately afterward. Your pulse, skin temperature, and blood pressure are lowered by a good laugh. These physiological signs of decreased tension can last for up to forty-five minutes. Laughter, then, is a way you can buy time to get your anger under control.

Some people were raised by parents who tolerated laughter only at certain times and places and under certain conditions. Their parents may have conveyed a limited tolerance of laughter by saying things such as, "Grow up, stop acting so silly," "Okay, enough's enough, straighten up now," or, "Knock off the laughter, it's time to be serious now." If you grew up hearing many comments like these, you may feel that spontaneous laughter is often inappropriate. Consequently, you may be looking at life so seriously that you miss much of the humor surrounding you. When you allow yourself to experience the joy of spontaneous laughter, it will be easier for you to see the humor in your life and use that humor to help manage your anger.

You don't have to belly laugh or act like a clown to appreciate the humor around you. The choice between vocalizing your laughter and keeping it to yourself is based on how close you want to be with others. Sharing a laugh often leads to feelings of goodwill and cooperation. Comedian Victor Borge defined laughter as ". . . the shortest distance between two people." How true! It is difficult to feel angry toward someone when you are laughing with him or her—it removes the tension barriers and decreases your anger arousal.

Extraverts get the most benefit from their laughter by sharing it with others, because laughing with another person means sharing an intimate experience, and they like being close to people. The more laughter you share, the closer you feel toward the person with whom you share your laughter.

Introverts, however, often feel more comfortable chuckling quietly to themselves. Internal laughter can be just as effective at helping you manage your anger as a full-throated belly laugh. You can learn to appreciate the humor in your life without sacrificing the social distance that is comfortable for you.

People who use their sense of humor usually convey a sense of acceptance and a willingness to consider other people's opinions. Conversely, people who don't use their sense of humor usually project an attitude of: "There's only one right way—mine"! Humorless people are often angry people.

I had a colleague in Atlanta who was almost always serious. Once in a while he would laugh at a joke that *he* told, but he would stop anyone else from telling a joke. His favorite phrase was, "Let's get to work now." When his controlling behavior provoked my anger and frustration, I would look for the humor in his extreme seriousness. My internal laughter served as an "emotional buffer zone" between myself and the provocation. This enabled me to view the situation from a more objective, less emotional viewpoint, and I was able to keep my anger at a manageable level. Controlling and domineering people, like this colleague, rarely give themselves permission to play, and they strongly resent it when others do.

Life is a blend of both humorous and serious events. The more capable you are of seeing the humor in various situations, the more capable you'll be at managing your anger. There won't always be humor in every situation you encounter, but when you make the effort to look for it *everywhere* you go, you will be amazed at how much humor there is in your life. The more you focus on finding humor, the more apparent it will be to you.

You wouldn't think that victims of an armed robbery would find humor in their predicament, but as the following example illustrates, humor can show up in the most unexpected places.

> After my family and I and the rest of the pizza-parlor patrons were forced by four gunmen to hand over our money, we were all herded into one restroom and instructed to remain there for thirty minutes, or we'd be shot. One of the patrons, thinking he was making a lifesaving suggestion, said in a very authoritative voice, "We can con-

serve what little oxygen we've got in here if we all stop talking!'' When he told us he had acquired this air-saving tip from a newspaper comic strip, we all had a good laugh, especially after we had discovered the restroom had direct access to an air duct. Although the patron's tip proved useless, the laughter it generated gave us temporary relief from the anger and fear we were experiencing.

When you don't see anything humorous about a situation, you can decrease the intensity of your anger by redirecting your focus to something humorous outside the situation. If it is practical for you to get away from the scene of the provocation, there is a wide variety of things you can do to put some humor into your life. For instance, you can go for a walk or take a short ride with a friend and talk about humorous things. If you don't feel like talking, you can put some cheer into your life by watching something funny, such as *Candid Camera* reruns, or by reading something funny, such as any of the humor sections in *Reader's Digest*. After you've laughed for a while, you'll notice that the intensity of your anger is much lower than it was before.

When you can't get away from the source of your anger, such as when you are at work or stuck in traffic, make yourself laugh. Think about something funny you heard on TV or radio, recall a humorous remark, visualize a humorous comic strip, or use your creativity to imagine a humorous scene.

Humor is the gateway to a broader perspective. Think of the number of times you've heard people say, ''Twenty years from now we'll probably be laughing at this.'' In other words, what seems so maddening now may seem funny once there has been time to put it into perspective. As Will Rogers once said, ''Everything is funny as long as it is happening to somebody else.'' It is your perspective, your point of view, that determines how serious or how humorous something is. When you are on the lookout for humor in a given situation and you find it, you can see that situation in a new perspective right away. This prevents, minimizes, or in some cases eliminates your anger. Humor helps you get control of your anger because it gives you time to get it down to a manageable level by redirecting your focus away from the provocation. That is one reason why children, realizing that their parents are upset with them, often try to make their parents laugh.

The more you are able to laugh at yourself and free yourself from having to be dead serious all the time, the better you'll feel about yourself. The better you feel about yourself, the easier it is to see humor in your life. The more you focus on humor, the more objective you'll view anger-provoking situations. The more objective you are when you are angry, the more you can control your anger. The more control you have over your anger, the more you can make your anger work for you.

CHAPTER THIRTY-FIVE

Treat Yourself to a Favorite Activity

he favorite activity technique is primarily an anger preven-
on technique. It helps reduce the frequency and intensity
f your anger.

As you saw earlier, your reaction to anger-provoking
tuations is strongly influenced by your self-esteem and
elf-respect. The more you like yourself, the more protec-
on you have against other people or situations provoking
our anger. The better you feel about yourself, the less
ritating other people will seem to you.

Making the time to do something *you* enjoy is one way of
lling yourself, "I am important. I deserve to enjoy this
oment to the fullest. I am doing this for me." Participating
a physically and/or mentally beneficial activity increases
our resistance to anger-provoking situations.

You don't expect your car to run smoothly when it has an
npty fuel tank, dead battery, or overheated engine, so you
do your best to prevent those conditions from occurring.
ou take the time to put fuel in the gas tank, check the

battery and maintain adequate amounts of antifreeze. Unfortunately, you may be taking better care of your car than of yourself. Do you put off *charging your own battery?* Do you keep driving yourself until you feel you need to *blow off a little steam?* The less care you take of yourself, the more frequent and intense your anger will be. The more often you charge your battery, the more energy you'll have to make your anger work for you.

You can use the favorite activity anger prevention technique without increasing the variety of your activities. You don't have to learn a new sport, take a trip, or go to more movies in order to benefit from this technique. Rather, you need to give yourself permission to enjoy to the fullest whatever mentally and/or physically healthy activity you choose.

It is important to remember that what is relaxing and therapeutic for *you* may not be so for your spouse or friend. Conversely, having participated in an activity with someone you like doesn't necessarily mean you have participated in an activity that will recharge your battery. If you need some alone time, and you have to spend your day working with a group of people, you may benefit from taking time to play a video game or finding a quiet spot to read. On the other hand, if you are energized from being around other people but spend much of your day somewhat isolated from adult interaction, you may prefer to play cards with some friends or participate in some type of group activity.

Avoid the temptation to sabotage this technique by saying, "I'm too busy; I don't have the time; I'm too tired; I don't feel well." Remember, when you catch yourself saying things like this, you *are* too busy! When you feel short of time or energy, choose an activity that doesn't require much time or physical exertion. Even taking an extra minute in the shower or tub to enjoy the warm water soothing your body may be just the prescription you need.

How to Implement the Favorite Activity Technique

When you give yourself permission to make time for yourself, whether you take just enough time to listen to a song on the radio or you take a whole day to relax at your favorite getaway, remember to:

- appreciate those moments
- recognize their importance
- say to yourself, "I deserve this"
- allow yourself to enjoy what you're doing

For example, if you're playing a game, allow yourself to focus on the game—the activity itself—more than on the outcome. Free your mind of any thoughts about uncompleted tasks. They don't get completed by worrying about them. Therefore, when you decide to get away from a task, allow yourself to move away mentally as well as physically.

Presidents Eisenhower and Ford took time to play golf. President Kennedy took time to go sailing. President Reagan took time to ride horses. Other presidents have taken time for tennis, jogging and fishing. Yes, you already have more than enough to do and too little time in which to do it. But look at it this way: if the world doesn't fall apart when the president of the United States makes time to enjoy his favorite activity, then the world can tolerate your taking occasional time-outs for yourself.

The favorite activity technique is an effective way for you to reduce the frequency and intensity of your anger. You benefit from it not necessarily by participating in more activities, but by getting more enjoyment out of whatever activity you choose.

CHAPTER THIRTY-SIX

Communicating with "I Messages"

How can you let someone know you are angry withou
eliciting that person's anger? Use an *I Message*. As orig
nally defined by author Thomas Gordon, I Messages hav
three basic components. They describe:

- your *feeling*
- the *offensive behavior*
- the *reason* for your feeling

Constructive anger management is based on constructiv
communication. When you express your feelings wi
nonjudgmental I Messages, you open the door to unde
standing and reconciliation. When you express your feelin;
with derogatory and accusatory *You Messages*, you open t
door to hurt, anger, denial, and retaliation.

Communicating with I Messages minimizes the possib
ity of putting other people on the defensive because you a
not blaming others for your feelings. Instead, you a

accepting *full responsibility* for your feelings and for the reasons behind those feelings. You Messages, however, increase the likelihood that the other person will feel defensive. *You Messages blame the other person's behavior for being directly responsible for your feelings.*

The following sentence contains all three components of an I Message:

> "I get angry [your feeling] when you walk away while I'm talking to you [the offensive behavior], because I feel my ideas aren't getting the attention they deserve [the reason]."

I Messages reflect an *internal locus of control*. When you express your anger with an I Message, you are putting the ownership of your anger on yourself, *not* on the other person. In the sample I Message above, notice that the speaker took full responsibility for his anger by accepting responsibility for his *feeling* and the *reason* for that feeling.

By contrast, You Messages reflect various *thinking errors* and an *external locus of control*. As you can see in the following example, You Messages place the blame for your anger away from yourself and onto another person.

> "You S.O.B., you really tick me off when you walk away while I'm talking to you. When are you going to wise up and realize there are plenty of people who have ideas that are just as good as yours?"

Criticizing Without Condemning

When you communicate with I Messages, your criticism limited to the description of the particular behavior or attitude that you find troublesome. But when you use You Messages, not only are you criticizing the person's behavior, you are criticizing the whole person.

A three-year-old, having just taken a sip of Kool-Aid, said apologetically, "Daddy, I didn't know it would taste like this." Her father, wondering what didn't taste right about it, took a taste and immediately realized that he had forgotten to put in the sugar. Without knowing what she had done, this three-year-old girl had used an I Message to let her father know something was wrong with the Kool-Aid. She had not judged her father's cooking abilities or put him down by raving on about his incompetence. Instead, she took responsibility for the problem by stating that the taste of the Kool-Aid didn't match *her* expectations.

If she had approached her father with a You Message such as, "Daddy, this Kool-Aid tastes awful. You must have done something wrong. Why can't you make it taste good like Mommy does?" Her relationship with her father might have temporarily become just as sour as the Kool-Aid.

I Messages are an excellent way for you to communicate your angry feelings and make others aware of your needs without provoking their feelings of defensiveness. Thus, Messages can actually help you strengthen your relationships with others. (Be careful, however, about disclosing your feelings of hurt and helplessness to people who are extremely self-centered and emotionally detached. These people will either laugh at such disclosure or use them against you. But, as long as you are careful about what you disclose to these people, I Messages will elicit less anger than You Messages, especially when your I Messages are stated in a straightforward, adult-to-adult, unemotional manner.

Communicating Your True Intentions

The difference between an I Message and a You Message is the difference between *assertiveness* and *aggressiveness*. Messages are assertive. They are used when you have no *intention* of inflicting hurt or emotional pain on the recipient of your message. In order for I Messages to be truly assertive, however, you need to be aware of *how* you are communicating your message. Your nonverbal communication (body language) needs to be as free from blame as your spoken message. Effective I Messages are communicated in an adult-to-adult manner, using a calm, gentle, but firm and matter-of-fact tone of voice. You Messages, on the other hand, are aggressive. You Messages are used when you *intend to hurt or put down* the person to whom you are speaking. They are communicated in a parent-to-child manner, usually in an agitated, hypercritical, demeaning tone of voice.

In some situations you may feel you need to buy time before you are able to make an assertive statement. Sometimes you will be so angry and so unaware of your intentions that your comments will be aggressive rather than assertive. In those situations, take time to calm down and get in touch with your intentions, so that you can be assertive. In other situations, you may feel too shy to say what you want to say. In those situations, take time to build up your courage so that you can be assertive.

I Messages don't need to be worded perfectly to be effective. It is important, however, that your tone of voice reflects respect for the other person, and you make it clear that your intentions are to resolve the conflict rather than to hurt or get even. When your tone of voice and intentions are appropriate, I Messages are an effective way of expressing criticisms that lead to constructive changes in the other person's behavior.

Making Requests Without Building Resentment

An I Message is a much more effective method than a You Message for *influencing people to change*. People willingly comply to an I Message because they interpret it as a plea for help. On the other hand, people comply reluctantly and resentfully to a You Message because they interpret it as a demand for change.

When you communicate your desire for change by using aggressive You Messages such as: "How could you do anything so dumb as to . . ." or, "You'd better stop doing that or else . . ." the recipients of these messages may change their behavior temporarily, but they will resent your trying to control them with verbal put-downs and demeaning remarks. In the long run, victims of this type of verbal abuse become less willing and less inclined to cooperate with people who use these aggressive You Messages.

I Messages Go Undercover

As we've seen, anger is often the outer covering for several layers of emotion, including feelings of frustration, hurt, and helplessness. The formulation of I Messages involves defining the behavior and the specific emotional effect that behavior has on you. Thus, communicating with I Messages helps you peel away the external layers of your emotion and discover what is at the heart of your anger.

Remember, I Messages help you manage your anger in three ways. First, they help you get in touch with your intentions so you can express your anger assertively. This helps you avoid eliciting other people's anger. Second, I Messages are an effective way to influence change in others, including changes in their anger-provoking behaviors. And third, I Messages clarify your feelings and desire for change, without evoking the listener's feelings of anger or resentment or desire for retaliation. Thus, I Messages help to strengthen the emotional bonds between you and the listener, and to decrease the frequency and intensity of future angry encounters that either you or the listener may provoke in each other.

CHAPTER THIRTY-SEVEN

Keeping an Anger Diary

An anger diary is a written record of your anger experiences. It documents the progress you are making in managing your anger, and, like the fishbowl technique, it increases self-awareness. The more regularly and accurately you record in your anger diary, the more you will gain from the process.

Anger diaries are most effective when you:

- record your entries at the same time each day
- record *all* situations that provoke your anger

Anger diaries typically include brief but specific descriptions of:

- the date, time, and place of each anger-provoking experience
- the person(s) and/or condition(s) involved
- the external events that provoked your anger

- your negative and positive self-talk immediately preceding, during, and after the anger-provoking experience
- how you behaved in response to the provocation

They also include your perception of the intensity of your anger and your evaluation of how well you managed it. For instance, did you feel enraged, or were you merely annoyed? Did you communicate in an assertive adult-to-adult manner, or were you loud and aggressive? Did you use restraint or were you verbally or physically abusive? The chart at the end of this chapter shows two entries from an extremely self-serving person's diary. The first entry was recorded when the individual was beginning his anger management training and the second entry was made eight months later.

The Benefits of Keeping an Anger Diary

Anger diaries enable you to step back, put your anger-provoking experiences into perspective, and prepare for future provocations by helping you become more aware of:

- *where* your anger occurs most frequently
- *external factors* such as who, and what conditions, anger you most intensely
- how your *internal responses* either increase or decrease your anger

The first step in keeping an anger diary consists of making a commitment to improve your anger management skills and record your anger experiences. For most people, once they begin documenting their experiences the more serious they become about monitoring and controlling their anger responses.

The process of keeping an anger diary can also help you analyze and reflect more objectively on the impact of your *self-talk, intentions, expectations,* and perceptions on the intensity, duration, and frequency of your anger.

Anger diaries can be a great source of reinforcement and encouragement. Therapists often ask their clients to keep anger diaries because these journals provide valuable information that can be used as a basis for acknowledging their clients' improvements. Additionally, anger diaries help them suggest to their clients specific ways to reduce inappropriate responses to anger-provoking situations. But you don't have to participate in therapy to benefit from keeping an anger diary. When you commit yourself to using some of the other anger management techniques described in this book, and your diary consistently includes accurate descriptions of your anger experiences, it will provide you with concrete evidence of the reductions in the intensity, frequency, and durations of your anger and the improvements in your anger management skills.

The Anger Diary

Describe each anger experience and rate the intensity of your anger and the level to which you managed your anger by using the two scales on the opposite page.

Date & Time	Place	Person(s) or Condition(s) Involved	The Provocation (External Events)	Self-Talk (Internal Response)
9/12/87 7:50 A.M.	Car	Fear of being late for work again	Running late and traffic was extremely sluggish	"Thanks to that stupid b——, I'm going to be late again!"
5/23/88 7:35 A.M.	Car	Concern for being to work on time	Traffic was sluggish	"Relax...take a deep breath... that's better, you don't have to be in a big hurry. You have plenty of time to get to work without having to rush."

Intensity of Emotion				
1	2	3	4	5
Annoyed	Irritated	Angry	Furious	Enraged

Anger Management Level				
1	2	3	4	5
Nonexistent	Poor	Adequate	Good	Excellent

Action Taken	Duration	Rate Intensity	Rate Management
Blasted horn, gave obscene gesture, and swore at slow driver	4 hours	5	1
Used positive self-talk	2 minutes	2	5

CHAPTER THIRTY-EIGHT

Self-Hypnosis

Can you recall a time when you were so involved in a television program that you didn't hear someone ask you a question? Or when you were so interested in a book you were reading that you lost track of time? If so, you've experienced self-hypnosis.

The self-hypnosis procedure that follows involves nothing more than a combination of relaxation, self-awareness, and self-talk skills. It begins with muscular relaxation because it is easiest to learn how to focus your *mental* attention when you aren't experiencing *muscular* tension. As you become more skilled with self-hypnosis, you will be able to focus your mental energy and visualize yourself managing your anger successfully without going through this formal relaxation procedure.

The deeper you allow yourself to go into a hypnotic state, the more power your conscious mind can derive from your subconscious thoughts. *Subconscious thoughts* are the silent messages that affect your everyday behavior without your being consciously aware of them. They consist of faded memories of knowledge and experiences you have accumulated throughout your lifetime, and they are reflected in your attitudes, beliefs, needs, goals, and desires. If everything you have ever learned were immediately accessible, you would not be able to function. You wouldn't have any way to filter out a specific thought from your entire lifetime accumulation of thoughts. Fortunately, your mind has a built-in "filing system." The thoughts you need on a moment by moment basis are readily available as your *conscious thoughts*. The rest of your thoughts are kept in the well-organized storehouse of your mind, your subconscious, until you need to retrieve them.

Here is an example: Your conscious mind has not been thinking of any specific numbers or names while you've been reading this page, but once you are asked to think of your address and phone number, you are able to transfer those numbers from your subconscious mind to your conscious mind. Or, when asked to name at least one of your grade-school teachers you can retrieve that information.

Self-hypnosis enables you to modify your subconscious thoughts so that they are in harmony with your conscious efforts to achieve control over your anger. When you want to improve your anger management skills, or any other skill, you need to practice and be committed to your goal both consciously and subconsciously. If your conscious self-talk is saying, "I know I can do it, I've got what it takes, nothing can stop me now," but your subconscious thoughts are filled with doubt and disbelief, you will *not* be effective in your self-improvement endeavor. But when your subconscious and conscious thoughts are in harmony with each other, you will succeed.

You can learn to use self-hypnosis to control your anger by following these five simple steps:

- induce your hypnotic state
- prepare for your posthypnotic suggestion
- make your posthypnotic suggestion
- prepare for your next hypnotic experience
- return to your conscious thinking

For your convenience, the following script has been designed so that you may read it into a tape, if you wish. Using a recording allows you to keep your eyes closed and stay relaxed whenever you want to use this self-hypnosis procedure. When recording this script for future use, record only the parts that are indented and single-spaced. Do *not* record anything that is in bold print or enclosed in parentheses.

Most people prefer recording their self-hypnosis tapes as if they were talking to another person, so the following script uses the pronoun "you." If you prefer to record your tape as if it were all self-talk, simply substitute the pronoun "I." For example, instead of saying "*You are* letting go of *your* tension," say, "*I am* letting go of *my* tension." The effectiveness of your self-hypnosis tape is influenced greatly by your tone of voice. As you read the following script, do it slowly, using the most soothing, low, rhythmic voice possible.

Induce Your Hypnotic State

(Relax)

Begin the self-hypnosis process by choosing a comfortable place to sit or lie down and allow yourself to relax. (5-second pause) Your body is now totally supported. You feel comfortable and in complete control of your mind and body. (5-second pause)

(Breathe Deeply)

Take a slow, deep breath, pushing your stomach out as you inhale and holding your breath as you count to three.

One . . . two . . . three. As you exhale, let go of any energy-draining, unnecessary tension (3-second pause) Notice the warm, relaxed, comfortable feeling you are experiencing . . . a feeling of tranquility, inner strength, and peaceful alertness. (3-second pause) You are in full control of the pace and duration of your relaxation. (3-second pause)

(Select a Signal)

(Select a word or short phrase that is calming to you, such as, "Relax," "Stay calm," "Let go," or whatever is soothing to you, and insert it wherever "———" appears in the script. As you say your chosen word or phrase, associate it instantly with deep relaxation. The more calmly and comfortingly you say this word or phrase, the easier it will be for you to go deeper and deeper into relaxation. This word or phrase will be your personal signal to relax and continue the self-hypnosis process.)

As you say "———," you feel your relaxation getting deeper and deeper. "———." (2-second pause) "———." (3-second pause) "———." (5-second pause)

(Close Your Eyes)

If your eyes are still open, allow them to close. (5-second pause) Now that your eyes are closed, you feel no need to open them. Your eyelids are feeling heavier and heavier. Your eyes are closed and relaxed, and your eyelids feel very heavy. You have no need or desire to open your eyes at this time. (5-second pause)

(Relax)

"———." (3-second pause) Your eyes and the muscles in your face are relaxing. (3-second pause) Your jaw is loose and your tongue is lying comfortably limp in your mouth. (3-second pause) Your breathing is slow and rhythmic. (3-second pause) Each breath is slow, deep, calming, and rhythmic. (3-second pause) The steady rhythm of your breathing is soothing and relaxing (10-second pause)

(Scan)

As your breathing continues to be slow and rhythmic, turn your focus inward to your thoughts, feelings, and bodily sensations. (3-second pause) Your body is completely relaxed, and your mind is free of external distractions, but you are fully alert. As you scan your mind and body, locate any unnecessary tension and release it as you exhale. (5-second pause)

(Let Go)

Feel yourself letting go of any remaining tension and becoming more and more relaxed. Your breathing is slow and rhythmic. (3-second pause) You feel warm, heavy, and relaxed in your head and neck (3-second pause), shoulders, arms, hands, and fingers (3-second pause), chest, abdomen, back, and buttocks (3-second pause), hips, thighs, calves, ankles, feet, and toes. (5-second pause)

(Imagine a Peaceful Place)

Now, allow yourself to focus your thoughts on a mental image of a place that is peaceful, relaxing, and tranquil. (5-second pause)

(You will increase the effectiveness of your self-hypnosis experience by using the same image each time.)

As you focus on your special, peaceful place, you feel warm, secure, and in control. (3-second pause) Your muscles continue to feel relaxed, heavy, and free from any desire to move. (5-second pause)

With each slow, deep, rhythmic breath you take, you feel more and more centered (2-second pause) and more and more in control. (3-second pause) You feel heavy, relaxed, and warm. (3-second pause) You are in complete control (3-second pause) You feel calm, peaceful, warm, and secure. (3-second pause) Your feeling of relaxation is becoming deeper and deeper. (3-second pause) You are feeling more and more relaxed. (3-second pause) Your mind is becoming clearer and clearer. (10-second pause)

Prepare for Your Posthypnotic Suggestion

(A posthypnotic suggestion is what you are suggesting to yourself to do *after* you complete the self-hypnotic process. The more relaxed you are when you make your suggestion, the more effective it will be.)

(Measure Your Readiness)

You are relaxed enough for your subconscious mind to accept your posthypnotic suggestion when you agree with the following statements. Your thought processes seem slower than usual. (3-second pause) Your hands and fingers feel warmer. (3-second pause) Your muscles feel heavy and warm. (3-second pause) You feel so relaxed both physically and mentally that you have little or no desire to move around. (3-second pause) You are able to focus your attention and release any distracting thoughts without effort or struggle. (3-second pause) You are aware of your inner mind's openness to positive suggestions from your conscious mind. (3-second pause)

(Determining the Depth of Your Hypnotic State)

Now see yourself at the top of a private escalator, which can take you deeper and deeper into your hypnotic state. (5-second pause) You feel mentally alert and focused, and more and more relaxed. (3-second pause) There are many places along the way where you can get off . . . but for now you are enjoying the relaxing ride. (3-second pause) When you choose to remain in a light hypnotic state you will get off near the top. (3-second pause) When you choose to remain in a medium hypnotic state you will get off midway. (3-second pause) When you choose to remain in a deep hypnotic state you will ride this imaginary escalator all the way to the bottom. (3-second pause) At whatever level you choose to get off this escalator, whether it is near the top, in the middle, or at the bottom, your subconscious mind will be influenced by your positive, posthypnotic suggestion. (5-second pause)

Make Your Posthypnotic Suggestion

(Stating Your Suggestion)

(When you make your posthypnotic suggestion, repeat it three times. Each time you say it, say it slowly and with conviction, so that you are emphasizing the positive action you will take when you are out of your hypnotic state.)

Now you are fully relaxed (3-second pause), alert (3-second pause), and in complete control. (3-second pause) Your inner mind is open to your positive posthypnotic suggestions, as you say: "I WILL manage my anger constructively." (5-second pause) "I WILL manage my anger constructively." (5-second pause) "I WILL manage my anger constructively." (5-second pause)

(Affirming Your Suggestion)

Your subconscious mind is affirming your positive, posthypnotic suggestions as you say: "I WANT to manage my anger constructively." (3-second pause) "I EXPECT to manage my anger constructively." (3-second pause) "I will ALLOW myself to manage my anger constructively." (3-second pause) "I DESERVE to manage my anger constructively." (5-second pause)

(Communicating your Subconscious Approval)

(You can determine whether your subconscious mind really approves of and accepts your posthypnotic suggestion by using "finger talking." Ask your subconscious mind to give you a signal of confirmation by allowing the *index finger* on your dominant hand to raise when it is in agreement with your suggestion, or is responding positively to your questions. Since finger talking is an involuntary movement, your finger will probably tremble or wiggle, then lift very slowly, almost as if it were being pulled on a string, like a puppet. If you were to lift your finger consciously, its movements would be smoother and quicker. When you use finger talking while you are sitting down, your hand should be resting palm down on the arm of your chair or in your lap.)

You can communicate your subconscious mind's approval of your posthypnotic suggestion by allowing your "yes" finger to lift in response to the following two questions: "Is my subconscious mind willing to let me know that I can manage my anger in a constructive manner?" (3-second pause) "Can I express my anger assertively, and let others know how I'm feeling, without being hurtful or putting others down?" Allow your "yes" finger to lift without using any conscious effort to do so. When it lifts, you will know that your subconscious mind has accepted your positive, posthypnotic suggestion. (30-second pause)

(Visualizing Your Success)

Now, using your imaginary fishbowl, create a mental picture of someone provoking your anger. (5-second pause) See yourself managing your anger constructively . . . responding to the other person in an assertive, nonhurtful manner. (3-second pause) You have no intention of putting the other person down. (3-second pause) Your voice is calm. (3-second pause) You are in control of your emotions. (3-second pause) You are responding in an appropriate, assertive manner. (3-second pause) You feel proud of your constructive handling of the situation. (3-second pause) You are confident that you can manage your anger constructively whenever it is provoked. (5-second pause)

Prepare for Your Next Hypnotic Experience

While you are still in your relaxed, fully alert hypnotic state, you can think about allowing yourself to go into an even deeper hypnotic state the next time you use self-hypnosis. (3-second pause) With increased use of this self-hypnosis process, you will be able to go into deeper and deeper hypnotic states and your posthypnotic suggestions will be even more effective. (5-second pause)

Before you begin your return to conscious thinking, allow yourself at least thirty seconds to enjoy the warm, soothing, tranquil feeling of your hypnotic state. As you allow yourself to enjoy your feelings of increased self-esteem and self-control, you feel powerful, energized, and secure. (30-second pause)

Return to Your Conscious Thinking

(If you'd prefer to remain relaxed for a while, take a nap, or get a full night's sleep, then instead of reading the rest of the script, just assure yourself that when you are ready you'll be able to awaken fully rested, alert, and energized. However, if you need to return to your conscious thinking as soon as you complete this hypnotic experience, then use this final phase to help you return to your activities feeling fully alert and energetic.

When you are ready to begin counting, say a number each time you exhale, and increase the volume of your voice with each successive number. Read the last paragraph at a faster rate than you have been reading the rest of the script, and allow your voice to sound increasingly more energetic.)

* * *

When you begin to count you will feel increasingly more and more alert and energetic. (5-second pause) You will feel energized in your head, neck, shoulders, arms, hands, and fingers. (3-second pause) You will feel energized in your chest, abdomen, back, and buttocks. (3-second pause) You will feel energized in your hips, thighs, calves, ankles, feet, and toes. (3-second pause)

As you progress with your counting, your eyes will begin to open and your muscles will begin to feel more and more energetic. By the time you reach "five," you will be completely alert and have the power, self-confidence, and determination to return energetically to your activities with an open-minded, positive attitude. (start counting)
1......2.....3....4...5.

How Self-Hypnosis Helps with Anger Management

Self-hypnosis enables your subconscious thoughts to reinforce your conscious efforts to control your anger. Self-hypnosis allows you to visualize yourself successfully managing your anger, thereby strengthening your self-confidence and self-esteem. Remember, the better your self-esteem, the more confident and successful you'll be in expressing anger in effective, assertive ways and the easier it will be to cope with other people's expressions of anger.

CHAPTER THIRTY-NINE

Systematic Desensitization

Some feelings are incompatible with anger. For instance, it is nearly impossible to feel happy and angry simultaneously. Feeling relaxed is also incompatible with anger because it is difficult to feel angry when your muscles are relaxed and you're visualizing calm and pleasant situations. Consequently, the more capable you are of staying relaxed during an anger-provoking situation, the easier it will be for you to keep your anger at a manageable level.

Systematic desensitization enables you to decrease the intensity of your anger by teaching you to be more relaxed in certain anger-provoking situations. The process of systematic desensitization was developed by Joseph Wolpe, M.D., author of *The Practice of Behavior Therapy*. He designed an orderly way of reducing or eliminating people's sensitivities to anxiety-provoking situations. He did this by helping them learn to remain calm and maintain a sense of deep muscle relaxation while they imagined various stressful situations. After his clients could successfully imagine a mildly anxiety-provoking incident without feeling tense or anxious, they gradually learned to stay relaxed while visualizing a hierarchy of situations that would normally evoke increasing amounts of anxiety. The following outline shows how systematic desensitization can be used as a self-help process for anger management. However, many people find it helpful to have a counselor or therapist guide them through it.

Step 1: Choosing a Topic for Your Anger Hierarchy

Make a list of five situations that most frequently provoke your anger and select one of the items from that list as the topic for your anger hierarchy. (Hierarchies consist of a number of anger-provoking situations arranged in order from least to most anger-provoking.) An anger diary is a likely source of choices for a topic, but if you haven't been keeping one, just think about what situations seem to provoke your anger most often, then choose one of them as the topic you'd like to work on first. For example, one of my clients frequently became angry while driving his car (as you can see by reading excerpts from his thinking log in chapter 42.) He also had difficulty coping with the anger provoked by his wife, children, boss, and in-laws. He decided to base his hierarchy on the anger he felt while driving his car because that is where he experienced the most frequent and intense anger.

Step 2: Choosing the Items for Your Hierarchy

Once you have selected your topic, think of ten to twenty anger-provoking situations pertaining to your topic. Write each situation down on a separate 3 x 5 card.

Step 3: Arranging Your Anger Hierarchy

Arrange your 3 x 5 cards in the following order: place the least anger-provoking situation on the top and the most anger-provoking situation on the bottom.

Step 4: Verifying the Order of Your Hierarchy

To make sure you have correctly arranged your anger-provoking situations according to how much they provoke your anger, close your eyes and briefly visualize each situation one at a time. Notice how angry you are as you imagine each situation and compare your reactions with the following range of emotional intensity. Do your emotional reactions become increasingly intense as you progress through your hierarchy . . . or do they fluctuate back and forth?

1	2	3	4	5
Annoyed	Irritated	Angry	Furious	Enraged

Next, rearrange the items in your hierarchy so they progress from least to most anger-provoking. Then number each item in your hierarchy in rank order.

For example, my client who frequently became angry while driving rearranged his hierarchy into the following order.

Rank Order	Level of Intensity	Situation
1	1	It is dark and raining. Suddenly you notice a bicyclist riding on the shoulder of the road who isn't using any lights or reflectors.

2   2

You are in a hurry to get to an appointment. When you try to start your car you discover you've left your lights on and the battery is dead.

3   2

After waiting for a traffic signal to change, you get about halfway through a busy intersection and your car stalls, forcing you to restart it.

4   2

After carefully parking your brand new car away from others, a driver recklessly pulls in close to you. He carelessly swings open his door, allowing it to bang into your car and chip the paint.

5   3

You are driving along a congested freeway. You get trapped behind a large truck. Before you can pass it, the truck accidentally flips up a rock that hits your windshield and cracks it.

6   3

You get up as soon as the alarm goes off, hurry through your shower, get dressed, eat breakfast, and leave the house in record time. Just as you begin to anticipate how impressed your boss will be to see you getting to work so early, you get stopped at a railroad crossing and have to wait over ten minutes while a long freight train changes tracks.

7   3

You haven't had a vacation in two years. Finally you make arrangements to take the family to Disneyland. Instead of enjoying the scenery along the way, your kids are busy screaming and fighting with each other. While trying to grab something from her brother, your daughter spills her food and milkshake all over the backseat of the car.

8	3	Along a stretch of the highway where there are no service stations in sight, your car unexpectedly runs out of gas. Your gas gauge has apparently malfunctioned.
9	4	As you're driving home from work, the driver in the next lane suddenly cuts in right in front of you. You slam on your brakes to avoid hitting him, and just barely escape being rear-ended.
10	4	When you return to your parked car you discover that someone has sideswiped it and left a huge gouge almost the full length of the car. They didn't leave a note and you can't find any witnesses.
11	4	Even though you are driving 55 in a 45 mph zone, someone is tailgating you and repeatedly giving you obscene gestures.
12	5	You're running late and really need to be someplace in a hurry. The elderly driver in front of you is creeping along way under the speed limit and has traffic stacked up as far back as you can see. Even though you are blasting your horn, he refuses to pull over so you can get past him.

Step 5: Learning to Relax

Before you begin the process of desensitizing yourself to the items on your anger hierarchy it is essential that you know how to relax.

Descriptions of two relaxation procedures, the rapid relaxation response and power relaxation, were provided in chapters 24 and 25. However, if you've never had any previous training in relaxation, or you find it difficult to relax, you may wish to have a professional person guide you through the classic relaxation procedure described by Dr. Edmund Jacobson in his book *Progressive Relaxation;* or follow the step-by-step procedure outlined in chapter 5 of *Stress Management* by Drs. Charlesworth and Nathan. Regardless of your method of relaxation you'll feel more relaxed when you do your relaxing in a quiet, comfortable, tranquil place where you can let go physically, mentally, and emotionally and be free of interruptions for at least fifteen to thirty minutes.

Step 6: Painting a Positive Mental Image

Select a positive mental image of the most restful, relaxing, and rejuvenating place imaginable to you. Perhaps your image is of a social gathering with some of your favorite people, a quiet mountain retreat, or a secluded sunny beach. Whatever the image, choose one that is automatically soothing and comforting to you. Then, whenever you begin to feel tense or angry, replace your negative thoughts with this positive mental image.

Step 7: Desensitizing Yourself to the Items on Your Hierarchy

Select a quiet, comfortable, tranquil place where you will be free from interruptions for at least fifteen to thirty minutes. Then let go of any tension and anger you may be experiencing until you feel completely relaxed. Once you are completely relaxed, look at the first item on your anger hierarchy. If you are able to visualize that first situation for fifteen to twenty seconds without experiencing any increase in tension or anger, continue the desensitization process by visualizing the second item on your hierarchy. If the first item does arouse your anger and make you feel tense, immediately stop visualizing that situation and replace that mental image with the positive mental image you created in step 6. When you feel relaxed once again, repeat the process by taking another look at the first item on your hierarchy. If this second visualization doesn't provoke your anger or make you feel tense, proceed to the next item on your hierarchy. However, if this image still provokes your anger, quickly change your focus back to your positive mental image. After you are feeling relaxed again, compliment yourself for engaging in the desensitization procedure, and wait until the next session to visualize that item again.

During the next session, if the first item continues to arouse your anger and make your feel tense, take some time to practice the relaxation procedures so it will be easier to achieve and maintain a state of deep muscle relaxation. Then replace that first item on your hierarchy with a less intense incident so you can succeed at remaining relaxed while visualizing an anger-provoking situation.

Step 8: Progressing Through Your Anger Hierarchy

Once you're completely relaxed and ready to begin a new session, begin by visualizing the highest item you've already visualized successfully, or the one just preceding it on your hierarchy. In other words, if you ended the previous session by successfully visualizing the fourth item on your hierarchy, then begin the current session by visualizing either item 4 or 3.

During a session if an item arouses your anger—for example, item 6—change your focus away from that imaginary situation to your positive mental image until you feel completely relaxed. Then return to the previous successful level on your hierarchy—in this case, item 5. Once you're able to visualize item 5, proceed with visualizing item 6 and continue up your hierarchy until your anger is aroused again. When your anger is aroused for the second time during the session, discontinue the process for that day by visualizing your positive mental image, returning to your fully relaxed state, and complimenting yourself for following through with your desensitization program.

The Benefits of Systematic Desensitization

The desensitization process provides a systematic way for learning to stay calm and relaxed when your anger is provoked. Although systematic desensitization involves imagining previously experienced anger-provoking situations, many people are able to apply the skills they learn through their visualizations to real-life situations. Remember, how you think is how you feel, and how you feel is how you behave. The systematic desensitization process teaches you to stop your angry thoughts and refocus on positive thoughts and images. This makes it easier for you to let go of your angry feelings, put anger-provoking situations into perspective, and control the intensity of your anger.

It is not necessary, nor is it even possible, to eliminate anger from your life. You may encounter many situations where you cannot avoid feeling angry. But the skills you acquire through systematic desensitization help you develop the self-control and self-discipline vital to effective anger management and constructive expressions of anger.

CHAPTER FORTY

Coping with "Faceless" Provocations

Face-to-face aggravations or indirect, passive-aggressive, manipulative behaviors aren't the only things that trigger feelings of anger. Sometimes angry feelings are triggered by "faceless" or "nameless" provocations we experience in particular situations. There are some situations just the very thought of which may arouse our anger. Crowded highways, congested city streets, lack of convenient parking, crowded sidewalks, subway violence, drug dealers, gangs, taxes, the threat of AIDS, the proliferation of muggers, pickpockets, and burglars, feelings of helplessness at work because of authoritative administrative policies or restrictive employee protection clauses—these are just some of the situations that provoke people's anger. You may or may not get angry with all of these faceless provocations, or perhaps you have some "pet peeves" that weren't mentioned. Regardless of the specific provocation, all faceless provocations present a common concern. They all represent situations that neither you nor I can single-handedly control or change.

When I need to get into Portland to give a presentation, and the freeway is like a parking lot, I wish I could push a button or say some magic word that would suddenly improve the traffic flow. When Carol saw the emotional, physical, and financial burden that patients and their families endured because of changes in Medicare regulations that led to early discharges and insufficient support services, she often expressed how powerless she felt in terms of getting the administrators of the hospital where she worked to change their discharge policy. Obviously one person cannot eliminate the threat of subway violence or street crime, nor can one person lower the tax rate or reduce inflation. True, one person can make an impact or be a creative force that eventually leads to change, but at the moment when these types of situations provoke your anger, it's not possible to wave a magic wand or do something that will result in a sudden correction or change in the situation. No matter how much you wish the circumstances were different, the desired change is beyond your immediate control. And it is that loss of control which is so anger-provoking and which must be dealt with in order to manage the anger that arises out of faceless provocations.

Unlike anger that is instigated by an individual as a result of his or her action or inaction, faceless or situational provocations cannot be resolved by confronting the person with whom you are angry and communicating your concern in an assertive, nonhurtful, adult-to-adult manner, because there is no individual to confront. For example, if you're upset with the subway system because it is too crowded, too dirty, or too dangerous, it doesn't do any good to talk to the subway. Subways can't notice changes in your tone of voice or in your body language, nor are they able to respond. That's part of what makes faceless provocations so frustrating. Anger-provoking situations, circumstances, or events are not capable of hearing or responding to anger. But that doesn't mean you have to "grin and bear it." Resolving anger triggered by situational or faceless provocations involves looking beyond what you cannot change and focusing on what you *can* change: your attitude, your perception, and your feelings about your life as well as about the situation itself.

The more emotional investment you have in a situation, or in your attitude or values that are affected by that situation, the more difficult it is to cope when that situation is out of your immediate control. The intensity of people's anger often reflects the extent of their emotional investment in the provocation. The more intense their emotional investment, the more intense their anger. Similarly, when there is a reduction in their emotional investment, there is a corresponding decline in the intensity of their anger.

For instance, if you are out for a leisurely sightseeing drive and you get stuck in slow-moving traffic, chances are your degree of anger would range from nonexistent to mild. On the other hand, if you were late for a meeting or an appointment and got caught in slow-moving traffic, chances are your degree of anger would range from moderate to intense. An obvious solution to reducing the frequency with which you get provoked by slow-moving traffic is to suggest a technique borrowed from time-management professionals—plan ahead and allow extra time for traffic congestion. If there is no congestion, you'll end up with spare time that you can use at your discretion. If there is congestion, you can relax, knowing that you have plenty of time to get to your appointment or meeting.

But what if you didn't have the time to plan ahead? What if you intended to allow extra time in case you encountered heavy traffic, but one thing led to another and you got away later than you had planned, and now traffic is very heavy? In spite of your best intentions, there you are stuck in heavy traffic, feeling that the problem is beyond your control. What can you do to cope with your anger and frustration, your overpowering feelings of helplessness, hopelessness, and despair? *Stop*. Stop filling your mind with irrational thoughts (self-talk) that tend to intensify your negative feelings. Stop your worrying. Stop focusing on how awful the situation is, on how it ought to be, or how "they" should have a better highway system. Stop focusing on what is beyond your control and start concentrating on what you can control, what you can do, and what choices you can make right now. You can control your attitude. You can choose how you feel about the situation. You can control the intensity of your anger. You can choose whether you are mildly annoyed, completely enraged, or somewhere in between. You can control your sense of hopelessness, helplessness, frustration, and despair. You can choose to continue to hold on to those negative emotions or to begin letting go of them.

The highway connecting the town where we live and the beautiful Oregon coast passes through some very serene, pastoral landscapes, a picturesque forest, and over a beautiful mountain range. Given the "right" frame of mind, it is a lovely, relaxing drive, an opportunity for experiencing a refreshing change of pace and luscious scenery. Given the state of mind I take with me, more often than I care to admit, the trip is an hour of slow-moving vehicles hogging a narrow, inadequate stretch of road that provides nothing but an opportunity for venting my frustration and anger about the unmet need for better, wider, straighter roads over to the coast. It's up to me how enjoyable or how anger-provoking the trip is. The road doesn't improve on certain days, but my perception of it does.

Another skill that helps people cope with faceless or situational provocations is the process of recognizing, accepting, and taking action on their own choices. It is a process that is often overlooked by those who perceive it as difficult or undesirable. The strongest resistance tends to come from those who have an external locus of control, because usually they feel more comfortable blaming others for their problems than accepting responsibility for their own choices.

As indicated in chapter 13, people who have an external locus of control believe there is little or no connection between their attitude, desire, and behavior and the eventual achievement of their goals. These attitudes, beliefs, and behavior patterns are often the result of extreme and prolonged parental domination and the lack of opportunity to experience a sense of control over one's environment. When children feel helpless they often become bitter and resentful and typically develop a blaming attitude of "Why even try, it's out of my hands." The more adept they get at blaming others, the more difficult it becomes for them to focus on what they actually can control and the variety of choices available to them.

Usually, the less control people felt they had over their own lives during their developmental years, the greater their desire to control their environment (including everyone in it) as adults. Whenever circumstances or events diminish their sense of control (such as bad weather, changes in policies at work, traffic congestion, or concern about personal safety), people with low self-esteem and tendencies toward an external locus of control are particularly vulnerable to feelings of pessimism, powerlessness, ineffectiveness, helplessness, and anger. They are often more dependent, insecure, self-indulgent, self-centered, angry, bitter, and hostile than people with an internal locus of control.

People with an internal locus of control have more self-confidence. It is easier for them to accept that their attitudes, perceptions, desires, faith, and actions influence their chances of reaching their goals. They are more willing to take ownership of and responsibility for their feelings and actions, and they realize that their choices and actions impact the quality of their life.

If you tend to have more of an external than an internal locus of control, it helps to think of that tendency as a challenge rather than as a liability or an excuse. Even though I have a tendency toward an external locus of control, that doesn't exempt me from needing to take responsibility for my behavior and my attitude. Whatever your tendencies, or your upbringing, you are still free to choose how you will respond to anger-provoking situations. It just may take more of a conscious effort for you than it does for someone else.

If you live or work with someone who tends to have an external locus of control, recognize that what may appear as a minor or insignificant irritation to you may be extremely frustrating to him or her. Carol has learned that when I have enough time and space, I can reduce my anger to a manageable level and redirect my energy into constructive action.

Many of the constructive anger management techniques described thus far in part 3 for coping with angry feelings and angry people can be equally as effective for coping with situational or faceless provocations. To adapt the techniques to these types of provocations, just shift your focus from coping with other people's comments and behavior to coping with your internal self-talk and attitude.

There are certain things you can control, whether you're stuck in a horrible traffic jam or you're confronted by a rigid, authoritarian administrative policy. Regardless of the situation and how out of control it appears to be, you still have mastery over your attitude, perception, perspective, plan of action, beliefs, faith, dreams, and goals. Sometimes it's hard to recognize that you have that control, and sometimes you may question the value of maintaining it, but it's there waiting for you to grasp it, like a life-preserver floating on a stormy ocean.

When your self-esteem is low, you may not recognize all the options for taking control that are available to you. The better you feel about yourself, the clearer you will see the many shades of gray that exist between the obvious extremes of black and white. It may seem as if the only choices are having complete and full control of the situation (white), or no control at all (black). When your self-esteem is raised, it is easier to see the variety of ways you can have some sense of control (gray). For example, you can't control how many cars are on the freeway at the time you need to be using it, but you can control your *attitude* about the traffic congestion and your *behavior*. You have the choice of "awfulizing" the situation or viewing it as "normal rush-hour traffic." You have the choice of being tense and uptight, clenching the steering wheel, honking and gesturing at other motorists, or of relaxing and using the time to play one of your favorite tapes. Building and maintaining your self-esteem is the cornerstone to coping with situational anger and faceless provocations. (See chapter 30 for *how* to do that.) The better you feel about yourself, the easier it is to recognize the control you do have and the choices you can make even in the midst of thoroughly provoking situations.

Modifying your self-talk is another way to gain a sense of control. If your self-talk sounds negative, pessimistic, or discouraging, give yourself permission to change it into positive, encouraging, optimistic self-talk. The reality of the anger-provoking situation won't change, but your perception of it will. Self-talk is a tool you can always use to your advantage, or you can allow it to destroy your outlook on life. You are in control of your self-talk. What you say to yourself in the privacy of your mind is your business and your secret gift to yourself. You have the opportunity to choose whether you treat yourself to pleasant, self-affirming thoughts or derogatory, self-deprecating thoughts. You have control over the decision whether to tell yourself everything that is wrong with the situation and everything that may go wrong with it in the future, or whether you encourage yourself to consider some of the ways you might be able to tap your creativity to overcome or cope with the provoking circumstance.

The process of reframing (described in chapter 29) is

another technique that can increase your sense of control and help you cope with faceless, situational anger. For instance, instead of dreading your daily battle with rush-hour traffic, reframe that part of your day as your time to escape the demands of home or work. By taking rush-hour traffic out of its "I'm going to be miserable" frame and putting it in a new "I can make the best of this" frame, you free your mind to consider all the opportunities and options available to you. Perhaps you'll want to start by making only minor, cosmetic changes to the frame, then gradually allow yourself to make bigger, more obvious changes. For instance, instead of immediately reframing misery-inflicting rush-hour traffic in a "I can make the best of this" frame, you may prefer to touch up the "misery" frame so that it becomes "I might get upset," then, "I can stay calm during rush-hour traffic," until eventually you reframe it as, "I can make the best of this." Recently, while driving down the freeway to get to one of her classes, Carol heard on the radio that there was an accident a few miles from where she was that had traffic at a standstill. She immediately chose to reframe the situation as, "Here is my opportunity to prove to myself how positively I can reframe the situation as an opportunity to begin reading the book I have with me." Much to her dismay, by the time she pulled up behind the last car in line and got out her book, the traffic started moving again. Although she probably had an underlying sense of relief that she wasn't going to be late for her class, her immediate reaction was, "This is awful. The traffic is moving already. There goes my chance to see how well I could have reframed this anger-provoking situation." With practice you too will be able to focus on reframing potentially anger-provoking situations into possibilities that seem less anger-provoking to you.

The technique of putting the situation into perspective is similar to the reframing process, but it has a slightly different emphasis. Whereas reframing enables you to gain a sense of control by looking at a situation from different angles, or in a new light, putting it into perspective gives you a sense of control by helping you compare the relative pros and cons of a particular situation with those of other situations. For instance, you may feel bitter about having to face the hassles on the highway during peak commuting times, but compare that with some people's experience of not being able to find employment. You may not be able to put every anger-provoking situation into a new or positive perspective, but just knowing that you have that option can help increase your sense of control and confidence.

If you're having difficulty putting a situation into perspective, or using the reframing process, there are other things you can do to help yourself cope with the provocation itself or the feelings of anger triggered by it. Many people benefit from emotionally disengaging and adjusting their expectations. (See chapters 28 and 30 for further explanation of these techniques.)

Since you are the one who controls the extent to which you are emotionally invested in the source of the provocation, you are your own best resource for providing yourself with some emotional distance and for reducing the emotional energy you are putting into it. During my years as a wrestling, basketball, and football coach, it was easy to see, but hard to accept, that I couldn't control the emotional investment each player was willing to make. I wanted each member of my team to meet or exceed *my* standards for the appropriate level of emotional commitment they were willing to make to the sport, to the team, and to winning. No matter how hard I exhorted my players to increase their involvement, the fact remained that they were the ones who made the final decision regarding their level of emotional investment. Through my countless words of encouragement and the example I set with my own obviously high degree of emotional involvement, I influenced their decision, but eventually I realized I couldn't make that decision for them.

Even though as a coach I was frustrated by the realization that I couldn't force a certain level of enthusiasm onto anyone else, I was thrilled with the flip side of that realization: I was free to choose how emotionally involved or uninvolved I was in any situation. No matter how entrapped I felt by a particular situation, or how anger-provoking it appeared, I was free to decide how much or how little it was going to impact my life. No matter what the situation, I was the only one who could decide how emotionally invested I would become. I could choose to become deeply invested in a particular situation and see it as awful, deplorable, or unbearable; or, I could choose to limit my emotional involvement and, as a result, view the same situation as merely unfortunate, undesirable, or inconvenient. If you are struggling with a particular situation, it may help to remind yourself that there is no built-in, preset level of emotional investment required of you. It is up to you to determine how emotionally entrenched you are. You set the controls, and you can change your level of emotional involvement with faceless provocations whenever you want.

Many types of situational or "faceless" provocations involve other losses in addition to the loss of control. In some situations, especially those that involve crime or the potential for criminal activity, there is a sense of loss of personal freedom and loss of innocence. People often feel indignant at the perceived injustice associated with these types of situations, and the greater the distance that exists between how they feel the situations should be and how they really are, the greater their sense of indignity, frustration, and anger. One way to facilitate the process of emotionally disengaging from anger-provoking situations is by adjusting your expectations of those situations. Allowing yourself to adjust your expectations does not mean you have to give up your dreams or desires. There is a difference between changing your expectations and altering your desires and dreams. For instance, you may wish that you could go for a leisurely walk in a big city at night without any risk of getting mugged, or you may wish you could get onto the freeway during rush hour and have a lane all to yourself, but such dreams aren't very realistic. By accepting the reality of the situation and adjusting your expectations until they more closely approximate that reality, it's easier to reduce your level of involvement and become emotionally disengaged.

People who realize that muggers prefer the protection of darkness, or that freeways are usually the most congested during the rush hours, are going to be less shocked when muggings occur at night or freeways are clogged at certain times of the day, but they may still remain actively involved in working toward making our cities safer, improving our nation's freeways, or finding alternative modes of transportation. Allowing yourself to accept the reality of a situation and adjusting your expectations to fit that reality enables you to reduce your emotional investment in an unrealistic expectation. This allows you to be sufficiently disengaged emotionally so that you can redirect your energies into positive, nonhurtful actions.

When you are faced with a reality that you cannot tolerate, adjusting your expectations is not your only option. You also have the choice of how you will react to that situation. You can rant and rave, become passive and despondent, or you can channel the energy from your anger into constructive actions. Even when the anger-provoking situation itself is beyond your direct control, you can always control how that situation will affect your life. Only you can choose what impact that situation will have on you. You can choose whether to allow the negative aspects of the provocation to play over and over again in your mind, until the vision of new, positive directions in your journey of life becomes obscured, or you can use the energy from your emotions triggered by the situation to sharpen your focus on the positive paths you can take.

Founders of groups such as Mothers Against Drunk Driving (MADD) and Crime Victims United (CVU) experienced realities that they found intolerable, but they realized that until intense, dedicated efforts were put in toward creating changes, those harsh realities would remain the same. Members of MADD realize that people who drink and drive are putting themselves and others at risk for serious injury and death. So, instead of expecting that there won't be any more accidents and fatalities caused by drunk drivers, they put their time and energy into creating stiffer penalties and changing public attitudes toward drinking and driving. Through their efforts, the number of people who drink and drive has been reduced, and consequently they have reduced the number of alcohol-related traffic deaths. Even though they can't replace their loved ones who've been killed by drunk drivers, members of MADD are regaining a sense of purpose for their own lives through their efforts to change the public's attitude toward drunk driving. Because of the unwillingness of members of CVU to accept the reality of victims of crime having fewer rights than the perpetrators of crime, and their dedication to redirecting the energy from their anger into creating a new reality, new laws have been passed that protect and increase the rights of victims. Members of CVU can't replace their loved ones who have been killed by convicted murderers, but they are finding at least some comfort in their commitment to create a system that protects and ensures the rights of future crime victims and their survivors.

Finally, you can recover your sense of control over situational or faceless provocations by choosing to *let go* of the anger you experienced in connection with those provocations. As seen in chapter 27, the process of letting go is a very individual matter. No one can take away your intense feelings of anger, hurt, and vindictiveness. It is your choice whether you cling to these feelings or let them go. This may seem like an overwhelming task and awesome responsibility, but hopefully you will grasp it as the wonderful opportunity it is to regain and retain control over your own feelings, attitude, and behavior. Even when your anger has been triggered by a specific circumstance, situation, or faceless provocation you still can choose the intensity, duration, and direction of your anger. By choosing to remain intensely uptight and angry, you may have difficulty discovering, recognizing, or appreciating any of the positive aspects of your life. On the other hand, if you choose to let go of the bitterness born out of your anger, allow yourself to resolve the resentment, hate, and frustration you encounter, you'll find it's easier to focus on what's enjoyable to you.

Just as you cannot always avoid anger-provoking individuals, you cannot always avoid anger-provoking situations. What you can avoid, however, is the pain that comes from allowing faceless or situational provocations to keep you from living the life you deserve. You can't always eliminate the source of your anger, but you can control how intense your anger will be, how long you will feel angry, and what you are going to do with your anger. There will be those times when situations, systems, or prevailing attitudes provoke your anger and create roadblocks along your journey of life. You can choose to keep your focus on the external source of the provocation and what you *can't* control, and allow those roadblocks to develop into seemingly unsurmountable barriers; or, you can focus on what you *can* control—your attitude, perceptions, self-talk, and beliefs— and use your internal powers to reduce those roadblocks to temporary detours. It's your choice.

CHAPTER FORTY-ONE

Systematic Approach to Defusing Hostility

As I awake each morning, I'm not usually thinking, "Gee, I hope I'll have an opportunity today to be confronted by several mean and nasty people. If I'm really lucky, maybe their anger will escalate into rage, and they'll direct their hostility toward me. Who knows, I might even get physically assaulted." Such thoughts certainly don't provide much motivation for getting out of bed.

Even though hostility isn't something you or I would normally seek out, especially if it's going to be directed at us, it is nice to know that when we are confronted by a hostile person, there are some constructive alternatives to ineffective shout-down tactics that people often use.

When we become the target of someone's hostility, we often feel as if we are being attacked. Consequently, the instinctive response is to defend ourselves against any further assault, by either counterattacking or getting away from the hostile person. The commonly held belief is: the best defense is a good offense. A counterattack can occur so quickly that it may seem as if it were an uncontrollable, reflexive, "knee-jerk" reaction. But, instead of extinguishing a little spark, counterattacks usually fan the flame and intensify the other person's hostility.

For instance, when Jessica was angry with Nathan and called him a power-hungry tyrant, he wanted to lash out with an equally hurtful remark. When Robert slapped Penny, her first instinct was to hit him back. Even though Nathan and Penny don't usually strike back verbally or physically, they probably have a conscious or unconscious desire to do so. For most of us, it is understandable that we might want to hurt the person who has wounded us.

Primitive man dealt with hostility by choosing instantly whether to fight or take flight. This "fight or flight" reaction was an instinctive, reflexive, lifesaving tactic. However, in modern, "civilized" societies, most people have been taught that it is not right to hurt others. We grow up hearing clichés like, "two wrongs don't make a right," or "turn the other cheek." In spite of these teachings, it's often very difficult not to feel the desire to strike back, seek revenge, or hurt the person or persons who have hurt us. If we retaliate, however, we may get a temporary sense of satisfaction, yet at the same time we may also feel a sense of guilt. The degree of guilt depends on our ability to empathize with others. That is why ESSs (described in chapter 42), who are extremely self-centered and lack empathy for others, have the hardest time resisting the desire to retaliate.

In responding to a hostile person, the emotion of fear also plays a big role in deciding whether to retaliate in a hurtful manner. The more likely it seems that the hostile person will respond with increased hostility to our hurtful behavior, the less likely we are to retaliate in an obviously hurtful way. When we believe the hostile person's reprisal may be life-threatening, we may decide to withdraw immediately. For example, most people held at gunpoint may desire to retaliate, but that feeling is often overshadowed by their sense of intense helplessness and fear. Battered children or women typically feel angry and vindictive toward their abuser. But understandably, for many of them, there is an even stronger feeling of fear that any retaliation on their part will only increase the intensity of their batterer's hostility. In situations where people are afraid to hurt the person who harmed them, they may aggressively display their anger, frustration, and hostility onto someone or something else. Among other things, this displaced aggression may take the form of breaking things, slamming doors, or striking walls. The hostility may also be turned inward and expressed in passive-aggressive ways such as pouting, "conveniently" forgetting to follow through with their commitments, or refusing to talk.

Within the last few years, I have watched in amazement as large buildings have been reduced to a pile of rubble and a cloud of dust, without causing so much as a scratch or a ding to adjoining buildings. Due to the skill of demolition experts, charges are strategically placed so that the building caves into itself instead of exploding outward as it would with a traditional dynamite blast. These controlled explosions (known as implosions) illustrate how technology can transform a potentially destructive energy source (dynamite) into a useful renovation tool.

Similarly, the surge of adrenaline you feel when you are the target of someone's hostility can be your energy source for initiating the defusing process, or it can be used to launch a counterattack and escalate the hostility. The choice is yours.

Often, when I receive a written request to give a workshop on defusing hostility, the request will read: "Would you be available to give a workshop on *diffusing* hostility?" I find that error rather interesting, because it captures the essence of the problem. Far too often, hostility is *diffused* (poured out and caused to spread freely) rather than *defused* (made less dangerous or tense). As long as people are unaware of positive ways to maintain and restore their sense of personal control in the face of hostility, it is only natural that they resort to instinctive, defensive tactics, even though such tactics often result in increased rather than decreased hostility.

Fortunately, you can learn how to break out of the self-defeating, "attack, counterattack, attack, counterattack" cycle. There is an effective, positive way to defuse hostility that utilizes many of the constructive anger management skills presented earlier in part 3.

Evaluating the Defusing Process

There are three basic rules of defusing hostility. The first rule is to be *self-aware*. (See "Applying Self-Awareness to the Defusing Hostility Process," below.) Be conscious of your feelings, intentions, and expectations (remembering not to expect too much rational or responsible behavior from some-one who's hostile); body language and demeanor (appear firm, in control, respectful, and nonthreatening); make eye contract; and keep your tone of voice and communication style matter-of-fact, adult-to-adult, slow, and controlled. The second rule is to *focus* on the other person's *feelings*. The third rule to abide by is to *respond according to the prescribed sequence:* reflect on the other person's feelings before responding to his other concerns or initiating any problem-solving.

Applying Self-Awareness to the Defusing Hostility Process

Whether it's in person or on the telephone, before you take any action or make any response to someone's hostility, use the fishbowl technique (see chapter 21) and self-talk to help you be aware of what *feelings* you have about that person's hostility and what your *intentions* are.

Self-awareness is an essential part of the defusing process, especially when the person's hostility is directed at you. The more carefully you monitor your feelings and intentions, to make sure you are calm and have no intention of hurting the hostile person, the more effective you will be at defusing his or her hostility. You can tune in to your feelings and determine whether your intentions are hurtful or nonhurtful by listening to your self-talk. Listen to this sample self-talk and see how it touches on feelings:

> "This person's outburst is starting to irritate me. I need to emotionally disengage, stay calm and in control. It feels good to be calm and in control."

Note how affirming it is to state your feelings "as if" you were already experiencing them, as discussed in chapter 22, rather than in the "I wish . . ." format.)

Next, listen to how self-talk focuses on intentions:

> "My intentions are to help this person calm down and regain his self-control, and to maintain my position of calmness, self-confidence, and self-control."

Be aware of how you are approaching the hostile person. You will be most effective when you come across as calm, confident, firm, respectful, and nonthreatening. Your controlled, self-assured approach indicates: "I respect you as an individual, and I am *not* intimidated or manipulated by your anger."

Be aware of your eye contact. Good eye contact, whether real or imagined, helps you focus on the individual and be more attentive to his or her needs. If the hostile person is on the telephone rather than facing you in person, visualize yourself giving the person good eye contact.

Finally, it is extremely important to be not only constantly aware of what you are saying, but of *how* you are saying it. As mentioned in chapters 18 and 22, you can increase or decrease the effectiveness of your communication according to how you say what you're saying. One of the most difficult aspects of dealing with hostile people is maintaining your emotional balance, because they aren't concerned with your well-being. Hostile people are not operating from a fully rational point of view. Their anger is so extreme that they usually aren't thinking about the consequences of their behavior. In order for you to be able to interact with them in a rational manner, you'll need to help them reduce their anger to a manageable level. The quickest and most effective way to do that is for you to maintain your emotional balance, by remaining emotionally disengaged and responding to them in a calm, respectful, nonthreatening manner. Your tone of voice, the pace, pitch, and volume of your speech, as well as your choice of words and word emphasis, are what the hostile person uses to evaluate how calm, respectful, and threatening you are toward him or her. If you say the "right" thing, without being aware of *how* you are saying it, the hostile person will pick up on any lack of congruence and any lack of control on your part and consider these discrepancies as justification for perpetuating or increasing his or her hostility.

The Defusing Sequence

The defusing process is comprised of three basic steps, taken in a specific sequence:

Step 1: Accurately *reflect* the hostile person's predominant *feeling*, then wait for him or her to respond.

Step 2: Accurately *restate* the hostile person's predominant *feeling* (you may wish to include some secondary feelings in addition to the predominant feeling), *paraphrase* his or her *concern*, then quietly and patiently wait for his or her response.

Step 3: Accurately *restate* the hostile person's *feelings and concern* and *initiate the problem-solving process*.

Only after the hostile person has completed his or her response to your Step 2 statement and you've waited two to five seconds before reconfirming his or her feelings and concern, is it appropriate to make your first, brief, Step 3 problem-solving response. For example, "It sounds as if you're angry and frustrated [feelings] with the poor service you received [concern]. What do you think needs to be done to resolve this situation [problem-solving]?"

Sometimes it seems as if it takes an unbearably long time for the hostile person to respond, but it's important to be patient and give him or her ample opportunity to respond. If the person you're defusing doesn't have any ready solutions, or is reluctant to express them, you might suggest one or two possible options. For example, "Have you considered putting your concerns in writing?"

When you are the specific target of someone's hostility, there are a couple of things you can do to get the focus off of you while you are defusing the person's hostility. One is to get the hostile person involved in looking for a solution instead of concentrating on the causes of his or her hostility. This can be accomplished by changing the style of your Step 3 response. Instead of taking responsibility for coming up with possible solutions to the hostile person's problem, it is often very helpful to say something such as, "What would be helpful to you at this point?" The other thing you can do to help reduce the tension is to apologize. When the need for an apology is obvious, requested, or implied, offering a *sincere* apology usually gives a real boost to the defusing process and in the long run benefits you as well.

Let's take a look at the interaction between Tom and Sam and see how they take each phase of the defusing process one step at a time.

Tom yells at Sam: "You filthy bastard! You're nothing but a lowdown slimy scumbag! Who do you think you are, you stupid son of a bitch! Nobody messes with me! *No one! Never!*"

"You're really angry," Sam states matter-of-factly, while looking directly at Tom. [Step 1 response]

Notice how Sam's response consisted of a short, concise reflection of Tom's predominant feeling. He reflected back the essence of Tom's feelings, then he quickly stopped talking, so that Tom could respond. If your reflection of a hostile person's feelings is on target, chances are that person will begin to feel attended to and may begin to behave a little more rationally. Notice how Tom's next comment is a little calmer than his initial outburst. Since Sam was nonthreatening and nonhostile to him, Tom begins to let down his guard a bit and provide some clues about the nature of his frustration.

"You bet I'm angry, and I'm not going anywhere until I get what I came here for, even if nobody gives a damn about my needs," Tom grumbles.

"Sounds as if you're angry and frustrated about your needs not getting met around here," Sam reflects with sincere concern. [Step 2 response]

Again, Sam's response was short and to the point. He restated Tom's predominant feeling, recognized an additional feeling, and paraphrased Tom's concern. He said just enough to let Tom know he was listening, then quietly waited again for Tom to respond. Sam refrained from interjecting his own values, opinions, or defenses. He was careful to summarize and paraphrase, rather than "psychoanalyze" and try to find some deep, hidden meaning behind what Tom had said. By responding only to the verbal and nonverbal information that Tom provided, Sam enabled Tom to feel a sense of autonomy and dignity. If Sam had tried to "read into" what Tom had said, Tom may have felt threatened or as if Sam had invaded his personal space. You can limit your risk of mistakenly reflecting a feeling or concern that the hostile person denies or doesn't recognize, by limiting your interpretation of his or her feelings and concerns to those that the hostile person shares or makes evident through their behavior.

Notice how Sam's response in Step 2 set the stage for Tom to be more explicit about the source of his frustration.

> "You're darn right. Why, just yesterday..."
> Tom explains.

After Tom explained what had triggered his intense frustration and anger, and Sam had reflected Tom's feelings and concern, it was finally appropriate for Sam to initiate the problem-solving process.

> "Obviously you're frustrated and angry about the way you were treated here yesterday. What do you see as some ways to resolve this situation?" Sam inquires after listening attentively to Tom's complaint. [Step 3 response]
> "Well," Tom suggests, "for starters, I could..."

Tom's nonhostile reply to Sam's statement in Step 3 illustrates the positive consequence of following the prescribed order of the defusing sequence and accurately reflecting feelings before proceeding to any problem-solving. Going through the first two steps of the defusing sequence gave Tom an opportunity to begin to see Sam as a possible advocate. "After all," Tom may have thought, "it seems as if Sam is trying to understand what I'm saying." If Sam had skipped over the first two steps of the defusing process and jumped right into the problem-solving phase, Tom may have held on to his preconceived notion that Sam was his adversary, and he may have rejected or sabotaged Sam's problem-solving efforts.

Sam demonstrated that he understood and respected Tom's feelings before he tried to initiate any problem-solving. This eventually helped Tom be less hostile, more rational, and more receptive to Sam's problem-solving efforts.

The Importance of Reflecting Feelings

In many situations, accurately reflecting the hostile person's feelings, without offering excuses, explanations, or defensive statements, is sufficient to defuse the hostility and provide a foundation on which you can engage in a constructive, nonhurtful interaction. When dealing with friends, relatives, or certain business associates, reflecting their feelings not only serves to defuse their hostility, but an accurate reflection may eventually result in restoring intimacy and reestablishing a more mutually satisfying relationship.

Although you probably have little or no interest in restoring or developing a sense of emotional intimacy with many of the hostile people you encounter, being able to reflect their feelings and reduce the intensity of their hostility may not only make your life more pleasant (by reducing the likelihood that they'll want to hurt you), but it helps them feel that some of their needs have been met. When you reflect hostile people's feelings and stay out of "power struggles" by choosing not to argue with them, you protect yourself from getting trapped in the "attack, counterattack..." hostility cycle. Thus, reflecting feelings often encourages "win-win" encounters and interactions.

Even though you may have a "perfect" solution to the person's problem, the best response you can give a hostile person is a short, concise, respectful, accurate reflection of the predominant feeling he or she has just expressed. Skipping over the feeling in order to respond to the hostile person's concern often leaves him or her feeling frustrated and misunderstood. That is because the specific complaint isn't necessarily the cause of the hostility. Hostility can evolve over a period of time as a result of repeated instances of unmet needs, unresolved frustrations, and feelings of being disrespected and unappreciated. The feelings that result in hostility are often deep-seated and are not easily removed by offering a quick solution to a stated problem. Hostile people feel more attended to, and are more receptive to your attempts to defuse their hostility, when they feel they are understood. The most efficient, effective, and long-lasting way to convey that understanding is by calmly, quietly, and respectfully reflecting their feelings as accurately and precisely as you can.

One way to determine how well you are reflecting a person's predominant feeling is to observe the length of your response. If your response is longer than six to eight words, your reflection of the hostile person's predominant feeling may be obscured. Practice reflecting just *one feeling*, then quietly waiting for the other person to respond. It may seem strange at first to give such a short response, but when it comes to defusing hostility, remember, less is more. The less you say initially, the more effective you'll be.

Tips for Reflecting Feelings

While listening to what a hostile person is saying, observe his or her nonverbal behavior and be attentive to all the emotions he or she is expressing or implying. By making a mental note of the general theme or overall tone of the person's feelings, you increase the likelihood that you will give an accurate reflection of that person's primary feeling.

Precede your initial response with a two- to five-second pause. Delaying your response and giving good eye contact are two of the most effective ways to demonstrate your respectful concern and sincere interest in the hostile person's feelings.

Hostility often arises out of feelings of not being respected or valued. Generally, the more you can do to increase hostile people's perceptions of you as their advocate, the easier it is to decrease their hostility. However, a word of caution is in order here. If you are dealing with people who tend to be chronically angry or are extremely self-serving (see chapter 42 for a description of ESSs), it is important to reflect their feelings in a nonthreatening, firm, and respectful manner, being careful not to use a soft, sympathetic tone that they have a tendency to interpret as weakness. They frequently misinterpret and take advantage of kindness and sympathy, even to the point of converting it into an increase in hostility. Since you don't always have the luxury of knowing in advance with what kind of hostile person you will be dealing, the least risky and most effective approach to take is one that is firm and respectful. It's best to reserve your sympathy for your friends and acquaintances whom you are confident you can trust to respond to it in a favorable way.

Special Cases: Working with the Extremely Hostile Person

Some individuals actually *enjoy* using their hostility to manipulate, exploit, and hurt others. Because of their limited amount of empathy or feelings for others, it is extremely difficult to defuse their hostility without using a show of force. This show of force usually consists of a number of professionals such as police or psychiatric aides who have been trained to deal effectively with extremely hostile people. When the hostile person is extremely self-serving, self-centered, and emotionally detached, it often takes a team of professionals approaching the hostile person in organized unison before he or she will begin to exhibit less hostility.

When approaching people who are out of control with

their hostility, it is important for the police, psychiatric aides, or other professionals involved in the process, to demonstrate that there are *rational* people *in control*, who will not allow the hostile individual to hurt him- or herself or others. It is important that all of the professionals involved in the defusing situation approach the hostile person in an organized, calm, firm, nonchallenging, emotionally neutral, adult-to-adult manner, without being physically or verbally violent or abusive. Each professional must portray a definite sense of self-confidence and self-control without appearing threatening. Any act or expression of violence, verbal or physical abuse, or bullying, used in an attempt to control extremely hostile people, will generally ignite the intensity of their hostility and lead to an increase in their desire to retaliate and be vindictive. Correctional officers and psychiatric aides are particularly affected by the ESS's characteristic habit of holding grudges for a long time.

Realistically, due to budget constraints, sufficient numbers of trained staff are not always available to provide an adequate show of force. When there are only one or two correctional officers or psychiatric aides available to defuse a large, strong, mentally ill ESS, who has a long history of being physically assaultive and is currently worked up into an extremely agitated and hostile state of mind, the staff has to concentrate on protecting other inmates/patients, themselves, and the hostile person. Obviously, in situations such as this, eliminating the threat of danger or violence by physically restraining the hostile person takes precedence over engaging in the three-step defusing process. Many correctional and psychiatric facilities lack the funds to hire a sufficient number of trained staff to manage hostile people correctly and effectively. Unfortunately, where these under-staffed conditions exist, some staff, patients, or inmates have been severely injured or killed.

There are also situations where police may need to use

their weapons in order to protect themselves or others, but the use of a weapon should be considered only as a last resort. When a person is endangering himself or others, and there aren't enough police available to provide an immediate and sufficient show of force, commercial sprays are sometimes used to subdue and temporarily eliminate the threat of violence. Professionals, including police and psychiatric aides, should use the least restrictive or invasive approach available to them that will ensure their own safety and enable them to help the hostile person reestablish a sense of self-control and begin the defusing process. Even when people are behaving in an extremely hostile manner, it is important to take them seriously, treat them with respect, and remain calm. Responding violently to their actions only perpetuates and intensifies the "attack, counterattack, attack, counterattack" hostility cycle.

Final Reminders for Defusing Hostility

Unless you are faced with the extreme situations just described, you will usually find that you can defuse most people's hostility quite effectively by remembering to:

- *Be self-aware*. Pay particular attention to your feelings, intentions, tone of voice, body language, and demeanor. Use the fishbowl technique (see chapter 21) and listen to your self-talk to maintain constant self-awareness.
- *Focus on feelings*. Maintain your emotional balance and stay out of power struggles by focusing on the hostile person's feelings and not allowing yourself to get distracted by his or her irrational, hurtful behavior and remarks. (Obviously, hostile people have the potential to inflict harm on you or themselves, and you have to be alert to this, but in order to defuse their hostility you need to remain calm, be respectful, and focus on their feelings.)

- *Follow the defusing sequence.* Each step is important, but their effectiveness depends on your taking them in the prescribed order. Skipping over step 1 usually sabotages and prolongs the defusing process. On the other hand, the intensity of most people's hostility can often be lowered just by reflecting their feelings.

PART FOUR

Anger Management Techniques for Professionals

CHAPTER FORTY-TWO

Working with the Extremely Self-Serving Personality: Keeping and Analyzing "Thinking Error" Logs

It's important to take a special look at the Extremely Self-Serving (ESS) personality type because of the impact they have on society. Although ESSs represent only a small portion of the overall population—less than five percent—they commit the majority of violent crimes in this country and are the most destructive and abusive with their anger. ESSs *want* their anger and they're extremely reluctant to let go of it. They have become accustomed to using their anger to intimidate others and get their own way. ESSs have no interest in managing or controlling their anger. They feel they have a right to be angry, bitter, and negative about anything that doesn't go their way . . . and a right to express it as aggressively or violently as they choose.

In terms of the attached-detached continuum described earlier, ESSs are very near the detached end of the continuum.

Their degree of detachment, along with their self-centeredness, irresponsibility, and lack of empathy for others, intensifies the negative influence that thinking errors

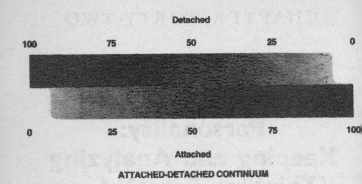

ATTACHED-DETACHED CONTINUUM

have on their behavior. This, in turn, makes their undesirable characteristics even more offensive.

In addition to the undesirable characteristics of the Self-Serving personality described in chapter 19, ESSs are extremely grandiose, hostile, and assaultive. They are also notorious for their chronic cheating, fighting, and lying. The philosophy of an ESS is, "I want what I want, when I want it, and I want it *now*!"

Many theories have been suggested as explanations for the development of the Extremely Self-Serving personality. Following are just a few of the more popular theories.

Sociological Theories

These theories presume that people would not develop ESS personalities if certain influences could be altered or avoided. Among these influences are:

- parental influences such as abuse and neglect; lack of nurturing and bonding; lack of assertive authority fig-

ures in the home; failure to instill appropriate standards and values; insufficient guidance and modeling in appropriate ways to cope with stress and express anger; an overly permissive and protective attitude interfering with the child's development of self-discipline
- substance abuse by family members, especially parents
- peer pressure to conform and participate in inappropriate activities
- social inequities resulting from racial discrimination and social or political injustices
- inadequate educational system, as evidenced by a high dropout rate, lack of special programs for students with special needs, and promotion of students for social rather than academic reasons
- Feelings of helplessness, hopelessness, futility, despair, low self-esteem, bitterness, and anger, resulting from poverty and unemployment

Environmental Theories

These theories contend that the ESS personality develops as a result of environmental conditions such as:

- overcrowding and urbanization creating undue pressures and intensifying people's feelings of stress, anxiety, and hostility
- geographical location and climate affecting people's moods
- the media (television, newspapers, magazines, comics, pornography) condoning and glorifying violence and aggression

Genetic Theories

These theories propose that people are predisposed toward having ESS because of certain factors determined by their genes. Among these factors are:

- certain body types and lack of attractiveness
- temperament
- endocrine disorders such as high testosterone levels, hypoglycemia, and premenstrual syndrome (PMS)
- mental deficiency
- brain damage or dysfunction
- abnormal brain waves, epilepsy

Mental Illness Theories

These theories attribute the development of the ESS to various types of mental illness or disorders. These include:

- neuroses, psychoses, and affective disorders (such as depression and bipolar disorder)
- attention deficit, impulse control, and explosive disorders

Although many of the preceding theories have been widely accepted by the general public and the professional community, they have not been substantiated by research. For every study indicating support for these theories, there have been other studies refuting them. Of all the theories that have been proposed as possible explanations for what causes someone to develop an Extremely Self-Serving personality, the most plausible seems to be parental neglect and abuse.

The process of forming an emotional attachment (bond) occurs during a child's first five years of life. Children who are neglected and/or abused by their parents during these early years aren't able to form the kind of emotional attachment with their parents that normally serves as the basis for developing trust and emotional closeness with others later in life. Instead, they become emotionally detached and basically mistrustful of other people's motivations. Angry over their lack of nurturing, neglected children often hold on to their anger throughout life. Having convinced themselves that their hurtful behavior is justified because they feel hurt, ESSs perpetrate that type of twisted logic through the use of thinking errors.

Neglectful and abusive parents fail not only to provide their children with the opportunity for bonding, but they fail to provide them with appropriate role models for coping with angry feelings and angry people. Children of abusive parents learn through experience that anger is expressed in impulsive, hurtful, aggressive ways.

Obviously, not all neglected and abused children grow up to be emotionally detached and extremely self-serving people. Research has shown that in families where one or more children develop an Extremely Self-Serving personality, there are often other children in those same families who mature into responsible, caring adults. These differences in outcome could be attributed to differences in temperaments, support from older siblings, relatives, etc., and differences in treatment from one child to the next.

As Samenow and Yochelson, authors of *The Criminal Personality, volumes I and II*, concluded: focusing on the projected causes of the Extremely Self-Serving personality perpetuates and reinforces the ESS's inappropriate behavior. Searching for the causes may actually be counterproductive. People who focus on the reasons for the ESS's behavior tend to overlook the ESS's need to accept responsibility for their behavior. These people often become *bleeding hearts* who look upon ESSs as victims rather than as victimizers. Bleeding hearts actually reinforce the ESS's inappropriate behavior and *stroke their deviance* by regarding the ESS's self-centered, irresponsible, nonempathic behavior as an unavoidable consequence of poor parenting, overcrowding, congenital abnormalities, or mental illness. According to Samenow and Yochelson, unless ESSs are helped to change their thinking, any changes ESSs make in their behavior will be only temporary. Consequently, the task of any treatment program for ESSs, whether it is conducted within an institutional setting or on an outpatient basis, is to help them correct their *thinking errors* and develop a more responsible and empathic attitude.

People who have an Extremely Self-Serving personality are the most resistant to learning how to cope with angry feelings and angry people. They are intolerant of others' expressions of anger, yet they insist on holding on to and using their own anger for personal gain. Most ESSs require a professionally guided approach to anger management before they will begin to replace their inappropriate expressions of anger with appropriate expressions. This approach takes a long time—sometimes several years—before lasting changes are established. In some situations the ESS has become so habituated to his thinking errors, and to manipulating others with his anger and irresponsible behavior, that permanent positive changes cannot be guaranteed.

Depending on the severity of the ESS's detachment, inpatient treatment may be necessary. Inpatient treatment provides professionals more control over the ESSs and makes it easier to monitor their behavior. Professionals need to be cautious, however, about assuming that changes in an ESS's behavior indicate changes in his or her thinking. The ESS may just be using the system or playing games to gain an early release from the program. Unless the ESS has changed his thinking, he may revert back to his irresponsible, hurtful, or criminal behavior as soon as he is released. Only time will tell if lasting changes have been established.

When working with ESSs it is important to avoid being manipulated or controlled by their expressions of anger or their maneuvers to avoid accepting responsibility for their behavior. You may find it is easier to maintain control over the therapeutic environment by complying with the following guidelines.

Be a Responsible Model

ESSs may eventually model how you interact with them. However, when they choose to use you as a role model, they will model only *what you actually do,* not what you say you are going to do. That is why it is important that what you say and what you do are congruent and consistent. If you express your frustration, irritation, or anger in authoritative, punitive, physically aggressive, or loud and demanding ways, ESSs interpret this with their own private, twisted logic as permission to continue their inappropriate, irresponsible, or violent expressions of anger.

You can also provide ESSs with an inadequate and inappropriate role model by responding to them in overly permissive ways. By overprotecting ESSs and excusing them from taking responsibility for their behavior, you relinquish control and reinforce their S.I.N. (self-centered, irresponsible, and nonempathic) behavior.

When permissive professionals are kind, warm, and caring they often mistakenly assume that ESSs will respond by automatically choosing to behave appropriately. Instead, ESSs interpret the professional's kindness, warmth, and caring as weaknesses that they can and usually do easily exploit by continuing to act irresponsibly and inappropriately. The leniency of permissive professionals and other bleeding hearts actually strokes ESSs' deviance and intensifies their inappropriate behavior.

You can provide ESSs with an appropriate role model by using a democratic approach and responding to them in a calm, quiet, assertive, respectful, firm, slow and controlled, matter-of-fact, adult-to-adult, emotionally neutral manner. When you consistently use constructive methods of confronting, disciplining, and communicating with ESSs, they will be more likely to associate nonhurtful, assertive behavior with feelings of anger and will be more apt to express anger in constructive ways. The democratic approach not only provides ESSs with an appropriate role model, it helps them to decrease their irresponsibility and increase their self-control, self-discipline, and responsible behavior.

Stay Emotionally Disengaged

By remaining emotionally neutral and objective you can maintain control and maximize the effectiveness of your interactions with and treatment of ESSs. If you are feeling provoked, angry, or extremely pleased with ESSs, these feelings might indicate that you have become overinvolved or are being manipulated by them. You can prevent ESSs from manipulating or exploiting you by maintaining your professional stance and remaining emotionally distant and objective. It is important that you do not:

- overidentify with ESSs
- want or need approval from ESSs
- validate your worth according to how well ESSs like you or how much improvement they are making

Set Firm, Fair Limits

Whenever possible, it is preferable to have ESSs assist in the establishment of the rules and regulations governing your interactions with them and in the development of the consequences for infractions of those rules and regulations. When it is not possible or practical to include them in this process, or when they refuse to provide any input, you will need to complete it by yourself. Regardless of the ESS's input in establishing the consequences, it is important that you always follow through with administering the consequences in a fair, firm, and consistent manner.

Stay in the Power Position

When interacting with ESSs it is always important for you to feel you are in control and actually be in control. You can accomplish this by:

- offering your hand first if you're going to shake hands
- designating a place for the ESS to sit and requesting that he or she sit there
- sitting on a chair slightly higher than the ESS's and maintaining good eye contact
- sitting up straight in your chair so that you support your lower back
- staying relaxed and calm, taking slow deep breaths when necessary
- speaking in a calm, firm, assertive, adult-to-adult, emotionally neutral tone of voice
- never, never *never* wanting or needing anything from the ESS

Be a Scientific Observer

ESSs can talk a good game and often use their feelings to support the fantasy that they are the victims. It is important to avoid overidentifying with their problems and getting sucked into their scams. You can do this by remaining objective and not accepting their feelings as excuses for their inappropriate behavior. You will be more effective when you observe and respond to the obvious manifestations of ESSs' thoughts as evidenced by their conversation and behavior, or by the statements they may be trying to make with their clothing, hairstyle, makeup, or jewelry. It is also important to be aware of any incongruence between what they are saying and how they are saying it.

Be Aware of Thinking Errors

Remember that ESSs justify and reinforce their self-centered, irresponsible, nonempathic behavior by relying on thinking errors. The most effective way to confront ESSs with their thinking errors is by holding a *reality mirror* up to them and requiring them to keep *thinking error logs*. (The thinking error log process is explained later in this chapter.) The reality mirror process consists of confronting the ESS with his thinking errors. This is accomplished by explaining in a firm, assertive, adult-to-adult, emotionally neutral tone of voice precisely what he is doing whenever you notice that he is using a thinking error (i.e., being vague, minimizing, blaming, or justifying). When done consistently, the reality mirror process helps ESSs recognize their hurtfulness and become aware of alternative methods of thinking. Eventually, ESSs may become motivated to develop more responsible behavior.

Be Aware of the ESS's Magical, Distorted Thinking

Notice how ESSs tend to reason about the same way five-year-olds do. Although most five-year-olds will comply with their parents' requests, they usually do so without understanding or considering the reasons for the request. Similarly, when you ask ESSs to do something they may do it, but most of them will do it without understanding or considering why you asked them to do it. Remember, ESSs want what they want, when they want it, and they want it now! The are emotionally detached from other people. As far as they are concerned, the world revolves around them; if they want something, they should be able to have it. They don't consider the long-term consequences of their actions. So, naturally, they don't stop to consider the reasons behind your requests.

One of the most effective ways to reduce ESSs' self-centeredness and increase their emotional attachment to others is by increasing their empathy. This is done by having the ESSs participate in a thinking error group where they are required to discuss their thinking logs and give and receive constructive feedback with their peers.

Recognize How ESSs Manipulate and Control with Anger

Remember, ESSs use anger to intimidate and control others. Although they are extremely skillful in provoking real and intense anger in others, their anger is often merely a tool for getting what they want. ESSs don't necessarily have short fuses, they just light their fuses more often. They should not be encouraged to yell, scream, or redirect their anger by pounding pillows, since ventilating anger allows them to rehearse their anger and strengthen their anger habit. However, ESSs should be encouraged and reinforced for expressing anger in appropriate, nonhurtful, nonmanipulative ways.

Stay out of Power Struggles

Engaging in any type of power struggle with ESSs—verbal, nonverbal, or physical—reduces your credibility, control, and effectiveness with them. ESSs don't mind losing a privilege or receiving a particular consequence for their misbehavior if in the process they are able to elicit your frustration or anger. They interpret their ability to elicit an emotional outburst from you as a sign of *winning a battle* and demonstrating their power and strength. ESSs are excellent at planting *emotional land mines* for you to trip over. They use excitement and power to ward off boredom. With ESSs' twisted way of thinking, they believe they are all-powerful when they can intimidate you with anger or provoke your anger. If you allow them to push your emotional button and knock you off your emotional balance, they see you as weak and susceptible to manipulation.

In terms of your ability to be effective with ESSs, it is not important or necessary for them to like you, but it is essential that they respect you. The key to maintaining their respect is to remain cool, emotionally disengaged, and communicate with them in an emotionally neutral, respectful, firm but fair, adult-to-adult manner.

Keep the Focus on the ESS

ESSs are notorious for shifting the focus away from their irresponsible behavior and onto the problems of others. They are masters at knocking professionals off their emotional balance, perpetuating the power struggle and disturbing the therapeutic relationship by provoking the professional's anger. Consequently, it is very important to keep the focus on the ESS and not allow him or her to shift the focus onto someone else.

Require Specificity

Another way you can maintain control of your interactions with ESSs is by asking specific questions and expecting specific answers. You will be more effective in obtaining specific answers by using leverage than by shouting or making emotional demands for an ESS to give you a specific response. As a professional, your sources of leverage may include remaining emotionally neutral and disengaged; terminating the interview; withholding a designated privilege; or, if you're conducting an outpatient group, contacting the ESS's parole officer.

When professionals accept anything other than a specific answer they reinforce the ESS's irresponsibility, lose control of the interaction, and reduce their effectiveness. ESSs have several ways of not giving specific answers. Sometimes they use passive-aggressive tactics such as giving vague responses, joking, acting confused, looking the other way, or giving you the silent treatment. Other times they may use aggressive techniques such as glaring or staring at you, or trying to intimidate you by screaming or shouting their refusal to answer.

Regardless of the tactics they use to avoid giving specific responses, you can calmly shift from asking questions to giving feedback. This shift is made by describing the ongoing process and the methods the ESS is using to obstruct the interview. For example, you might say, "I noticed that I've asked you three times about...and you haven't answered the question," or, "It's interesting that when I asked you about your...you were looking down at the floor, tapping your foot, wringing your hands, and basically not paying attention. But you haven't given a direct answer to my specific question."

Use Thinking Logs and Thinking Error Groups

A thinking log is a written record of a person's actual, unabridged, unedited thoughts. Thinking error groups are specifically designed therapy groups for ESSs. They are most effective when they are limited to eight to twelve clients and are co-led by two professionals. Thinking error groups usually meet three to five times per week when conducted on an inpatient basis, and once a week when the group consists of outpatients. When thinking error logs are used as part of the group process, ESSs are required to record their thoughts as they occur for approximately ten minutes a day. One of the easiest and most effective ways for ESSs to record their thoughts is to use a tape recorder and then transcribe the tape. ESSs may vary the time of day they select to record their thoughts, but they must make an entry every day.

When ESSs record their thoughts accurately, without omitting or revising any of their thoughts, thinking logs reveal the specific thinking errors they are using. Usually certain patterns of thinking errors begin to emerge. As the sessions proceed, their thinking logs may reveal increases in their sense of responsibility, empathy or respect for others, and improvements in their ability to plan ahead, reason, and control their anger and hostility. Professionals need to be wary, however, of expecting ESSs to readily comply with the rule of not editing their thoughts. ESSs are extremely sensitive to criticism and are untrusting of others, so they are very resistant to recording their actual thoughts or sharing them with others. More likely than not, ESSs will try to edit their thinking logs before they turn them in. An obvious indicator of dishonesty in their thinking logs is the discrepancy between their behavior and their reported thoughts. Remember, how you think is how you behave. If you've observed an ESS's irresponsible behavior, his thinking log should include the thinking errors that correspond with the observed behavior. When such discrepancies occur, the ESS should be confronted either by you or members of the thinking error group.

Confrontations are most effective when the person doing the confronting observes the following guidelines:

- show concern for the person you are confronting by being respectful, direct, honest, and sincere
- have the intent of helping the ESS correct or reduce his thinking errors
- stay focused on one issue at a time
- confront in a calm, rational, assertive manner
- be aware of your verbal and nonverbal messages; make sure what you say and how you say it are congruent and consistent with your intent to help

When receiving constructive confrontation, it is best to:

- listen attentively and with an open mind
- look at the person giving the confrontation and give him or her your complete and undivided attention
- wait to respond until the person has finished speaking
- show empathy by considering the other person's perspective (this is difficult for ESSs to do when they begin

treatment, but it is an important skill for them to acquire)

- let the person know you've heard and understood what's been said, by using a calm, nondefensive, respectful tone of voice to paraphrase what you heard

Sample Thinking Logs

The following transcripts illustrate the thinking log process. The first transcript is taken from a client who frequently became angry in his car on his way to work. His assignment was to say his thoughts out loud into a tape recorder as he drove to work, then transcribe his tape at night. The thinking errors in brackets are the labels given to his statements when he shared his log with the thinking error group. It is worth noting that this client shared at least a dozen obviously edited thinking logs before he finally transcribed this tape, which contained relatively few omissions or revisions of his thoughts. The second example illustrates how the client's thoughts eventually included fewer thinking errors and more positive self-talk after several months of participating in a thinking error group.

Transcript 1

"Okay, lady . . . faster . . . speed up. [instancy] We're going to miss the light. [Failure to assume responsibility] *No!* Oh s——! Nice going, you dumb b——! [anger] You were out in the intersection when the light turned yellow; why did you stop and back up? Dammit! I'm in a hurry! [lack of empathy]

"I had a chance to be early today. I could have impressed my boss and some of the other guys who have been on my case lately. [victim stance] And what do *you* do? You f—— coward! I can't believe it. [anger and blaming] I shouldn't have to take this long to get to work. I *hate* it! [uniqueness] Every d—— day the traffic is so f—— sluggish. And you, you b——! People like you are what make it that way. If it weren't for you I could have been on time today! [anger, blaming, failure to assume responsibility]

"Okay, the light's green now, lady, come on . . . make things flow! Are you deaf or somethin'? Can't you hear my horn? Come on, lady, get out of my way! [power] You drive like a timid ninety-year-old incompetent fool. *Move it!* [anger] Why . . . why . . . why are you in my way? [victim stance] I want to be on time. Come on, lady, *Move!* [instancy]

"What am I supposed to do? [victim stance] I can't go to bed when the kids do just so it will be easier to get up earlier. I'd miss my favorite TV shows. [I can't] D——! I'm too good for this job. I'm going to get a job that pays some big bucks and doesn't make me punch a time clock. [superoptimism] I'm sick and tired of punching that d—— time clock. Absolutely *hate* it! I hate having to worry about pleasing that idiotic boss of mine. [failure to assume responsibility] He makes such a big deal out of being on time. So what if I'm ten or fifteen minutes late a couple of times a week. Big deal! [minimizing] Besides, what guarantee do I have he'll ever give me a raise even if I do get to work on time? [lack of trust]

"I feel like a loser. I'm never going to get ahead. . . . I'm falling further and further behind. Too many bills. What have I done with my life? I've been stuck—trapped in this same dead-end job for sixteen years. What a waste! I can't seem to please anyone. My wife is always nagging me. My kids are always upset about not having this or that. I can't win. I can't even bowl worth a d—— anymore. Second place . . . what good is that! I want to be number one! [zero state]

"*Hurry up*, lady . . . you're going 10 mph under the speed limit! The least you can do is drive the posted speed! [instancy]

"Thank goodness! That b—— finally turned off. Okay, I can relax now. I'm almost there. I would've been to work already if that lady would have known how to drive worth a d——. [blaming and excuse-making] I'll just tell my boss I had to take my dog to the vet. . . . No, that won't work. I'll tell him my wife woke up sick, and I had to help her. . . . Yeah, that's it, my wife got sick. That ought to keep my boss off my a——. [excuse-making and lying]

"Hey, what does that guy in back of me think he's doing? Back off a——hole! This isn't a race track for C—— sake! [anger] How self-centered can you get! You dirty b——! What's your big hurry? [lack of empathy] I feel like slowing down, just to p—— him off! Ha! How's that, you self-centered idiot! [anger and lack of empathy]

Transcript 2

(The client recorded this entry in his thinking log after he had completed eight more months of professional treatment.)

"Come on, fella, move it. I didn't get up this early to miss every stinkin' light. Great, that's just great . . . now I missed another one. Son of a b——! Okay, hold on here. So you missed a light. It's not the end of the world. You can handle it. Just take a deep breath . . . that's it . . . one . . . two . . . three . . . four . . . five . . . That's the way, just relax and think positive.

"Okay—green light! Let's go! Come on, gramps! My G—! How do guys like you get a license? D——! I lost my positive attitude already. Okay, I'll just start over. Relax . . . take a deep breath . . . that's better . . . you don't have to be in a big hurry. You left early so you would have plenty of time to get to work without having to rush. Wow, who's that? What a knockout . . . wonder where she works. Gee . . . What does that truckdriver think he's doing? I oughta show him what I think of people who cut in front of me like that! S——! There I go again. Come on, calm down. You're almost there, don't blow it now. You can stay calm. That's the way. Think positive. Hey, that guy coming up behind me really looks like he's in a hurry. I'd better pull over and let him get around me if I don't want him right up next to my bumper all the way to work.

"There, that feels better not to have to worry about that guy. I'm glad I'm not in as big a hurry as he was. It feels good to allow enough time for getting to work. I feel a lot more relaxed.

The Role of Thinking Logs as an Anger Management Technique

Thinking logs and thinking error groups are not foolproof techniques for helping ESSs develop skills for coping constructively with angry feelings and angry people. Just as you need to learn to recognize basic shapes and perform simple arithmetic computations before you can master geometry, ESSs need to learn to reduce their self-centeredness and irresponsibility, and increase their empathy for others, before they will be very effective at managing their anger. And thinking error groups and the use of thinking logs are the most effective methods developed to date for helping ESSs develop the prerequisite skills for effective anger management.

CHAPTER FORTY-THREE

Assertiveness Training Through Role-Playing

Role-playing is the process of behavior rehearsal and acting out a real or imagined interaction between two or more people. It is a very effective anger management technique because it:

- strengthens most people's self-confidence
- increases most participants' understanding of themselves and others and helps them modify their attitudes toward others
- helps the participants gain new insights into their own style of confrontation
- teaches the participants how to confront others in constructive, nonhurtful, assertive ways

People who tend to be fairly passive and nonassertive benefit from role-playing because it allows them to practice specific assertive expressions of anger in a realistic way within the safety of a therapeutic environment. Clients feel relatively safe rehearsing assertive confrontations through role-playing because they are confronting a therapist rather than the actual person they are learning to confront.

Role-playing is beneficial to people who tend to be overly aggressive because it gives them the opportunity to practice expressing anger in assertive ways; acquire insights into their own and other people's thoughts and feelings; increase their empathy for others; and decrease their aggressiveness.

People who already tend to be fairly assertive also benefit from role-playing because it helps them manage anger even more effectively. By participating in the role-playing process, assertive people often become more aware of how others may be perceiving them and develop a more insightful, objective understanding of others.

The ideal setting for conducting a role-play is within a group of approximately eight to twelve people. By restricting the size of the group, clients participating in role-plays benefit in two ways. First, they benefit by receiving emotional support from other group members, and second, they benefit by feeling less self-conscious than they would if they were role-playing in front of a large group. There are some people, however, who may never feel comfortable role-playing in front of a group and need the emotional security and protection of role-playing within the privacy of the therapist's office. Others may feel comfortable role-playing in front of a group after they've had the experience of role-playing with their therapist.

There are several variations of role-playing. These evolved out of three basic forms: psychodrama or spontaneous role-playing; structured role-playing; and fixed-role therapy. The role-playing process described in this chapter is a variation of structured role-playing. It also includes some characteristics of spontaneous role-playing. For example, the therapist directing the role-play (therapist 1) has the flexibility to have the participants switch roles whenever he or she feels the need to emphasize or clarify a point or to increase the client's empathy for the other person (OP) involved in the interaction. Consequently, the following step-by-step role-playing procedure is a synthesis of spontaneous and structured role-playing.

Step 1

The therapists select a member of the group who has a specific incident in mind that he would like to role-play. Once this group member has been selected, the role-playing process begins by one of the therapists inviting the client (the selected group member) to close his eyes and visualize the designated situation as it actually occurred.

Step 2

After the client has visualized the situation, he helps the therapists get a clear picture of it by:

* describing the situation and the pertinent characteristics and typical responses of the other person (OP) involved in the interaction.
* role-playing the situation with therapist 2—therapist 2 plays the part of the OP, and the client reenacts his own role in the situation as accurately as possible

Step 3

In this step the client observes both therapists as they role-play the situation in a nonhurtful, nonanger-provoking, assertive manner. Therapist 1 takes the role of the client and models how to interact assertively with the OP, who is played by therapist 2.

Step 4

After the therapists have completed role-playing the situation, they encourage the client to share some of his reactions to the role-play by asking questions such as:

- Did therapist 2 portray the OP in a realistic manner?
- Did therapist 1 model a type of assertive confrontation with which you could feel comfortable? (If not, why not?)

Step 5

Therapist 1 asks the client to visualize the situation once again. The purpose behind this is to give the client the opportunity to see if he would want to incorporate any of the techniques modeled by the therapists. (Perhaps the client will visualize himself having better eye contact with the OP, using different words, or showing more empathy than he did in the original situation.)

Step 6

The client is given an opportunity to role-play the same situation two more times with therapist 2. During the first of these role-plays the client assumes the role of the OP and therapist 2 acts as the client. By assuming the role of the OP the client gains added insights into how the OP may be thinking and feeling when the client confronts him. These insights help the client to gain a broader and more objective perspective of the situation and develop more empathy for the OP.

Then the client and therapist 2 switch roles (the client is himself and therapist 2 assumes the role of the OP) and they role-play the situation once again. Therapist 1 continues as the director and facilitator of the process. During this role-play, therapist 1 subtly whispers or gestures certain cues and suggestions to the client. These may include words or actions that the client could say or do to be more assertive, or verbal or nonverbal expressions of approval or encouragement to the client for saying or doing something in an appropriately assertive manner.

After the client and therapist 2 have each played both parts of the situation, the client listens as therapist 2 shares how he felt as the person doing the confronting (the client) and as the person being confronted (the OP). Then the client shares the feelings he had as the person being confronted and as the person doing the confronting.

Step 7

At this point in the process, the client receives straightforward, supportive feedback from therapist 1 and therapist 2. When the therapists feel it is necessary to give the client some constructive criticism, the client is most likely to accept these criticisms without becoming hurt or defensive when they are sandwiched between two compliments. For example, one of the therapists might say, "You sounded very assertive when you said . . . [first compliment] Your eye contact could have been a little more direct at that point [criticism], but your tone of voice was appropriately firm and very adult-to-adult." [second compliment]

Step 8

After the role-plays have been completed and the client has received feedback from both therapists, the remaining members of the therapy group share their feelings about what they observed. Group members are asked to limit their comments to positive, supportive statements, or to recall some of their own experiences that they regard as similar to the client's. Members are encouraged to select experiences that aroused some of the same feelings the client has been expressing in the role-plays, such as feelings of apprehension, frustration, fear, depression, hurt, helplessness, or anger. When the client hears this type of feedback he typically feels as if he is being wrapped in a blanket of strength and support. Receiving sympathy and empathy from the other group members, and being able to hear how they experienced similar feelings, helps the client feel less isolated, vulnerable, and alone, and increases the client's feelings of self-worth, self-confidence, and sense of personal power.

Step 9

The role-playing process concludes by therapist 1 encouraging the client to proceed at his own pace and apply what he has learned to an actual situation when he feels ready and confident to do so. If the client expresses a need for more time to practice his assertive confrontation before he actually confronts someone, therapist 1 encourages the client to role-play the situation again at a future group meeting, or with an individual the client trusts and respects. If the client is particularly timid and reluctant to assert himself, sometimes it helps to establish a hierarchy with him, as you would in the systematic desensitization process, and role-play the least stressful situation with the client until that situation is no longer stressful for him. Then the therapist helps the client gradually continue the process, role-playing each situation in the hierarchy until the client can role-play the most stressful item without feeling anxious.

Role-Playing's Role in Anger Management

The process of role-playing helps many people strengthen their self-esteem, increase their empathy for others, and improve their assertive confrontation and anger management skills. However, people who lack either self-confidence or empathy may find role-playing to be more effective for them when they become an active participant in individual and/or group therapy designed to help them express anger in constructive, assertive ways.

Conclusion

What are you going to do with your anger? It doesn't matter if you are responsible for your angry feelings or if someone else made you angry. *You always have the choice of how intense your anger will be, how long it will last, and what you are going to do with it.* Do you want to hide or repress your anger, hoping that if you ignore it the anger will go away? Do you want to be hurtful with your anger, be vocally aggressive, or have an adult version of a temper tantrum? Or do you want to express your anger in an assertive, helpful way? It is up to you whether your anger is expressed indirectly, aggressively, or constructively.

The emotion of anger provides you with extra energy. You can choose to waste that energy by keeping it focused on your anger, or you can use it to help you reach for your goals. Throughout America, members of organizations such as Crime Victims United (CVU) have suffered the emotional pain of violent crime. But instead of focusing all their energy into their hurt and anger, they use the energy from their anger to reach toward their goal of justice for victims of crime. Members of Mothers Against Drunk Drivers (MADD) have been traumatized by the irresponsible behavior of drunk drivers. It is no accident that the name of their group is abbreviated MADD. Yes, they are angry, but they are directing their anger into educating others about the dangers of drinking and driving and the need for stiffer penalties.

Just as members of CVU and MADD have chosen to recognize their anger and use their anger-engendered energy to help them achieve their long-term goals, you too can choose what you will do with your anger.

APPENDIX A

The Twenty Most Important Aspects of Constructive Discipline

Guidelines for Assertive Parenting

1. Be a good **model**.

   Maintain congruent behavior. Develop self-awareness, self-pride, and a positive attitude, in order to be a good model to emulate.

2. Be in touch with your *intentions*.

   Do *not* discipline out of revenge, frustration, or anger.

3. Be *aware* of your verbal and nonverbal communications.

   Be aware of your tone of voice and your volume. Know whether you are talking adult-to-adult or parent-to-child.

4. Express *unconditional positive regard*.

   Set no conditions the child must meet in order to gain your acceptance.

5. Use *proactive discipline*.

   "Catch" the child acting appropriately and reinforce that behavior.

6. *Encourage* children for succeeding and/or striving to succeed.

7. Help the child develop *self-discipline*.

8. Have realistic *expectations* of the child's capabilities.

   Be firm, but flexible.

9. *Decide together* with the child upon the rules and regulations.

10. *Ignore* inappropriate behavior.

    Remember, children misbehave in order to acquire recognition. Children who have poor self-esteem may be misbehaving just to elicit your reaction and confirm their negative self-image.

11. *Seek assistance*.

    Ask the child for help in finding possible solutions to the problem.

12. *Make time* to discipline when you and your child are calm.

    Don't be impulsive. Be cautious about responding to your first impulses.

13. Give the child *choices* and *negotiate*.

    Decide on the most appropriate consequences for inappropriate behavior through a process of negotiations.

14. Follow through and *take action with agreed upon consequences*.

    Accept no excuses. Do not use idle threats. Develop trust by doing what you say you're going to do.

15. Focus on the child's *present behavior*.

    Comment on the child's *actions*, not his or her character.

16. *Don't judge* or accuse.

17. Focus and reflect on the child's *feelings*.

18. Use *I Messages*.

    Say, "I'm angry." *Not,* "You make me angry."

19. *Confer dignity*.

    Be warm, considerate, kind, fair, firm, and *consistent*. Say "I'm sorry," when you make mistakes.

20. Help the child develop and increase his or her sense of *self-respect, self-control,* and *independence*.

    Don't be overly protective.

APPENDIX B

Cause of Emotion: Comparative Theories

James-Lange

The earliest and most basic theory of emotion was developed by William James and Carl Lange almost one hundred years ago. Their theory suggested that emotions are initially experienced as a physiological reaction, then the brain labels that physical response as a specific emotion.

WILLIAM JAMES AND CARL LANGE
1890

Anger-provoking stimulus	→	Physiological reaction (stomach is in knots)	→	Brain registers your reaction & labels the emotion ("My stomach is in knots, therefore I'm angry")

Cannon-Bard

According to a later theory developed by Walter Cannon and Philip Bard in the 1920s, one part of the brain (the thalmus) responds to an anger-provoking stimulus by simultaneously alerting the brain's labeling center (the cortex) and the rest of the body. Their theory suggested that emotional arousal can be independent of physiological changes.

WALTER CANNON AND PHILIP BARD 1920

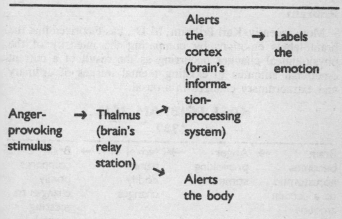

Anger-provoking stimulus → Thalmus (brain's relay station) →

Alerts the cortex (brain's information-processing system) → Labels the emotion

→ Alerts the body

Schacter

The first major cognitive theory of emotion was developed by Stanley Schacter in 1971. He theorized that the brain first processes both cognitive data (one's perception of the current stimulus and one's memory of past experiences) and physiological feedback from internal organs and skeletal muscles, then labels that information as a particular emotion.

STANLEY SCHACTER
1971

Anger-provoking stimulus → Physiological reaction →

Anger-provoking stimulus ↘ Memory of past experiences Perception of present stimulus ↗

→ Brain labels reaction as anger, joy, etc.

Pribram

More recently, Karl Pribram, M.D., has theorized that the brain labels emotions by comparing the intensity of the physiological changes occurring as the result of a current emotional stimulus to existing mental images of ordinary and extraordinary changes in arousal.

KARL PRIBRAM, M.D.
1980

Brain becomes accustomed to a certain amount of bodily changes	→	Anger-provoking stimulus	→	Novel or painful bodily changes	→	Brain compares bodily changes to existing mental images

→ →

→

Mental image

(Neurorepresentation)

Brain labels the comparisons as anger, joy, etc.

APPENDIX C

Summary of Catharsis Research Results

The following conclusions from various research studies illustrate the ineffectiveness of catharsis as an anger management technique.

- Children who play aggressively become more aggressive.

  S. Feshback (1956)

- Direct or vicarious participation in aggressive activities may actually increase aggression.

  A. Bandura and R. Walters (1963)

- Aggressive play has no cathartic value.

  S. Mallick and B. McCandless (1966)

- Verbal aggression toward the frustrator may actually increase the aggression toward him.

  S. Mallick and B. McCandless (1966)

- When we tell someone off, we stimulate ourselves to continued or even stronger aggression.

  L. Berkowitz (1970)

- Aggressive responses to anger-provoking situations are learned responses, not innate.

  J. Hokanson (1970)

- Aggressive behavior does not inevitably lead to a reduction in physiological tension nor to a reduction in aggressive behavior.

  J. Hokanson (1970)

- After observing the aggressive behavior in others in situations such as movies . . . the observer's level of aggression increases rather than decreases.

  A. Doob and L. Wood (1972)

- Violence on the movie or television screen often stimulates reactions that facilitate aggression.

  L. Berkowitz (1973)

- Ruminating about annoying incidents can increase subsequent arousal and aggression.

  A. Bandura (1973)
  E. Ebbesen, B. Duncan, and V. Konecni (1975)

- Talking out an emotion doesn't reduce it, it rehearses it.

  C. Tavris (1982)

APPENDIX D

Quick Guide for Coping with Angry People

1. PAUSE. Do NOT make any impulsive, hurtful response.
2. Take a "one second" SELF-AWARENESS break. Get into your FISHBOWL and become aware of:
   - What you see. Observe your body language and facial expression.
   - What you hear. Listen to your SELF-TALK and get in touch with your:
     - THOUGHTS (irrational and negative, or rational and positive?)
     - EXPECTATIONS (unrealistic or realistic?)
     - INTENTIONS (hurtful or nonhurtful?)
     - FEELINGS (negative or positive?)

If your feelings are POSITIVE and your intentions are NONHURTFUL, skip ahead to step 4. If your feelings are NEGATIVE and your intentions are still HURTFUL, proceed with step 3.

3. *Give yourself permission to RELAX and EMOTIONALLY DISENGAGE.*

- Treat yourself to some slow, relaxing *deep breathing*.
- Use *therapeutic counting* to help reduce the emotional impact of the angry person's remarks or behavior.
- *Scan* your entire body for any unwanted tension and allow yourself to *release* it, so that you feel *relaxed, calm,* and *in control*.
- *Refocus:* Focus on the positive outcome you desire, instead of on the emotional "sting" of the provocation. Don't take it personally.
- Treat yourself to positive, calming, affirming, reassuring *self-talk*.
- Put the situation into *perspective* by considering its ultimate importance to you.
- *Emotionally disengage* by visualizing yourself as an emotionally neutral, *impartial observer.*

4. *Show RESPECT for the other person's FEELINGS, and ACCEPT RESPONSIBILITY for your own feelings.*
   - *Listen* attentively.
   - Maintain good *eye contact*.
   - *Pause* (2–5 seconds) before responding.
   - *Confine your first response to a short, accurate reflection* of the other person's predominant *feeling*. Wait for his or her reply.
   - Restate the other person's feelings and paraphrase his or her *concern*. Wait for him or her to respond.
   - Reiterate other person's feelings and concern, then encourage him or her to get involved in *problem-solving*.
   - Choose to stay out of arguments and power struggles.
   - Be an appropriate, assertive *model*. Avoid being aggressive or passive-aggressive.
   - Respond in an *adult-to-adult* manner. Speak in a calm, matter-of-fact, respectful, firm, nonthreatening, nondefensive, nonjudgmental, emotionally neutral tone of voice. (A controlled, self-assured approach indicates, "I respect you as an individual, but I am *not* intimidated or manipulated by your anger.")

- Verbally *pace* the agitated person. Initially mirror his or her rapid rate of speech, then gradually moderate your speech until you are modeling a slower, calmer, more controlled rate of speech.
- Communicate your feelings with *I Messages*.
- Allow the other person to take ownership of his or her own feelings.
- Focus on adjusting your expectations and attitude (which you can change), rather than on the other person's attitude and behavior (which *you* can NOT change).

APPENDIX E

The Needs of Battered Women and Suggestions for How to Be Helpful

Needs

Living in an abusive relationship slowly erodes a woman's self-esteem and further entraps her in the battering cycle. The lower her self-esteem, the harder it is for her to recognize and strive for healthy alternatives. The following list outlines the basics of what battered women need in order to rebuild their self-esteem and free themselves from the cycle of abuse.

Battered women need:

- to feel respected, loved, and supported
- to feel they have control over their own lives
- to receive reassurance, sympathy, empathy, and understanding
- to have a safe place to live and sleep
- to be permitted to share their story as often as they desire, and to feel listened to and believed

- to be shown patience, tenderness, compassion, and commitment
- to reestablish trust (in themselves and others), self-worth, and self-confidence
- to reaffirm their sexuality
- to regain a sense of personal security and employability
- to receive emotional support and companionship from family, friends, and/or support group; and psychological and medical assistance from appropriate professionals
- to let go (eventually, at their own pace) of the anger, shame, sadness, and guilt associated with their abusive relationships

How to Help

As mentioned in chapter 3, battered women face many barriers to breaking free from the entrapment of abuse. The following list includes some of the basic forms of assistance that help battered women break out and stay out of the battering cycle.

You can help battered women by:

- encouraging them to seek out professional help and talk openly about the abuse
- providing reassurance that they can call or see their advocate whenever they need to
- encouraging them to let go of their "victim" image, accept responsibility for their role in the battering cycle, and set new goals for themselves
- helping them channel their rage into something positive
- teaching them how to be angry and express their feelings in nonhurtful ways
- helping them understand that anger does *not* have to be violent or lead to violence
- offering constructive alternatives to retaliation, such as

taking time out and using that time to "cool off" with nonhurtful anger management techniques

- assisting them to regain a sense of control and confidence by providing them with opportunities to experience success through encouraging them to make progressively more difficult decisions on their own.
- being patient, tender, and understanding; and, if you are a mate of someone who was battered in a previous relationship, obtaining her permission before gently touching her or making sexual advances

References

Introduction

Burns, David D. *Feeling Good: the New Mood Therapy*. New York: New American Library, 1980.

Coleman, James C. *Abnormal Psychology and Modern Life*. Glenview, IL: Scott, Foresman & Company, 1984.

Elliott, F. A. "Neurological Factors in Violent Behavior." In R. Sadoff, ed. *Violence and Responsibility*. New York: Spectrum, 1978.

Kaplan, Harold I., Alfred M. Freedman, and Benjamin J. Sadock. *Comprehensive Textbook of Psychiatry III*. Baltimore: Williams & Wilkins Company, 1980.

"Mapping Emotional Paths." *The Oregonian*. May 9, 1991, 1F.

Mark, V. H., and F. R. Ervin. *Violence and the Brain*. New York: Harper & Row, 1970.

Norris, Ronald V., and Colleen Sullivan. *PMS: Premenstrual Syndrome*. New York: Berkley Books, 1984.

Wolman, Benjamin B., ed. *The Therapist's Handbook: Treatment Methods of Mental Disorders*. New York: Van Nostrand Reinhold, 1976

Part One

Abramson, Lyn, M.E.P. Seligman, and J. D. Teasdale. "Learned helplessness in humans: critique and reformulation." *Journal of Abnormal Psychology* 87(1), 1978, 49–74.

"Abuse often continues." *Statesman Journal*, September 27, 1987, 6B.

Alberti, Robert E., and Michael L. Emmons. *Your Perfect Right: A Guide to Assertive Living*. San Luis Obispo, CA: Impact, 1986.

Albin, Rochelle Semmel. *Emotions*. Philadelphia: The Westminster Press, 1983.

Averill, James R. *Anger and Aggression*. New York: Springer-Verlag, 1982.

Bach, George, and Herb Goldberg. *Creative Aggression*. Garden City, NY: Doubleday, Anchor Books, 1983.

Baron, Robert. *Human Aggression*. New York: Plenum Press, 1977.

Berkowitz, Leonard. *Aggression: A Social Psychological Analysis*. New York: McGraw-Hill, 1962.

————. "Experimental Investigations of Hostility Catharsis." *Journal of Consulting and Clinical Psychology* 35(1), 1970 1–7.

————. *Roots of Aggression*. New York: Atherton Press, 1969.

————. "The Case for Bottling up Rage." *Psychology Today* 7(2), July 1973, 24–31.

————. "The Concept of Aggressive Drive: Some Additional Considerations." In L. Berkowitz, ed. *Advances in Experimental Social Psychology*. New York: Academic Press, 1965.

————. "The Expression and Reduction of Hostility." *Psychological Bulletin* 55(5), 1958, 257–82.

Callwood, June. *Love, Hate, Fear, Anger, and Other Lively Emotions*. Garden City, NY: Doubleday, 1964.

Camp, B., G. Blom, F. Herbert, and W. VanDoorninck. "Think Aloud: A Program for Developing Self-Control in Young Aggressive Boys." *Journal of Abnormal Child Psychology* 5, 1977, 157–67.

Cavanagh, Michael. "Anger: Something to Shout About." *U.S. Catholic*, March 1985, 36–39.

"Childswork/Childsplay: A Catalog Addressing the Mental Health Needs of Children and Their Families Through Play." Philadelphia: Center for Applied Psychology, 1991.

"Class Bully Likely to Break Law as Adult." *Statesman Journal*, August 17, 1985, 10A.

Daldrup, Roger. *Freedom from Anger*. La Selva, CA: Living Business, 1988.

Danesh, Hossain B. "Anger and Fear." *American Journal of Psychiatry* 134(10), October 1977, 1109–12.

Dollard, J. R., L. W. Doob, N. E. Miller, O. H. Mowrer, and R. S. Sears. *Frustration and Aggression*. New Haven: Yale University Press, 1939.

Doob, Anthony N., and L. E. Wood. "Catharsis and Aggression." *Journal of Personality and Social Psychology* 22(2), 1972, 156–62.

Duncan, Lois. "Violence in the Family." *Current Health* 2, November 1984, 3–9.

Dyer, Wayne W. *Your Erroneous Zones*. New York: Funk and Wagnalls, 1976.

Ebbesen, Ebbe, Birt Duncan, and Vladimir Konecni. "Effects of Content of Verbal Aggression on Future Verbal Aggression: A Field Experiment." *Journal of Experimental Social Psychology* 11, 1975, 192–204.

Ellis, Albert. *Anger: How to Live With and Without It*. Secaucus, NJ: Citadel Press, 1977.

Erikson, Erik H. *Gandhi's Truth: On the Origins of Militant Nonviolence*. New York: W. W. Norton, 1969.

Eron, Leonard D., L. O. Walder, and M. M. Lefkowitz. *Learning of Aggression in Children*. Boston: Little, Brown, 1971.

Eron, Leonard D., L. O. Walder, L. R. Huesmann, and M. M. Lefkowitz. "The Convergence of Laboratory and Field Studies of the Development of Depression." In J. DeWitt and W. W. Hartup, eds. *Determinants and Origins of Aggressive Behavior*. The Hague, Mouton, 1978.

Feshbach, Seymour, "The Catharsis Hypothesis and Some Consequences of Interaction with Aggression and Neutral Play Objects." *Journal of Personality* 24, 1956, 449–62.

Forman, S. "A Comparison of Cognitive Training and Response Cost Procedures in Modifying Aggressive Behavior of Elementary School Children." *Behavior Therapy* 11, 1980, 594–600.

Gaylin, Willard. *The Rage Within: Anger in Modern Life*. New York: Simon and Schuster, 1984.

Geen, Russell, and M. B. Quanty. "The Catharsis of Aggression: An Evaluation of a Hypothesis." In L. Berkowitz, ed. *Advances in Experimental Social Psychology*. New York: Academic Press, 1977.

Haer, John L. "Anger in Relation to Aggression in Psychotherapy Groups." *The Journal of Social Psychology* 76, 1968, 123–127.

Hatcher, Chris, and Philip Himelstein. *The Handbook of Gestalt Therapy*. New York: Jason Aronson, 1976.

Heppner, Mary J. "Counseling the Battered Wife: Myths, Facts, Decisions." *Personnel and Guidance Journal*, May 1978, 522–25.

Hokanson, Jack E. "Psychophysiological Evaluation of the Catharsis Hypothesis." In Edwin Megargee and J. Hokason, eds. *The Dynamics of Aggression: Individual, Group, and International Analyses*. New York: Harper & Row, 1970.

Hoskins, Lotte, ed. *I Have a Dream: the Quotations of Martin Luther King Jr.* New York: Grosset & Dunlap, 1968.

Janov, Arthur. *The Primal Scream.* New York: Delta, 1970.

Kahn, Michael. "The Physiology of Catharsis." *Journal of Personality and Social Psychology* 3(3), 1966, 278–86.

Kazdin, A., K. Esveldt-Dawson, N. French, and A. Unis. "Problem-Solving Skills Training and Relationship Therapy in the Treatment of Anti-Social Child Behavior." *Journal of Consulting and Clinical Psychology* 55, 1987, 76–85.

Kettlewell, P., and D. Kausch. "The Generalization of the Effects of a Cognitive-Behavioral Treatment Program for Aggressive Children." *Journal of Abnormal Child Psychology* 11, 1983, 101–14.

Kiester, Edwin Jr. "The Use of Anger." *Psychology Today* 18, July 1984, 26.

LaHaye, Tim. *Anger Is Choice.* Grand Rapids, MI: Zondervan, 1982.

Laiken, Deidre S., and Alan J. Schneider. *Listen to Me I'm Angry.* New York: Lothrop, Lee & Shepard Books, 1980.

Lazarus, Arnold, and Allen Fay. *I Can If I Want To.* New York: Warner Books, 1975.

Leakey, R. *The Making of Mankind.* New York: E. P. Dutton, 1981.

Lerner, Harriet, *The Dance of Anger.* New York: Harper & Row, 1985.

Lorenz, Konrad. *On Aggression.* New York: Harcourt Brace, 1968.

———. "On Aggression." In Edwin I. Megargee and Jack Hokanson, eds. *The Dynamics of Aggression: Individual, Group, and International Analyses.* New York: Harper & Row, 1970.

"Low Self-Esteem Can Trap Victims." *Statesman Journal,* June 20, 1989, 5B.

McKay, Matthew, Peter Rogers, and Judith McKay. *When Anger Hurts: Quieting the Storm Within*. Oakland, CA: New Harbinger Publications, 1989.

Madow, Leo. "Why You Get Angry—And What to Do About It." *U.S. News & World Report* 92(16), April 26, 1982, 74–5.

Magid, Ken, and Carole A. McKelvey. *High Risk: Children Without a Conscience*. New York: Bantam Books, 1987.

Mallick, Shahbaz Khan, and Boyd R. McCandless. "A Study of Catharsis of Aggression." *Journal of Personality and Social Psychology* 4, 1966, 591–96.

Marshall, John R. "The Expression of Feelings." *Archives of General Psychiatry* 27, December 1972, 786–90.

Miles, Rosalind. *Love, Sex, Death, and the Making of the Male*. New York: Summit Books, 1991.

Mitteager, Jim. "Confessions of a Wife Beater." *Women's Day* 49(11), 1986, 30–35.

Neidig, Peter H., and Dale H. Friedman. *Spouse Abuse: A Treatment Program for Couples*. Champaign IL: Research Press, 1984.

Olweus, Dan. "Stability of Aggressive Behavior Patterns in Males: A Review." *Psychological Bulletin* 86, 1979, 852–75.

"Pop, Pop, Pop the Stress Away," *Statesman Journal*, March 2, 1987, 3B.

Pribram, Karl H. "The Biology of Emotions and Other Feelings." In Plutchik, Robert, and H. Kellerman, eds. *Emotion: Theory, Research, and Experience, vol. 1*. New York: Academic Press, 1980.

Rackham. H., trans. *Aristotle: the Nicomachean Ethics*. Cambridge, MA: Harvard University Pres, 1962.

Revised Standard Version, *The Holy Bible*. New York: Thomas Nelson & Sons, 1952.

Rosenblatt, Daniel. *Opening Doors: What Happens in Gestalt Therapy*. New York: Harper & Row, 1975.

Rothenberg, Albert. "On Anger." *American Journal of Psychiatry* 128(4), October 1971, 86–92.

Rubin, Theodore Isaac. *The Angry Book*. New York: Collier, 1970.

Schachter, Stanley. "The Interaction of Cognitive and Physiological Determinants of Emotional State." In L. Berkowitz, ed. *Advances in Experimental Social Psychology*, vol. 1. New York: Academic Press, 1964.

Seligman, M.E.P. *Helplessness*. San Francisco: W. H. Freeman, 1975.

Stampfl, Thomas G., and D. J. Lewis. *Implosive Therapy: Theory and Technique*. Morristown, NJ: General Learning Press, 1973.

Stearns, Frederic. *Anger: Psychology, Physiology, Pathology*. Springfield, IL: Charles C. Thomas, 1972.

Steinmetz, Suzanne K. *The Cycle of Violence*. New York: Praeger, 1977.

Stoop, David. *Self-Talk: Key to Personal Growth*. Old Tappan, NJ: Fleming H. Revell, 1982.

Straus, Murray, Richard Gelles, and Suzanne Steinmetz. *Behind Closed Doors: Violence in the Family*. Garden City, NY: Doubleday, Anchor, 1980.

Southard, Samuel. *Anger in Love*. Philadelphia: Westminster Press, 1973.

Tavris, Carol. *Anger: The Misunderstood Emotion*. New York: Simon & Schuster, Touchstone, 1982.

———, ed. *Every Woman's Emotional Well-Being*. Garden City, NY: Doubleday, 1986.

Warren, Neil. *Make Anger Your Ally: Harnessing One of Your Most Powerful Emotions*. Brentwood, TN: Wolgemuth and Hyatt, 1990.

Wells, Theodora. *Keeping Your Cool Under Fire: Communicating Nondefensively*. New York: McGraw-Hill, 1980.

Williams, Redford. *The Trusting Heart: Great News About Type A Behavior*. New York: Times Books, 1989.

Part Two

Adler, Alfred. *The Practice and Theory of Individual Psychology.* New York: Harcourt Brace, 1927.

Ansbacher, H. L., and R. R. Ansbacher, eds. *The Individual Psychology of Alfred Adler.* New York: Basic Books, 1956.

American Psychiatric Association. *Diagnostic and Statistical Manual of Mental Disorders: Third Edition, Revised.* Washington, D.C.: American Psychiatric Association, 1987.

Atkinson, Rita L., Richard C. Atkinson, and Ernest R. Hilgard. *Introduction to Psychology.* New York: Harcourt Brace Jovanovich, 1983.

Bandura, Albert. *Aggression: A Social Learning Analysis.* Englewood Cliffs, NJ: Prentice-Hall, 1973.

————. *Principles of Behavior Modification.* New York: Holt, Rinehart, and Winston, 1969.

Bandura, Albert, J. Grusec, and F. Menlove. "Some Social Determinants of Self-Monitoring Reinforcement Systems." *Journal of Personality and Social Psychology* 5, 1967, 449–55.

Bandura, Albert, D. Ross, and S. A. Ross. "Vicarious Reinforcement and Imitative Learning." *Journal of Abnormal and Social Psychology* 67, 1963, 3–11.

Bandura, Albert, and Richard H. Walters. *Social Learning and Personality Development.* New York: Holt, Rinehart, and Winston, 1963.

Baron, Robert, "Reducing the Influence of an Aggressive Model." *Journal of Personality and Social Psychology* 20, 1971, 240–45.

Baron, Robert, and C. R. Kepner. "Model's Behavior and Attraction Toward the Model as Determinants of Adult Aggressive Behavior." *Journal of Personality and Social Psychology* 14, 1970, 335–44.

Becker, W. C. *Parents Are Teachers: A Child Management Program.* Champaign IL: Research Press, 1971.

Bennet, E. A. *What Jung Really Said*. New York: Schocken Books, 1966.

Berne, Eric. *Games People Play*. New York: Grove Press, 1964.

———. *Transactional Analysis in Psychotherapy*. New York: Grove Press, 1961.

———. *What Do You Say After You Say Hello*. New York: Grove Press; Bantam Books, 1973.

Billig, Michael. *Social Psychology and Intergroup Relations*. New York: Academic Press, 1976.

Bredemeier, Brenda Jo, and David L. Shields. "Values and Violence in Sports Today." *Psychology Today*, October 1985, 23–32.

Check, James V. P., Neil M. Malamuth, Barbara Elias, and Susan A. Barton. "On Hostile Ground." *Psychology Today*, April 1985, 56–61.

Darrach, Brad. "A Comic's Crisis of the Heart." *People* 29(7), February 22, 1988, 78–85.

Decker, Phillip J., and Barry R. Nathan. *Behavior Modeling Training*. New York: Praeger, 1985.

Dinkmeyer, Don, and R. Dreikurs. *Encouraging Children to Learn: The Encouragement Process*. Englewood Cliffs, NJ: Prentice-Hall, 1963.

Dinkmeyer, Don, and G. D. McKay. *Raising a Responsible Child*. New York: Fireside, 1982.

Dodson, Fitzhugh. *How to Discipline with Love*. New York: Signet, 1977.

———. *How to Father*. New York: Signet, 1974.

———. *How to Parent*. New York: Signet, 1970.

Dreikurs, Rudolf. *Discipline Without Tears*. New York: Hawthorn, 1972.

———. *Fundamentals of Adlerian Psychology*. Chicago: Alfred Adler Institute, 1953.

———. *Psychology in the Classroom*. New York: Harper & Row, 1968.

Dreikurs, Rudolf, and L. Grey. *A Parents' Guide to Child Discipline*. New York: Hawthorn, 1970.

Dreikurs, Rudolf, B. B. Grunwald, and F. C. Pepper. *Maintaining Sanity in the Classroom*. New York: Harper & Row, 1971.

Dreikurs, Rudolf, and Vicki Soltz. *Children The Challenge*. New York: Hawthorn Books, 1964.

Eron, Leonard D. "Parent-Child Interaction, Television Violence, and Aggression of Children." *American Psychologist* 37, 1982, 197–211.

―――. "Relationship of TV Viewing Habits and Aggressive Behavior in Children." *Journal of Abnormal and Social Psychology* 67(2), 1963, 193–96.

"Experts Swap Blame for Bad Schools." *Statesman Journal*, April 27, 1988, 1A.

Friedrich, Lynette K., and Aletha Stein. "Prosocial Television and Young Children: The Effects of Verbal Labeling and Role Playing Learning and Behavior." *Child Development* 46, 1975, 27–38.

Funkenstein, Daniel H., Stanley H. King, and Margaret Drolette. *Mastery of Stress*. Cambridge, MA: Harvard University Press, 1957.

Germain, Robert B. "Beyond the Internal-External Continuum: The Development of Formal Operational Reasoning About Control of Reinforcements." *Adolescence* 20(80) winter 1985, 939–47.

Gilmore, Susan K., and Patrick W. Fraleigh. *Communication at Work*. Eugene, OR: Friendly Press, 1980.

―――. *Personal Style/Programme Analysis*. Eugene, Oregon: Friendly Press, 1981.

―――. *Personal Style/Programme for Intimate Partners*. Eugene, Oregon: Friendly Press, 1982.

Ginott, Haim. *Between parent and child*. New York: Macmillan, 1965.

―――. *Between parent and teenager.* New York: Macmillan, 1969.

Glasser, William. *Reality Therapy*. New York: Harper & Row, 1965.

———. *Schools Without Failure*. New York: Harper & Row, 1969

Hall, Calvin S., and Gardner Lindzey. *Theories of Personality*. New York: John Wiley, 1970.

Hankins, E. Gary. "The Comparative Effectiveness of Adlerian Group Counseling with Homework and Adlerian Group Counseling without Homework in the Elementary School." Ph.D dissertation, Georgia State University, 1976.

Harris, Thomas. *I'm OK—You're OK*. New York: Harper & Row, 1967.

Hedrin, Sam. *Network*. New York: Pocket Books, 1976.

James, Muriel, and Dorothy Jongeward. *Born to Win: Transactional Analysis with Gestalt Experiments*. Reading, MA: Addison-Wesley, 1971.

———. *The People Book: Transactional Analysis for Students*. Reading, MA: Addison-Wesley, 1975.

Jung, Carl G. *Man and His Symbols*. New York: Dell, 1973.

Kandel, D. *Epidemiological and Psychological Development: A Longitudinal Study of Youth*. New York: Academic Press, 1982.

Keirsey, David, and Marilyn Bates. *Please Understand Me: Character and Temperament Types*. Del Mar, CA: Prometheus Nemesis, 1984.

Kipnis, David and Stuart Schmidt. "The Language of Persuasion." *Psychology Today,* April 1985, 40–46.

Kolb, Lawrence C. *Noyes' Modern Clinical Psychiatry*. Philadelphia: W. B. Saunders, 1968.

Kohl, Herbert. *Growing with Your Children*. Boston: Little, Brown, 1978.

Kreisman, Jerold, and Hal Straus. *I Hate You—Don't Leave Me: Understanding the Borderline Personality*. New York: Avon Books, 1989.

LaHaye, Beverly. *How to Develop Your Child's Temperament.* Irvine, CA: Harvest House, 1977.

LaHaye, Tim. *Spirit-Controlled Temperament.* Wheaton, IL: Tyndale House Publishers, 1982.

McBride, Angela Barron. *The Growth and Development of Mothers.* New York: Harper & Row, 1973.

Millon Theodore. *Disorders of Personality.* New York: John Wiley, 1981.

Morris, Larry Wayne. *Extraversion and Introversion.* Washington, D.C.: Hemisphere Publishing Corporation, 1979.

Moyer, K. E. "The Physiology of Violence." *Psychology Today* 7(2), July 1973, 35–38.

Myers, Isabel Briggs. *Introduction to Type.* Palo Alto, CA: Consulting Psychologists Press, 1980.

Patterson, C. H. *Theories of Counseling and Psychotherapy.* New York: Harper & Row, 1973.

Patterson, Gerald R. *Coercive Family Process.* Eugene, OR: Castalia Publishing, 1982.

———. *Families.* Champaign, IL: Research Press, 1971.

Patterson, Gerald R., and Marion Forgatch. *Parents and Adolescents: Living Together.* Eugene, OR: Castalia Publishing, 1987.

Peele, Stanton. "The Question of Personality." *Psychology Today,* December 1984, 54–56.

Phares, E. *Locus of Control in Personality.* Morristown, NJ: General Learning Press, 1976.

Rotter, J. "Generalized Expectancies for Internal Versus External Control of Reinforcement." *Psychological Monographs* 80(609), 1966.

Rushton, J. Philippe. "Effects of Prosocial Television and Film Material on the Behavior of Viewers." In L. Berkowitz, ed. *Advances in Experimental Social Psychology* 12. New York: Academic Press, 1979.

Satir, Virgina. *Conjoint Family Therapy: Revised Edition.* Palo Alto, CA: Science and Behavior, 1967.

————. *Peoplemaking*. Palo Alto, CA: Science and Behavior, 1972.

Schwartz, Arthur. *The Behavior Therapies*. New York: Free Press, 1982.

Shelton, John, and J. Mark Ackerman. *Homework in Counseling and Psychotherapy*. Springfield, IL: Charles C. Thomas, 1974.

Shiff, Eileen, ed. *Experts Advise Parents*. New York: Delacorte Press, 1987.

Siegel, Judith. "The Multidimensional Anger Inventory." *Journal of Personality and Social Psychology* 51, 1986, 191–200.

Silberman, Charles. *Crisis in the Classroom*. New York: Random House, 1970.

Soltz, Vicki. *Study Group Leader's Manual*. Chicago: Alfred Adler Institute, 1967.

Steiner, Claude. *Scripts People Live*. new York: Grove Press, 1974.

Swick, Kevin, and Stephen Graves. "Locus of Control and Interpersonal Support as Related to Parenting." *Childhood Education*, October 1986, 41–49.

Wolman, Benjamin B. *Clinical Diagnosis of Mental Disorders: A Handbook*. New York: Plenum Press, 1978.

Woolams, Stan, and Michael Brown. *TA: The Total Handbook of Transactional Analysis*. Englewood Cliffs, NJ: Prentice-Hall, 1979.

Part Three

Anderson, Jill. *Thinking, Changing, Rearranging: Improving Self-Esteem in Young People*. Eugene, OR: Timberline Press, 1981.

Beck, Aaron T. *Cognitive Therapy and the Emotional Disorders*. New York: International Universities Press, 1976.

Beck, Aaron T., A. J. Rush, B. F. Shaw, and G. Emergy. *Cognitive Therapy of Depression*. New York: Guilford Press, 1979.

Benson, H. *The Relaxation Response*. New York: William Morrow, 1975.

Bernhardt, Roger, and David Martin. *Self-Mastery Through Self-Hypnosis*. New York: New American Library, 1977.

Bleich, Howard, and Emily S. Boro, eds. "Systematic Hypertension and the Relaxation Response." *The New England Journal of Medicine* 296(20), May 19, 1977, 1152–55.

Bower, Sharon A., and Gordon H. Bower. *Asserting Yourself*. Reading, MA: Addison Wesley, 1976.

Caprio, Frank S., and Joseph Berger. *Helping Yourself with Self-Hypnosis*. Englewood Cliffs, NJ: Prentice-Hall, 1963.

Charlesworth, Edward A., and Ronald G. Nathan. *Stress Management: A Comprehensive Guide to Wellness*. New York: Ballentine, 1985.

Cousins, Norman. *Anatomy of an Illness*. Boston, G. K. Hall, 1980.

———. *The Healing Heart*. Boston, G. K. Hall, 1984.

Deffenbacher, Jerry, Kathleen McNamara, Robert Stark, and Patricia Sabadell. "A Comparison of Cognitive-Behavioral and Process-Oriented Group Counseling for General Anger Reduction." *Journal of Counseling and Development* 69, 1990, 167–72.

Dustin, Richard, and Rickey George. *Action Counseling for Behavior Change*. New York: Intext Press, 1973.

Ellis, Albert. *Humanistic Psychotherapy: The Rational-Emotive Approach*. New York: McGraw-Hill, 1974.

———. "The No Cop-Out Therapy." *Psychology Today*, July 1973, 56–62.

Erickson, Milton H., and Ernest L. Rossi. *Hypnotherapy: An Exploratory Casebook*. New York: Irvington Publishers, 1979.

Eron, Leonard D. "Prescription for Reduction of Aggression." *American Psychologist* 35(3), 1980, 244–52.

Evans, David R., and Margaret T. Hearn. "Anger and Systematic Desensitization: A Follow-Up." *Psychological Reports* 32, 1973, 569–70.

Foa, Edna B., and Paul M. G. Emmelkamp, eds. *Failures in Behavior Therapy*. New York: John Wiley & Sons, 1983.

Goldfried, Marvin, and Michael Merbaum. "How to Control Yourself." *Psychology Today*, November 1973, 102–04.

Gordon, Thomas. *Parent Effectiveness Training*. New York: P. H. Wyden, 1970.

Haley, Jay. *Advanced Techniques of Hypnosis and Therapy: Selected Papers of Milton H. Erickson*. New York: Grune & Stratton, 1967.

Harper, Robert A. *The New Psychotherapies*. Englewood Cliffs, NJ: Prentice-Hall, 1975.

Hassett, James. "Teaching Yourself to Relax." *Psychology Today*, August 1978, 28–40.

Hearn, Margaret T. and David Evans. "Anger and Reciprocal Inhibition Therapy." *Psychological Reports* 30, 1972, 943–48.

Heide, Frederick J. "Relaxation: The Storm Before the Calm." *Psychology Today*, April 1985, 18–19.

Henderson, Charles E. *You Can Do It with Self-Hypnosis*. Englewood Cliffs, NJ: Prentice-Hall, 1983.

Lazarus, Arnold A. "Basic Id." *Psychology Today*, March 1974, 59–63.

———. *Behavior Therapy and Beyond*. New York: McGraw-Hill, 1971.

LeCron, Leslie. *The Complete Guide to Hypnosis*. New York: Harper & Row, 1971.

———. *Self-Hypnotism: The Technique and Its Use in Daily Living*. Englewood Cliffs, NJ: Prentice-Hall, 1964.

Lochman, John. "Effects of Different Treatment Lengths in Cognitive Behavioral Interventions with Aggressive Boys."

Child Psychiatry and Human Development 16, 1985, 45–56.

Lochman, John, Peter Burch, and John Curry. "Client Characteristics Associated with Behavior Change for Treated and Untreated Aggressive Boys." *Journal of Abnormal Child Psychology* 13, 1985, 527–38.

Lochman, John, Peter Burch, John Curry, and Louise Lampron. "Treatment and Generalization Effects of Cognitive Behavioral Goal Setting Interventions with Aggressive Boys." *Journal of Consulting and Clinical Psychology* 52, 1984, 915–16.

Lochman, John, and John Curry. "Effects of Social Problem-Solving Training and Self-Instruction Training with Aggressive Boys." *Journal of Clinical Child Psychology* 15, 1986, 159–64.

Lochman, John, and Louise Lampron. "Teacher Consultation and Cognitive-Behavioral Interventions with Aggressive Boys." *Psychology in the Schools* 26(2), 1989, 179–88.

————. "Cognitive Behavioral Interventions for Aggressive Boys: Seven Month Follow-Up Effects." *Journal of Child and Adolescent Psychotherapy* 27(2), 1988, 226–32.

————. "Situational Social Problem-Solving Skills and Self-Esteem of Aggressive and Nonaggressive Boys. *Journal of Abnormal Child Psychology* 14, 1986, 605–17.

Lochman, John, Louise Lampron, Thomas Gemmer, and Steve Harris. "Anger Coping Intervention with Aggressive Children: A Guide to Implementation in School Settings. In P. Keller and S. Heyman, eds. *Innovations in Clinical Practice: A Source Book* 6, Sarasota, FL: Professional Resource Exchange, 1987.

Lochman, John, W. M. Nelson, and Joseph Sims. "A Cognitive Behavioral Program for Use with Aggressive Children." *Journal of Clinical Child Psychology* 10, 1981, 146–48.

McMullin, Rian E., and Bill Casey. *Talk Sense to Yourself.* Golden, CO: Counseling Research Institute, 1975.

Madow, Leo. *Anger: How to Recognize and Cope with It.* New York: Charles Scribner's and Sons, 1972.

Mann, Harriet, Miriam Siegler, and Humphry Osmond. "Four Types of Personalities and Four Ways of Perceiving Time." *Psychology Today* 6(7), December 1972, 76–84.

Meichenbaum. Donald, and Dennis Turk. "The Cognitive-Behavioral Management of Anxiety, Anger, and Pain." In P.O. Davidson, ed. *The Behavioral Management of Anxiety, Depression, and Pain.* New York: Brunner/Mazel, 1976.

Miller, Sherod, Elam W. Nunnally, and Daniel B. Wackman. *Alive and Aware: Improving Communication in Relationships.* Minneapolis, MN: Interpersonal Communication Programs, 1975.

Moody, Raymond A. Jr. *Laugh After Laugh: The Healing Power of Humor.* Jacksonville, FL: Headwaters Press, 1978.

Novaco, Raymond W., *Anger Control: The Development and Evaluation of an Experimental Treatment.* Lexington, MA: Lexington Books, 1975.

———. "The Cognitive Regulation of Anger and Stress." In Philip Kendall and Steven Hollon, eds. *Cognitive-Behavioral Interventions: Theory, Research, and Procedures.* New York: Academic Press, 1979.

Paul, Gordon L., and Donald T. Shannon. "Treatment of Anxiety Through Systematic Desensitization in Therapy Groups." *Jounral of Abnormal Psychology* 71(2), 1966, 124–35.

Peter, Laurence, and Bill Dana. *The Laughter Prescription.* New York: Ballantine Books, 1982.

Reik, Theodor. *Listening with the Third Ear.* New York: Farrar, Straus and Company, 1949.

Rhoades, George Franklin Jr. "The Effect of Stress Inoculation and Dogmatism upon Anger Management with Forensic Inpatients." Ph. D. dissertation, Western Conservative Baptist Seminary, 1981

Samalin, Nancy, and Martha Moraghan Jablow. "You Make Me So Mad!" *Parents*, January 1987, 53–57.

Simon, Irving. "A Humanistic Approach to Sports." *The Humanist*, July/August 1983, 25–27.

Smith, Manuel J. *When I Say No I Feel Guilty*. New York: Dial Press, 1975.

Stoop, David. *Self-Talk: Key to Personal Growth*. Old Tappan, NJ: Fleming H. Revell, 1982.

Thoresen, Carl E., and Michael J. Mahoney. *Behavioral Self-Control*. New York: Holt, Rinehart, and Winston, 1974.

Toch, Hans. "The Management of Hostile Aggression: Seneca as Applied Social Psychologist." *American Psychologist* 38(9), 1983, 1022–26.

Watson, David L., and Roland G. Tharp. *Self-Directed Behavior: Self-Modification for Personal Adjustment*. Monterey, CA: Brooks/Cole, 1972.

Wolpe, Joseph. *The Practice of Behavior Therapy*. New York: Pergamon Press, 1973.

Part Four

Ainsworth, M. D. S., M. C. Blehar, E. Walters, and S. Walls. *Patterns of Attachment: A Psychological Study of the Strange Situation*. Hillsdale, NJ: Erlbaum, 1978.

Bergin, Allen E., and Sol L. Garfield, eds. *Handbook of Psychotherapy and Behavior Change: And Empirical Analysis*. New York: John Wiley & Sons, 1971.

Blatner, Howard A. *Acting-In: Practical Applications of Psychodramatic Methods*. New York: Springer, 1973.

Bowlby, J. *Attachment and Loss, Volume 2*. New York: Basic Books, 1973.

Cleckley, H. *The Mask of Sanity.* New York: New American Library, 1982.

Cochran, John B., senior clinical forensic psychologist, Oregon State Hospital. Personal conversations, 1975–1988.

Corsini, R. J. *Role Playing in Psychotherapy: A Manual.* Chicago: Aldine, 1966.

Doren, Dennis. *Understanding and Treating the Psychopath.* New York: John Wiley & Sons, 1987.

Eysenck, H. J. *Crime and Personality.* London: Routledge & Kegan, 1977

Fagen, Joen, and Irma Lee Shepherd, eds. *Gestalt Therapy Now.* New York: Harper & Row, Harper Colophon Books, 1971.

Gibbons, D. C. *Changing the Lawbreaker: The Treatment of Delinquency and Criminals.* Englewood Cliffs, NJ: 1965.

———. *Society, Crime and Criminal Careers.* Englewood Cliffs, NJ: Prentice-Hall, 1968.

Goldstein, J. H. *Aggression and Crimes of Violence.* New York: Oxford University Press, 1975.

Harrington, Alan. *Psychopaths.* New York: Simon & Schuster, Touchstone, 1972.

Hollandsworth, James G. Jr., and Myles L. Cooley. "Provoking Anger and Gaining Compliance with Assertive Versus Aggressive Responses." *Behavior Therapy* 9, 1978, 640–46.

Kelly, G. A. *The Psychology of Personal Constructs.* New York: Norton, 1955.

Kelly, G. A., R. R. Blacke, and C. E. Stromberg. "The Effect of Role Training on Role Reversal." *Group Psychotherapy* 10, 1957, 95–104.

Lion, John. "The Role of Depression in the Treatment of Aggressive Personality Disorders." *American Journal of Psychiatry* 129(3), September 1972, 347–49.

Livingston, Roxanne. "Treatment of Criminal Personality" workshop, 1983.

MacDonald, J. *Psychiatry and the Criminal: Second Edition*. Springfield, IL: Charles C. Thomas, 1968.

Mann, J. H., and C. H. Mann. "Role Playing Experience and Interpersonal Adjustment." *Journal of Experimental Social Psychology* 6, 1959, 148–52.

Mann, L., and I. Janis. "A Follow-Up Study on the Long-Term Effects of Emotional Role Playing." *Journal of Personality and Social Psychology* 8, 1968, 339–42.

Matas, L., R. A. Arend, and L. A. Sroufe. "Continuity of Adaption in the Second Year: The Relationship Between Quality of Attachment and Later Competence." *Child Development* 49, 1978, 547–56.

Matson, Katinka. *The Psychology Today Omnibook of Personal Development*. New York: William Morrow, 1977.

Menninger, Roy, and Herbert Modlin. "Individual Violence: Prevention in the Violence Threatening Patient." In Jean Fawcett, ed. *Dynamics of Violence*. Chicago: American Medical Association, 1971.

Moreno, J. L. *Psychodrama*. New York: Beacon, 1946.

Reid, William H., Darwin Dorr, John Walker, and Jack W. Bonner. *Unmasking the Psychopath: Antisocial Personality and Related Syndromes*. New York: Norton & Co., 1986.

Revitch, E., and L. Schlesinger. *Psychopathology of Homicide*. Springfield, IL: Thomas, 1981.

Rimm, David, and John C. Masters. *Behavior Therapy: Techniques and Empirical Findings*. New York: Academic Press, 1974.

Rimm, David, George Hill, Nancy Brown, and James Stuart. "Group-Assertive Training in Treatment of Expression of Inappropriate Anger." *Psychological Reports* 34, 1974, 791–98.

Robins, L. "Follow-Up Studies." In H. Quay and J. Werry, eds. *Psychopathological Disorders of Childhood: Second Edition* New York: Wiley, 1979.

Roff, J., and R. Wirt. "Childhood Aggression and Social Adjustment as Antecedents to Delinquency." *Journal of Abnormal Child Psychology* 12, 1984, 111–26.

Samenow, Stanton E. *Inside the Criminal Mind.* New York: Time Books, 1984.

Shah, Saleem. "Dangerousness: A Paradigm for Exploring Some Issues in Law and Psychology." *The American Psychologist* 33(3), March 1978, 224–38.

Shelton, John. "Assertive Training: Consumer Beware." *Personnel and Guidance Journal* 55(8), April 1977, 465–68.

Szasz, Thomas. *Law, Liberty and Psychiatry.* New York: Macmillan, 1963.

Weiner, Irving B., ed. *Clinical Methods in Psychology.* New York: John Wiley & Sons, 1976.

Wohlking, Wallace, and Hannah Weiner. "Structured and Spontaneous Role Playing: Contrast and Comparison." *New York State School of Industrial and Labor Relations Training and Development Journal* 25(1), January 1971, 8–14.

Wolman, Benjamin. *The Sociopathic Personality.* New York: Brunner Mazel, 1987.

Yochelson, Samuel, and Stanton E. Samenow. *The Criminal Personality, Volume I: A Profile for Change.* New York: Jason Aronson, 1976.

———. *The Criminal Personality, Volume II: The Change Process.* New York: Jason Aronson, 1977.

INDEX

A

Abuse, 105
  advocate, role of, 20
  child, 8, 79–80, 101
  cycle of, 12–15, 17, 19, 21
  emotional consequences,
    16–17
  exercise for batterers, 22
  passive-aggressive anger and,
    28
  spouse, xv, 8, 13, 14–23
  stopping the cycle of, 12,
    21–22
  triggers of, 21
  verbal, 79
  who gets abused, 15–16
  See also Women, battered
Abusive relationships
  considering choices in, 17,
    18, 22
  four types of anger in, 20–21
  reasons for not leaving,
    18–20
  significance of control in, 16
ACLU, 81
Adult-to-Adult, 39, 72, 77, 84,
  90, 92, 142, 166, 170,
  174, 179, 189, 199, 255,
  259, 317, 320, 322, 333,
  337
Affiliation, 103, 120
Aggressive (active-aggressive)
  anger, 5, 24, 28, 95, 122,
    322
  behaviors of, 5, 24, 26, 95,
    122, 322
  breaking habit of, 46,
    50–59
  cathartic release and,
    45–46, 51–55, 57